Jon Frost is an experienced Customs officer of over twenty years' standing. He has served as a HM Customs Preventive Officer in London airports, an Operational Intelligence Specialist, an Investigation/Surveillance Specialist (Drugs), an Anti-Corruption Manager (Overseas) and National Intelligence Coordinator, and an Investigation Specialist for SOCA (Serious Organised Crime Agency). He is also experienced in army-trained covert surveillance (CROPs) for the long-term observation of criminal gangs and operations.

Anything to Declare? is the first book of a planned series of Jon Frost memoirs.

Anything to Declare?

Jon Frost

CONSTABLE • LONDON

In memory of

Vera Elsie Clack
8.9.27—5.8.2013

*The gentlest of women, who put Mark and I on
the right path for adult life.*

CONSTABLE

First published in Great Britain in 2015 by CONSTABLE

Copyright © Jon Frost, 2015

A CIP catalogue record for this book
is available from the British Library.

ISBN: 978-1-47210-942-2 (paperback)
ISBN: 978-1-47210-944-6 (ebook)

Typeset in Garamond by Photoprint, Torquay
Printed and bound by CPI Group (UK) Ltd, Croydon, CR0 4YY

Constable
is an imprint of
Constable & Robinson Ltd
100 Victoria Embankment
London EC4Y 0DY

An Hachette UK Company
www.hachette.co.uk

www.constablerobinson.com

Contents

Introduction:
As is the Custom

You know when you've just come back from holiday and, as you stagger knackered through the cold airport, in shorts and flip-flops, with your wonky-wheeled luggage trolley, and you get to the red/green/blue Customs channels and – even though you know you're not bringing anything back from abroad other than burned feet, hotel shower gel and a souvenir hangover – you still get that uneasy feeling walking through 'nothing to declare'?

Well, sorry for putting you through that but we're kind of glad you feel that way. Because it means we've created the right environment to ensure that the uneasy feeling will be much, much worse for the people that we really want to catch – the criminals and smugglers bringing in contraband that may seriously harm you and yours. We want them to get that horrible feeling: sweaty palms and nervous gulping is an easily spotted dead giveaway. And, if you saw the things that we would regularly find hidden on and in people, you'd probably agree.

Oscar Wilde, when going through New York Customs, made the most famous remark ever uttered to a Customs officer when he said that he had nothing to declare but his genius. It's a great line, but I'm surprised that the undoubted genius of Wilde didn't alert him to the fact that that's *exactly* the kind of smartarse remark that's going to have any Customs officer snapping on the old rubber glove with relish and saying, 'Right, sonny Jim, let's see exactly where you've hidden that genius . . .'

Anyway, like they say, as is the custom, I'll introduce myself: I served over twenty years in Her Majesty's Customs and Excise (HMCE), initially as a uniformed officer at London airports, then moving on to a role as a preventive Intelligence officer before promotion into the plain-clothes and undercover Customs Investigation Division. Later still, I moved to the Serious Organised Crime Agency (SOCA). Most of what I have seen and done has never been made public except for some of the larger drugs jobs, and even then very few people knew what occurred before the arrests took place. Between uniform, investigation work, overseas postings and covert operations, only the names have been changed to protect those involved.

Some of what we did should have never have happened and some things should never have been seen by anyone, but someone had to do the job and that was us.

Prior to the formation of the admittedly less effective SOCA, HM Customs Preventive & Investigation counted for more than 70 per cent of all UK drug, gun and porn seizures. Just one Customs Investigation heroin team would seize more heroin in a year than the whole of the UK's police forces (and there were six Customs heroin teams).

In more than twenty years, I have worked with the mad, the bad, the brave, the stupid, the spectacular and the heroic. The Customs officers I have known came from all kinds of backgrounds. It was quite rare for the department to recruit directly from school and it was unknown for a person to join the Investigation Division without having a good grounding in Customs, Excise or VAT. I have served with former policemen, engineers, soldiers, sailors, airmen, council gardeners, bouncers and even double-glazing salesmen. It was never the pay that drew these people in. Sometimes it was the glory or the power of wearing a uniform. For the ex-military guys, it was the worry of *not* wearing a uniform. Every officer had their own reason for joining. Mine was luck.

The work of Customs officers at ports and airports was and is essential. HMCE was regarded as the best Customs service in the world and, having worked around the world in many countries, I learned that it was true. Customs has always stated that it protects society – and, take my word for it, some of what Customs seizes on its way into this country would make your hair stand up and scream. In my time as a uniformed officer I seized many weird and wonderful things: passengers, aircraft, presidential aircraft, a working tank, cars, lorries, boats and coffins; and I uncovered wild animals, killer snakes, bush meat, animal porn, poisonous vodka, dodgy medicine, bootleg prescriptions, pirated pills, toxic alcohol, firearms, sidearms, swords, explosives, stolen gold, dirty money, blood diamonds, child pornography, dead parrots and every drug known to man (and a few as yet unknown). And that was all just from searching the living. The dead? Well, we searched them, too. We had to. It's amazing what you can hide in a coffin.

There were many aspects of the job that made you think twice about ever again putting your fingers anywhere near your mouth. Every single hiding place and hole in the human body has at one time been used by smugglers, and I'm afraid the poor old Customs officer has to sometimes look inside them. And, yes, even the dead ones. In fact, we sometimes preferred the corpses – especially on a Monday morning or when suffering from a hangover – as the dead don't argue, swear or spit at you.

When you've confiscated everything from a suitcase full of human hair to a live, urinating monkey hidden in the lining of a passenger's overcoat, you know you can never return to a normal line of work. And from being a uniformed officer I then went into plain-clothes and undercover Customs work and things really got . . . even less normal.

Over the years, there have been many so-called detection methods for criminals and criminal activity, from the low-tech reading the bumps on a human head to the high-tech airport Sniffer Arch (more of that later); from the lie detector test to actually using fruit flies to try to identify drugs (yes, it's true). But I don't think any method has yet been found that beats the knowledge, the experience, the suspicion, the gut instinct, the skill, the bloody-mindedness and the ever-twitching antennae of that uniformed human radar detector – the good old-fashioned Customs officer.

Unfortunately, or fortunately, this 'trusting no one' technique usually pays off. When I was at work in the airports, in front of me would be a long queue of incoming passengers (including smugglers), and behind me there were 88,000 square miles of Great Britain. We were all that stood between the two. So, when you next step off a plane, the Customs officer may be the first unfriendly face you see, but they are actually the last border defence that we have.

Just don't try to sneak in a monkey under your overcoat – we know the signs . . .

Part 1: In Uniform

1. Counting the Bodies Before Breakfast

There's an old Japanese proverb that says, 'If you sit by the river long enough, the body of your enemy will float by.' You could also say that, if you worked at an airport long enough, you would eventually see everything.

One day when I was on the early shift, I was just about to drive into the staff car park when I noticed a vehicle parked up in an unusual place. Next to the car park there was a dead-end road that hadn't yet been connected to wherever it was intended to lead. Down this road there was a Ford saloon that had both front doors wide open, as if its driver and passenger had got out in a hurry and legged it. And speaking of legs, on closer inspection there appeared to be a man's legs hanging out of the driver's door, and there also appeared to be a pair of woman's legs sticking out from the passenger's door. Maybe they were sunbathing or having a quick nap, but it seemed an odd place to do it.

Now, Customs runs airports (by ancient legislation, no foreign entry point into Great Britain can exist without Customs authority) – security do their bit and so can the police, but Customs officers are always on the lookout for smuggling attempts or dodgy goings-on and the telltale signs of either. So I thought this looked strange enough for me to have a closer butcher's.

As I slowly drove a little closer to the car, I could tell that something was seriously wrong. As well as the two pairs of legs sticking out of the car (which were immobile), both the front and rear windows were smashed – and yet the car didn't look as if it had been in an accident. At least I couldn't see any frontal impact.

As I got out of my car and walked towards the vehicle, all I could hear was the blood in my ears and the roar of incoming aircraft above my head. I slowly stepped nearer and called out a hopeful 'Hello', thinking that they would perhaps both sit up, startled, embarrassed that they'd been caught doing whatever they were doing. But something inside me wasn't surprised when there was no response. Now I could feel the tiny cubes of safety glass scattered around the car crunch underfoot. And, even though I had a bad feeling about this, when I got near enough to peer inside I was quite shocked at what I saw: the whole inside of the car was decorated with sheets of fresh blood, as if the interior had been reupholstered with a kind of dark, sticky red leather. I noticed for the first time that one of the man's shoes was off, lying on the floor, right next to a double-barrel shotgun. A quick assessment made it plain to me that the man had used the shotgun to completely blow off the head of his wife; and he'd then orally taken the same double-barrelled medicine himself. There was blood, bone and brain matter all around the inside of the car, and presumably four eyeballs and sixty-four teeth must have been scattered around inside there, too. I'd heard of shotgun weddings but this was my first experience of a shotgun divorce.

By now, the commercial jets above me weren't the only incoming flights I had to deal with. Obviously word, and the smell, had got round the local area and there seemed to be a busy flight path of flies and insects circling the car and making their approach for landing.

Well, serves me right, I thought – the curiosity of the Customs officer strikes again. Trust me to have a butcher's and find . . . what looked like a butcher's. That'll teach you, Jon, you nosy, suspicious old bastard. I was just glad that, technically, this was actually nothing to do with Customs. I could wipe my hands of it, if not my nostrils.

I was just getting ready to leave and call it in when the first police arrived, obviously alerted already by someone equally suspicious. The first officer came closer, looked in, turned green, and immediately bent over and noisily parked his breakfast all over his shoes. They went from being shiny black to multicoloured pebble-dash. The second officer smiled weakly at me, nodded, and to his credit he straight away got on with what he knew had to be done – secure and make safe the shotgun (which, as he picked it up, you couldn't help but notice, was dripping with something that belonged *inside* the human body but was now irretrievably *out*).

Great start to a Monday morning, I thought a little while later as I sat in the canteen eating a large fry-up. Oh, come on, don't hold that against me – as they say, breakfast is the most important meal of the day! (Though that young copper might have disagreed.)

And all this, remember, had happened *before* I'd actually clocked on, so technically I hadn't even been at work. Not for the first time, something encountered during the course of a day made me think: if that's the kind of thing that this job reveals to you even when you're off-duty, then you can imagine what you might have to look forward to when your shift actually does begin. Perhaps even more bodies floating past me in the river.

It's Monday mornings like that one that make me think back to how I got into this and where it all started.

2. The Tattooed Side of the Moon

Everyone, as they say, has to start somewhere. My starting place in Customs was at Stansted Airport on the 'old' side of the runway, that is, on the other side of the runway to the new high-tech 'greenhouse' terminal designed by Norman Foster at a cost of £100 million. What would become known as the old Stansted (but which was at the time new to me) was a pretty simple creation from the 1970s with single-storey buildings and Portakabins. The passengers, believe it or not, actually had to *walk* from the plane to the terminal. And the staff canteen was really no more than a glorified prefab Nissen hut from the time when Stansted was in the hands of the 8th Air Force of the USAAF (United States Army Air Force) during the Second World War. From looking at the regular canteen menu, I think they left some of their food behind as well.

But, having already served in the regular Army, I was used to food that wasn't exactly haute cuisine. After I had left the regulars, I'd joined the Territorial Army, which also allowed me to return to college in Cambridge. Near exam time, I was on TA duty in the officer's mess of the Royal Anglians when I'd been approached by an ageing captain who was a little drunk. He was apparently worried that I was heading for the dole in the next couple of weeks and informed me that Customs at Stansted Airport was looking for bench officers. For some reason, even though I'd never considered it before, the idea immediately grabbed me. And I wrote and posted a letter of interest within the next twenty-four hours.

As new recruits, our training consisted of three intensive months: first month, we were at our home airport of Stansted and we covered all the basics: law, rules and regulations (you needed to know the different Customs Acts of Parliament inside out), spotting potential targets, etc. Month two was spent on a residential training course, in my case held at a hotel in Eastbourne, away from our station, and here officers from all over the country were brought together for role-play training, advanced training in interviews and paperwork (note-books and witness statements), training in passenger stops and advanced lessons based on the first month's teaching. Our third month was at a different port or airport – Gatwick was my temporary posting – to the one where we were mentored all the time. Then a probation period continued for nine more months at the home station where we were assessed on how we carried out our duties with any cock-ups noted – strip searching the Queen, letting through a live monkey disguised as a hairy child, detaining someone for being in possession of a concealed banana . . . that kind of thing.

Our exams were an ongoing thing, structured very much like the military – explanation, demonstration, imitation, test. There was no computer-based training. In fact, we only had one computer and that was a secure Customs and Excise Departmental Reference & Information Computer (CEDRIC) terminal in the Intelligence office.

The failure rate was low for preventive training Customs officers because, although the uniform service was an attractive option to many people, when they discovered the hours and the exacting work required, most dropped out even before their training started. On top of this, the interview stage we'd been through to get there was tough. You had to show you had the right stuff to progress any further.

Like Judge Dredd, we had to know the laws inside out and back to front. I knew that, when I was operational, I wouldn't get time to sit and flick through the law books. The important front-line laws were: the Customs and Excise Management Act (CEMA, which was our bible), the Police and Criminal Evidence Act (PACE), the VAT Act, the Customs Consolidation Act 1876, the Misuse of Drugs Act, the Customs and Excise Tariff, the Firearms Act, the Convention on International Trade in Endangered Species (CITES), the Counterfeit Act and the Misdescription of Goods Act amongst others. So you can see that my bedtime reading at this time wasn't exactly a barrel of laughs. There aren't many chuckles to be had in the VAT Act.

The training was hard and intense and we were expected to learn quickly. There is a reason for this: HMCE was regarded as the best Customs service in the world. I trained with all

sorts, from the mad and the bad to the whip-smart and dis-
ciplined – drawn from all walks of life for all kinds of reasons.
The training hammers us all into shape and then nails us into
a stiff black (though officially 'Customs Blue') uniform with
bright gold braid and scary peaked cap (ominous X-ray stare,
officer's own).

After the first month's book and theory training, my tutor,
Mick, decided to let me loose to have a go on the general
public, just to see if I had what it takes. Mick was a very
experienced, long-in-the-tooth former Excise officer who had
moved over to Customs. He knew that all the theory in the
world won't tell you whether or not you're ready for harsh
reality – at some point, you've got to get stuck in and hit 'the
channels' (as we called the red/green declare/nothing-to-
declare exits). As I walked in uniform down the shining con-
course of a London airport for the first time, the polished
floor reflecting the strip lights above, I knew that I'd found
the right job and the right place to be. I was now officially a
HMCE Airport Preventive Officer (APO) working the bench
(search table) on incoming channels and airplane searches at
Stansted Airport.

On this particular day, an Amsterdam flight had just landed
and so I positioned myself behind a bench and tried to look
like I knew what I was doing, helped by the fact I was wearing my evil-looking HMCE-issue cap with its white cover and
steep shiny black peak and my black APO uniform decorated
with gold braid – the passengers didn't know that single gold
band on my sleeve meant I was only a newly appointed APO.
(They probably also didn't know that the historical reason

why the gold braid doesn't go all around the arm on a Customs officer uniform is because we donated the inside half of the braid to the military in the First World War.)

I stood there watching everyone file past knowing that, like when it comes to spiders, they're more afraid of you than you are of them. I remembered from my training that they said that spotting potential targets is like trying to find Willy Wonka's Golden Ticket. Although the training gave us guidelines in the area, in the end it quite often came down to experience. But, until you got that experience, you needed something to go on, so it was broken down into categories of suspicion:

a) Paperwork: Passports that showed trips to drug-source countries; flight tickets paid in cash; and diaries (some people are actually stupid enough to write down everything that they have been up to, including the illegal acts).

b) Dress: Are they wearing the right type of dress for the place from which they have just arrived? For example, wearing a business suit on a package flight from Ibiza is going to stand out. People mistakenly think that simply looking smart is enough to avoid suspicion. But it is better to look scruffily right than too smartly wrong.

c) Drug paraphernalia: Cannabis T-shirts, golden razor-blade necklaces, etc. seem almost *too* obvious – but they aren't.

d) General appearance: Many drugs users are employed as mules because they are cheap and can be paid in the product that they are smuggling, so telltale signs of a user are often the signs of a carrier.

e) Nervousness: Again, this seems obvious but it is more difficult to read because it is only a certain *kind* of nervousness that rings our alarm bells; mostly we expect people to be a little bit nervous when stopped by Customs.

f) Amsterdam: Just because it's Amsterdam. Nuff said.

On top of this, we would be supplied by our Intelligence teams with what we called 'Trend Alerts', that is, specific areas of suspicion that occurred during certain times and for certain reasons. For example, as I was beginning my training, there was a fashion for smuggling gangs to give British pensioners free holidays to Spain – and all the little grey-haired old ladies and gentlemen had to do in return was to bring back a package. It was based on the understandable idea that little old ladies seem more trustworthy. Unless, of course, you're a big, bad Customs officer who wouldn't trust a nun on a crutch.

Sometimes I knew that passengers made things easier for you by being . . . well, let's not beat around the bush . . . by being idiots. T-shirts with a big cannabis leaf on the front tended to get noticed, as did ones with 'Free The Weed' written across them. No sign is too obvious, so don't think that these passengers got a pass on the basis that you wouldn't wear a cannabis leaf T-shirt *and still* have a travel bag full of weed. Unsurprisingly, often the two went together. So walking through Customs in that kind of attire meant that you may as well have done it with your pants already around your ankles – it would have certainly saved time.

Contents of baggage also gave away massive clues, and clues so obvious you would think the passenger would see it themselves. Often they didn't. So packets of Jumbo Rizlas with some of the cardboard missing (torn off to make a homemade filter – a roach) on someone coming back from Amsterdam was enough to earn them a pull on the grounds of stupidity alone. And burnt spoons in the luggage may have been taken out, but the track marks up the arms could not be hidden – both obvious signs of heroin use. But one of the favourite giveaways was photographs showing the traveller toking on a big spliff.

Unfortunately, none of these obvious signs were present and none of the usual alarm bells were being rung by the passengers off the Amsterdam flight, so, on the basis that I had to stop someone, I eventually motioned to a young Dutchman to come over to me so I could conduct my first ever search. The passenger was a chap called Van der Mons who, it turned out, was a glasshouse erector working in the north. Which was sort of appropriate as the Dutch were among the first to heat larger greenhouses, using charcoal braziers – and we all know what is often grown in greenhouses in Holland.

I rummaged through his bag as if every single item hid a terrible secret – remote control exploding underpants? Socks impregnated with heroin (or was that just skin flakes)? Comb that doubled up as a flick-knife? Well, I didn't know; during training it was drilled into us to trust no one, be suspicious of everyone and search everything. What I found was an excess amount of tobacco and a telltale packet of Jumbo Rizla. With Mr Van der Mons's passport in hand, I wandered over to Mick and told him what I had found.

'So then,' he said, 'do you want an SOP?'

That was Search of Person. I didn't really know: did I really want to look up a stranger's arse this early in my career? But I knew that I did want a good result so . . . in for a penny. Mick took me over to the senior officer. By the book, I had to officially request an SOP, giving my reasons. This I did, and Mick and I escorted our Dutchman into a search room.

Now, I'm not a lover of the naked male form – I don't even like my own – but I didn't know then that over the next few years I was to see more naked men than the choreographer of the Chippendales. In the case of Mr Van der Mons, we politely asked him if he would strip down and Mick asked him to lift his bollocks.

'*Boll*-locks? Boll-locks? What are "boll-locks"?' he said, laughing.

'Er . . . *them* things,' said Mick, pointing to our Dutchman's testicles.

He happily complied, laughing all the time and occasionally shouting out, '*Bollocks!* Good! I like! Bollocks. Ha!'

We found about 9 grams of cannabis resin . . . but in his trainers, under the tongue – so all along all we'd needed to do was ask his shoes to open up and say 'argh'.

He was fined and sent on his way and, as for me, well I was the golden boy for having got a successful 'find' on my first pull – albeit a small find and albeit more by luck than judgement. Though, having said that, often on certain flights from Amsterdam, it would sometimes have been difficult *not* to pick someone who was carrying.

After this time on practical experience, I left the airport to join my friend and fellow trainee, Brian, and resume my uniform training until I was ready to hit the channels full time.

By the time Brian and I were at stage three of training a few months later, we were at Gatwick Airport and about to learn that there was truth in the old saying that there was more than one way to skin a cat . . . and smuggle a cat . . . and hide a cat in your luggage . . . and smuggle drugs in a cat, etc. You could also say that, if you worked at an airport long enough (or, if you were unlucky, even for just one day), you would eventually see everything. Twice.

So on a Monday morning, in summer, Brian and I entered the fray at Gatwick. There happened to be airport strikes all over Europe, so, on the way to our new office, we had to negotiate the large maze of bodies of all the delayed, sleeping passengers, trying to literally not step on anyone's toes . . . or fingers.

We had, it turned out, arrived at work half-an-hour after the arrival of a flight from America's West Coast and the passengers were just starting to wander through the channels after picking up their luggage from the ring of hell (i.e. baggage carousel), where it had been very carefully sorted by the airport's bag smashers (i.e. highly trained luggage handling personnel).

As we were being welcomed and briefed by the duty senior officer, I couldn't help but notice that Brian was staring hard over the officer's shoulder. I followed his gaze and there, standing at one of the exam desks, being 'chatted to' by one of our boys, was a vision of absolute loveliness: six foot two, long blonde hair, even longer legs, stiletto shoes and silk stockings with a seam running all the way up the back towards a short, figure-hugging silver lamé dress. A few seconds drifted by and the senior officer eventually shut up and turned around to see what had drawn our eyes. We remained at attention for a few seconds . . . until the passenger turned around to pick up her bag and we saw that she had a big, black, hairy walrus moustache; and, now that we looked closer, enormous hands and a large, bobbing Adam's apple.

Our senior duty officer smiled broadly and turned back to address us: 'I guess the San Francisco flight is in then. Welcome to Gatwick, boys.'

We soon got into the swing of things. I bagged a couple of small drugs jobs and Brian was spending his time sitting on a stuffer. That isn't as much fun as it sounds, by the way: 'swallowers' were the mules (smugglers) who swallowed their drugs packages and 'stuffers' . . . well, you can probably guess where they put theirs. With both swallowers and stuffers, it becomes a waiting game – that is, waiting for nature to take its course and the hidden contraband to come out.

And that's one thing they didn't put on the recruitment poster – '*Join Customs! Watch People Crap!*' You know how they say 'shit happens'? Well it's true, it does, and, when it did, we had to sift through it looking for drug-filled condoms by hand.

A week later, we were not only still tiptoeing over abandoned passengers again but we also had to fend off the advances of some religious sect's followers who had invaded the airport terminal and wanted to give us flowers and bless our aura-something. Brian, who was nearly twenty years older than me and an ex-hippy, said, 'Blimey! The sixties have reappeared overnight – I feel like I'm having some kind of strange flashback.' And then he went off to see if anything interesting had come out of his latest stuffer's . . . aura.

The airport staff and security were both in a flustered state about the religious sect invasion; even our lot – a bunch of usually unflappable Customs officers – were moved to lift an interested eyebrow at the goings-on. We got into our offices and were then dragged back out and into a team meeting that was being held by a very senior officer and some bloke from the Foreign Office. It appeared that within the hour some religious guru was arriving from India with about a hundred of his followers. Add that to the followers already in the airport and we had quite an impromptu religious festival on our hands. The briefing stated that we were to perform our normal duties as far as the arriving followers were concerned but it might be diplomatic to avoid the Big Guru. We didn't like this at first as it went against our professional nature and natural instinct to pull someone, especially if they expected special treatment; but then we were told that his hold bags on the plane *would* be scanned and searched, that he had no hand luggage and that he would be wearing not a lot more than a yellow sheet. So it would be pretty unlikely for him to get anything through.

Sat at the back of the meeting with his arms crossed like pirate swords was Officer Billy, nicknamed The Beast, so-called because of his undeniably mean nature. We loved him. And throughout the briefing we could hear his constant and hilarious mumbling: 'Bloody God-botherer and his bloody Bible bashers and this bloody jumped-up Foreign Office toady coming in here trying to tell us our job . . .' It went on and on but nobody took any notice except us and the senior officer.

The meeting ended and we all wandered out to the channels to see the arrival of 'the enlightened one'. All, that is, except Billy. The senior officer had decided that it was too much of a risk having Bill anywhere near our incoming Big Guru and so had sent him off on some task in the stores. Soon we could hear the chanting from all the arriving followers and this chant was then taken up by the followers behind us. The first to arrive in the channels were the guru's flower girls with large baskets of rose petals, spreading them on the ground. We had been told of this ritual – the Holy One's feet should not touch the floor, apparently. Fair enough. And then he finally appeared: a little chubby chap with a big grey beard and glasses and wearing what looked like cheap flip-flops. Surely, I thought, an impressive flip-flop is an essential part of any religious guru's outfit? Apparently not. He floated past us with a genial wave and headed for the automatic exit doors. I noticed our senior officer give a visible sigh of relief that the spectacle of Billy the Beast versus Big Guru had been averted.

Then, as the flower girls disappeared, throwing flowers behind them, there was a really loud bang as the storeroom door, which was right next to the exit, suddenly flew open – and there, in full uniform, including hat (black peak pulled down like a knight's visor), was Billy . . . with the biggest fuck-off broom I had *ever* seen. It was about six feet wide. He looked like a cross between the Terminator and Norah Batty. Cue very sharp intake of breath from one senior officer and several sharp intakes of breath from all attending Customs personnel. In a flash, Billy was out of the storeroom and following the flower girls, who had no idea that he was using his mega-brush to sweep a beautiful clean swathe right through the rose-petal pathway. As Billy disappeared from view, brushing vigorously in front of His now-quite-baffled Holiness, under the chiming of the followers 'peace bells' we could hear the low rumble of Billy's muttering: 'Frigging holy man my arse well learn what it's like for us lowly ones down here on earth you short-sighted beardy bastard oh yes you're in the real world now old son . . .'

The Amsterdam flights were always quite fruitful and the constant work was a good way for a newly qualified officer to put training into practice and, it turns out, to accidentally run into people you hadn't seen since school.

On this particular day, I had just arrested a Dutchman for smuggling 6 kg of cannabis resin concealed within large soup cans. Which is pretty clever. But we knew that there were numerous places in the Netherlands where you could get this illegal canning professionally done. The one flaw in the plan is that people don't often travel with large jumbo catering cans of soup – it's not exactly essential travelling gear and it's heavy – so their presence alone is a bit of a giveaway.

This passenger had on him six large cans of so-called vegetable soup. I had already opened one and X-rayed the other five so I had no doubt that we had six kilos. The guy was arrested and put into custody, and he asked for the on-call solicitor. Luckily for him, the solicitor arrived within twenty minutes, which broke the average time by about an hour. I couldn't believe my eyes when an acquaintance, Richard Smith, walked through the door as the on-call solicitor. We had never been friends. In fact, he hadn't liked me and the feeling had been mutual.

I greeted him pleasantly enough but his first words to me were: 'I think you can drop the Richard bit and call me Mr Smith. I am a solicitor, you know.'

Martin, our duty officer, who was well known for his dislike of solicitors, looked up from his paperwork. Now he was interested. I knew I couldn't lose face here so I replied, 'In which case, you call me Officer Frost. After all, I am a Crown-commissioned officer.' Martin smiled and went back to his paperwork.

Things didn't really get better from then on. Smith got his client to go 'no comment', so the interview was very short. To finish off the job, we just needed to open the remaining cans and confirm the contents weren't exactly the kind of stuff approved by Heinz – even in Amsterdam. I brought all five cans into the interview room so that we could open them in front of the Dutchman. I opened the second can and pulled the cannabis blocks out from the soup. As I was drying the blocks on some kitchen paper, I casually passed the can opener to Smith and asked, 'Would you mind popping that one open for me, Mr Smith?' After a moment's hesitation, he opened the can in a few seconds and then lifted out the cannabis on to some more kitchen paper on the table. As he passed me back the can opener, I handed him a blank witness statement form.

'What is this for?' he asked in a snotty tone.

'It's for your witness statement for the prosecution, Mr Smith,' I replied. 'It has to go on the record exactly who opened which cans . . .'

I left the interview room and he stormed out after me, his face now burning red. 'You bastard!' he shouted, his nose only two inches from mine. 'I can't represent him now. You fucking set this up! Where's your duty officer? I want to complain. This means big trouble for you!'

I pointed in the direction of the venomous, solicitor-hating Martin.

Once I had cleaned up all the soup off the drug blocks, I wandered into the main office just in time to hear Martin's response to the complaint against me.

'Well then, Richard!' he said. 'It sounds like my officer carried out his duty as he should and you, son, are a bit of a twat for opening the can. Now, sir, could you sit over there and write out your statement?'

Smith's final words to us on his way out were that this was not the last we would hear of it. The duty officer told me not to sweat about it. I was still a touch worried, though, and tried to explain that it hadn't been a deliberate ploy to get him to open the can, just a genuine request for help.

'Course it was, son,' he said with a smile and a wink. 'Of course it was.'

Robert was another acquaintance. He had spent the last two years of his schooling in a cannabis stupor before just managing to get into college to study an 'ology'. It was there that he got involved in the new and expanding rave culture. His drugs usage moved from the downer cannabis to the hallucinogenic LSD. I hadn't seen him in a while but what I didn't expect to see was him being escorted into the green channel by a couple of policemen a few years after our last meeting. Luckily, I was in a position to avoid being involved, yet still be available for advice.

Apparently, Rob had been given the usual security pat down at departures by BAA security. During the pat down, the security officer had felt a body pack on Rob and had got him to lift up his jumper, so revealing a few thousand ecstasy and LSD tablets. He was on his way to Tenerife to make his fortune as a dealer. By the time Rob was delivered to us, he was screaming threats left and right. What surprised me was Rob's supposed defence that he was shouting out to anyone who would listen: 'But I'm going *out* of the country, you fuckers! I'm not bringing the stuff *in*!'

The illegality of the exportation of controlled drugs is exactly the same as the importation of them. I don't know whether years on drugs from a young age had affected his powers of reasoning but he did genuinely believe that because he was taking the consignment out of the country he shouldn't be in any trouble. As if he was doing everyone a favour by taking the gear out. He was so sure of his legal position that he refused a solicitor and later defended himself in court. And, as the old saying goes, the man who defends himself in court has a fool for a client. Rob got three years.

One person I wasn't particularly surprised to see again was our Mr Van der Mons, as he came through the airport off another flight from Amsterdam, but I was *very* surprised by his reaction and by what he proceeded to do. While standing in the passport line, he spotted Mick and me. Now, I didn't know it at the time, but I was about to get the best and most unusual reception I could ever get from a passenger whose arse I had once looked up – he started smiling broadly at us and waving wildly. Then, at the top of his voice, he started shouting, '*Bollocks!* Good! *Ha-ha*. Bollocks! *Good!*'

Mick and I looked at each other, a little puzzled. Well, quite a lot puzzled, actually. All the other passengers in the queue shared our bafflement – they looked at each other, then looked at Mr Van der Mons, then looked back at us. It was like a mass breakout of synchronized frowning. I assumed they were wondering how brave, or foolish, you'd have to be to start shouting 'Bollocks!' at a Customs officer.

But that wasn't all our flying Dutchman had in store. As he came through the green channel, he bounded over to where Mick and I were standing, undoing his belt and unzipping his trousers as he approached. Then he spun round and Mick and I – like a couple of astronomers looking at the night sky at a certain time of the month – were bathed in the unmistakable glare of a full moon.

By this time, the rest of the passengers were split between a mixture of hysterics and horror. But all of them might have wondered why Mick and I were just chuckling. What they couldn't see was that on his bared right cheek there was a brand new tattoo – a British bulldog smoking a large joint and, needled in irreversible ink underneath, were the words 'BOLLOCKS! GOOD!' I actually thought, 'Good lad – fair play to you, son.' He returned to the queue to a smattering of applause and with a cheery double thumbs-up back to us.

I suppose, if nothing else, it did prove that our Mr Van der Mons must have smoked a shitload more weed than we ever actually caught him with.

3. DOA: Dead on Arrival

If you can (and some can't), please try to die in your home country. Obviously better if you don't die *at all* but, just in case, I thought I'd mention it.

Repatriation of a human body back to the UK is complicated and very expensive (currently about £4,500 for Spain to the UK). To us, as Customs officers, repatriated bodies and body parts were simply freight and they even appeared on the aircrafts' airway bills listed as such. Which may come as a surprise to trusting passengers, who are too used to being fooled by the clever skills of the pilots and the cabin crews into feeling that the airline does really care about them. But it will come as no surprise to the pilots and the cabin crew, who secretly refer to the passengers as SLF – or self-loading freight. That's you, that is, that they're talking about. And me, too, when I fly. We are just pieces of baggage with legs that are occasionally viewed as mildly preferable to the other baggage because we walk ourselves on board; but often viewed as less preferable to the other baggage because we complain and get drunk. There is no suitcase in existence (outside one that explodes) that aircrews could hate more than a human passenger.

But, if you are a smuggler, a human corpse represents not a symbol of human loss but simply a good vehicle for contraband importation. Even so, we didn't often check the dead as we knew it would take quite a widespread and very professional organization to pull off smuggling in this way. So what makes it so complicated?

Well, if Billy Bobbins gets pissed on cheap plonk and does a backflip off his tenth-floor hotel balcony in Tenerife while singing 'Come on England!' and finds that he misses the swimming pool below by a good fifty feet (and which, by the way, with a Brit abroad, would be classed as a 'death by natural causes'), then the result is that the body has to be embalmed within forty-eight hours. Traditionally, it tends to happen quickly in hot countries, for the obvious reason that before refrigeration the dead would soon turn ripe. Scotland, on the other hand – *nae* problem. Granddad could pop his sporran there and you could prop him up in his favourite chair for a few weeks for company. One of the benefits of a cold climate.

After a death abroad, next comes lots of paperwork: death certificate, embalming certificate, certificate of transportation, freedom from infection certificate. Once all these certificates are in place, they have to be checked by the local authorities and copies sent to the British Embassy. Next comes the physical stuff: the body must be sealed by a Spanish Customs officer in a zinc-lined coffin. Zinc is used to create a hermetic seal and also because it still allows the coffin to be X-rayed.

The body can be clothed but under no circumstances is anything allowed to be put in the coffin, even personal mementoes of the deceased.

The coffin will then be transported to the airport where it is placed within a specific cargo container and registered with its own airway bill. The choice of which airline to carry the deceased is either by special freight plane or – and this is the option most often used – by a normal everyday passenger jet. So, that's right, a normal holiday jet can, and often does, carry corpses. Often when there is someone on a plane crying for most of the flight, it's because they know that down in the hold they are bringing home evidence of an ended life.

For those who bring the deceased back in a coffin rather than propped up in a seat wearing wonky sunglasses, once they are into the UK, all the paperwork is examined and only then is the coffin released. Between arrival and release, we at Customs can examine the contents . . . if we really want to.

During my early months at the airport, I was often thrown in at the deep end and some tasks were, I knew, to test my mettle and mental reserves. My tutor Mick's evil smile usually informed me that whatever he had in mind was going to be amusing for others and a lot less so for me. Still, what was I to do, pack it all in and go running home to my mother?

'Right, we're off to the freight shed,' Mick said one day. He didn't expand on this but I'm sure now that all the other guys in the office were aware of what lay in store for me.

The freight sheds and Customs freight office were on the other side of the airport, a fifteen-minute drive. The freight staff and the passenger Customs staff rarely mixed. We thought that we were superior as we dealt with real people, and they countered with the fact that cargo didn't sweat or act nervous so they had the harder job because they had to solely use their investigative minds to find contraband.

We were joined in the car by my senior officer who said that he had some admin work to do in the freight office. That was, I thought, bollocks for sure – he was coming to watch my pain.

We drove straight into the freight shed and parked near the Customs clearance cage. As we got out of the car, I couldn't miss my target for the day. There, in the middle of the shed, was a large, shiny brass-handled casket. The strip lights were reflected in the dark polished wood. The cargo handlers had unpacked it from its flight container and forklifted it on to a narrow exam bench, a bit like balancing a shoebox on a matchbox. Because of its size and the overhang of the width, as you approached it from certain angles it looked like it was almost floating in mid-air.

The senior officer headed off towards our offices as Mick and I stood either side of the boxed-up deceased. Mick smiled, 'Okay then, off with the lid and let's see what we are dealing with.'

It took me about five minutes to remove all the decorative screw covers and then the screws themselves. Together, Mick and I lifted off the heavy, zinc-lined lid to reveal the occupant. The first thing that hit me was the smell of embalming fluid, and with its composition being a mixture of formaldehyde, methanol, ethanol and other solvents, the smell was quite distinctive. Then came the body. The chap was chubby and well dressed with a great shock of ginger hair.

'Right then, Jon, how do you feel?' asked Mick.

How did I feel? I thought for a few seconds: how should I feel? The chap looked as if he was asleep yet smelled like a hospital sluice room.

Mick, standing on the opposite side of the coffin, continued, 'We are going to search the coffin but, in this case, we are not going to search the corpse.' Well, that was a relief anyway. 'I want you to reach in and roll him towards you. Now, this is not going to be easy as there is not much room in there, so you will have to use a bit of force.'

I put my right hand on his cold head and grabbed his right arm with my left hand. Mick looked impressed – I had not bottled out. 'OK, on my count, roll him towards you . . . Three, two, one, roll!'

As I pulled his arm, there was a loud human cry of '*Aaaarrrgghhh!*' The world suddenly went into very slow motion . . . and then speeded up: FUCK ME – the bloke must be alive! With a loud shout of my own, I let go and flew backwards. What I didn't know was that the cry had come from the senior officer who had just crept up behind me, so as I flew backwards I clattered slap-bang into him and we both went sprawling on the floor. Fifteen stone of me knocked him clear off his feet and we both hit the ground with a crunch.

Still on the floor, I could hear laughing. The freight staff and the cargo handlers had all come out to watch Mick and our senior officer play this trick on me. The officer was star-fished out on the floor, covered in scalding coffee from the cup he'd been holding and, with a fracture to his drinking arm, screaming blue murder at me. I was lying on top of him and screaming blue murder at Mick, and my right arm was in the air holding – I suddenly noticed to my shock – what was obviously the dead man's bright-ginger wig. I must have grabbed it as I flew backwards.

The other thing I couldn't help but notice – and this was something else I must have inadvertently grabbed and pulled at in the shock – was that the deceased's right arm was now stuck up in the air, sticking straight out of the coffin like he was giving some eerie Nazi salute from beyond the grave.

Mick was chuckling uncontrollably and, as a result, he was struggling to hold on to the heavily lined coffin lid, which was about to topple out of his hands. I got to my feet but didn't help him – I thought that was the least he should suffer. I pressed the Nazi salute back down into the coffin like pushing a giant lever, and I was just grateful it didn't spring back up again of its own accord. That *would* have been scary.

And though I tried it all different ways, turning it this way and that, pulling it backwards and forwards, spinning it around from right to left, lifting it up and putting it back down again . . . I was never really completely happy with the way that big orange wig went back on.

4. Fear of Flying . . . with Bloody Good Reason

One of the fascinating things about working inside certain professions is the fact that they give you the fish's-eye view of a swan's arse. Meaning, while the swan looks calm and serene up top, underneath its legs are going ten-to-the-dozen, and sometimes looking beneath the surface is where you find the truth. Ask any chef who's ever worked in a kitchen what he's seen going on in there, and you'll probably never eat out again. Similarly, once I'd seen some of the aviation industry from the inside, I wondered if I'd ever again fly. It might seem odd coming from someone whose working life revolved around airports, but I have to admit to not being a fan of planes myself: they're dangerous in the air and often even more dangerous on the ground.

Funnily enough, the word 'airport' itself was coined by a British Customs officer. The first ever engine-powered aircraft flight over the English Channel was made in 1909 by a French flyer, Louis Blériot, who landed in fields near Dover Castle, claimed his £1,000 prize money for the achievement and overnight became world famous. And you might well think 'bloody typical!', but guess who was waiting for him when he landed at Dover? That's right, a Customs officer! I love the fact that even at the end of a record-breaking world's first journey there would still be a little guy in a uniform licking the end of a pencil and saying, 'Now, sir, if you could possibly just sign here . . .' But the fact is, even though Blériot still had to make a Customs declaration, the officer only had forms with the words Sea Port (as commercial air travel didn't yet exist). So he crossed out the word 'Sea' and above it wrote 'Air'. A new word was born. The dutiful officer also had to make do with reporting the plane as a yacht and describing Blériot as its master.

Still, it could have been worse, Blériot could have mentioned that he'd stopped off in Amsterdam and ended up going down in history as the victim of the first ever Customs airport strip search.

I quickly discovered how shockingly little some areas of aviation had come on since Blériot's time. There was a scary unforeseen consequence of the end of the Cold War: the skies became full of very old, very badly maintained former USSR and Eastern European aeroplanes with coughing engines, the craft also usually full of hard-smoking, coughing passengers – if one of these planes had burst into flames, no one would have noticed; they would have all probably lit another fag from the flames. But, as a bit of light relief, it gave staff at the airport endless entertainment watching these things lurch out of the sky like elderly asthmatic ducks. Once a week, we would get a Balkan Bulgarian Airlines ski flight coming in from Vàrna. The plane was always the same, an old and knackered Tupolev plane that must have been one of the first out of the factory. We were surprised that it didn't have an outside toilet, Roman numerals on the side and a chimney for the engines. It was the kind of aircraft that would make you want to rediscover the joys of train travel.

So, every time the Balkan Bulgarian flight arrived, myself and a few other officers would go out on the tarmac and wait for it. The reason for the rare occasion of a Customs officer stepping outside the channels was twofold. First, the boarding officer had to be there to inspect the weapons in the cockpit. I have no idea why the pilots carried a couple of pistols, locked in a safe, as no hijacker in their right mind would want to hold up this bucket airline – and if they did their first ransom demand would have been to get the plane to a repair shop. There was more chance of it blowing up of its own volition than with a terrorist bomb.

The second reason for the Customs officers gathering outside was the amusement provided by the plane itself. This was still at a time when Stansted Airport was operating from the old terminal and, as such, the passengers had to walk down the stairs that had been physically wheeled out on to the tarmac (nothing motorized here!), and then they had to walk to the terminal. It was hilariously low-tech. But not as low-tech as the Balkan Bulgarian plane.

So it was for the final act of passenger disembarkation that we all gathered to watch. The aircraft was so decrepit and aged that, as passengers disembarked, the plane's hydraulics would start to expand, making the plane rise higher and higher in violent jumps. By the time the plane had jacked itself up to a good three or four feet, it meant that there was a reciprocal three- or four-foot drop from the aircraft to the top of the stairs. And just who was left on the aircraft that had to try to jump this gap to safety? Our patience was paid off every single time.

Now, to state that the hostesses were helpful would be an outright lie. They really did see their passengers in the way that other cabin staff only jokingly refer to them, as SLF – self-loading freight. Their method of off-loading the last passengers was done with a heavy helping hand: the cabin crew escorted them to the exit, like walking the condemned to the gallows. It was a magnificent sight to behold and always drew a healthy and appreciative crowd of airport staff.

The moral of the story: don't go skiing in Eastern Europe, and, if you do, make sure when you are back in England that you get off the plane first.

It wasn't only semi-bankrupt former communist countries that ran big birds made from bent tin through the skies. Switch Air was an American-owned cheap airline, or what they call 'bucket shop'. In this case, that was an insult to the quality of most buckets. Switch Air had one plane, a DC8 Super that had seen better days and the better days it had seen were already millions of miles in the past. Its regular once-a-week flight went between London and Florida and cost just over £100 for a return ticket. Which was about ninety-nine quid too much. It was bloody dire on board and the plane had a frightening history of breaking down. The airline was economical in the extreme. On its first arrival with us, I was on a shift doing plane walk-ons, so I boarded the flight along with our dog-handler Mickey and his mutt Arthur to give the plane and the crew a once-over and to make sure they knew that UK Customs meant business at this airport.

The first thing to hit us was the smell of human waste. It smelled like a Turkish prison lavvy at the height of summer during a violent outbreak of diarrhoea. We quickly learned that it was because all the toilets were overflowing with excrement and urine. In order to save money, the airline had not paid to have its bilges pumped in the States. So between me, the dog and the dog-handler, it was a close-run thing to see who got off the plane first. Because its sense of smell was far more sensitive, the dog won by a nose.

A couple of weeks later, the same aircraft – which we had now christened Turd Airways – came into land in its usual way, descending like a homesick brick. On landing, it somehow managed to blow two of its tyres. It wasn't a simple task to inflate them again because aircraft tyres are filled with nitrogen so that they don't burn and explode with the heat of landing. Now, for some reason, the mad captain (we decided he must be mad to fly this old shed) decided to call for a full emergency evacuation, which was completely unnecessary. We couldn't work out why he'd done it, and decided that he probably just wanted a laugh at the passengers' expense.

So sirens went off everywhere screaming blue murder, and police and fire engines roared out of their sheds with everything flashing – including the crew, still pulling on their pants – and they all sped towards the plane in the expectation of actually getting to use their kit (there's nothing more eager than a bored fireman jump-started by a fire bell).

I happened to be patrolling around at the time in our little boarding car, so when this screaming motorcade of bells and blue lights on red alert sped past I thought that I would mosey on over and take a look. The doors of the DC8 were wide open and I was just in time to see the emergency slides deployed – these are the large plastic inflatable ramps used to slide passengers down to the supposed safety of the runway. I was surprised that this airline even had slides that worked, although, knowing this outfit, they were probably connected to the toilets.

I saw that standing in the doorway was a very heroic-looking passenger, ready to take the lead and be the first to take the escape route to safety. Now, there's a right way and a wrong way to use aeroplane emergency slides – you have to lower yourself to the lip and slide down slowly – but you would probably only know this if you'd been told by the plane's crew. Surprise, surprise, this passenger evidently hadn't been told anything, so he took a massive leap into mid-air and hit the inflated slide right in the middle. All the emergency crews standing by looked at each other, and then quickly looked back, knowing what was coming next. The slide bowed down a good fifteen feet, stretching almost to the tarmac, and then, like a bungee rope at full stretch, it *twanged!* – and shot the poor guy out of the slide with such speed that he rose in the sky like a homesick angel and then landed a good fifty yards away on the bare tarmac. We all winced at the sound of the wet *smack*. He was immediately carted off to hospital with two shattered ankles, making this cheap bucket-airline flight of his an awful lot more costly.

Afterwards, I wondered what it would have looked like if someone had taken a photograph of the scene at that precise moment: an aeroplane with two flat tyres surrounded by emergency vehicles, flashing lights, policemen, firemen, airport staff and Customs officers (one in a buggy) . . . and every single face looking up to the right, into the sky, as if watching a bird. But there is no bird. There is instead a middle-aged man with a wide-open mouth (and no shoes), wondering how he managed to get to an altitude currently higher than that of the plane he flew in on.

But you never have a camera around when you need one, do you?

As Stansted Airport dragged itself into the twenty-first century, there were many things that had to be repaired or replaced to enable it to call itself a modern airport. First, of course, came the new terminal. An amazing piece of modern engineering designed by Sir (now Lord) Norman Foster, who must have been playing with straws or pipe cleaners when he came up with the design. Next on the list was the runway. Although it wasn't the longest in the UK, it had the accolade of being the first UK runway to have a space shuttle land on it in 1983 (albeit a shuttle having a piggy back on a 747 jumbo jet). All runways have to be relaid at some time and the process is quite spectacular, and they are always relaid at night so that the airport can be shut down. The old runway has to be lifted so the new one can be laid and the teams usually manage about thirty feet a night. It doesn't sound very much, but then the runway, believe it or not, is about four foot deep, and it has to be dry and ready for planes by 8 a.m. the next morning. It's one thing for you to leave a cheeky shoeprint in some wet pavement concrete, but a fully laden passenger jet ploughing down into soft tarmac would not be good publicity.

One of the biggest tasks at Stansted was the rebuilding of the fuel farm. The old one was never going to be adequate for the new airport and long-haul aircraft. The whole farm had to be rebuilt with new piping and storage facilities. The stored aviation fuel was kept in what used to be called 'gasometers' and these huge tanks would provide enough internal pressure so that there was little further pumping needed. The rebuild took months and the final stage was to test the whole operation prior to filling the system with Avgas (aviation gasoline). We had received prior notice that on the due date the water was to be turned off for the whole terminal building. This was due to the fact that the gasometers were to be filled with water to check for leaks and to measure pressure through the pipes to the aircraft stands. Pretty simple, you'd think.

The day arrived and most of us turned up at work with bottled water; others would just wait till lunchtime and then fill up with beer. Everything was going tickety-boo. The tanks were filled and the pipes were ready to take the flow. Then Bang! Boom! Boom! Gush! The stopcocks gave up the ghost and exploded, one so violently that it embedded itself in a brick wall. The domestic pipes then took the full pressure, blowing taps off sink basins. Metal junction covers shot into the air and then the whole airport flooded with some pretty disgusting water as the drainage system collapsed. You could say the shit hit the fan . . . and the walls, and the floor, and the ceiling, and just about everything else. The ultimate dirty bomb.

It could not have been more of a hugely successful disaster if it had been planned by some evil Marvel super-villain called Doktor Turdfest – we had a brand spanking new £100 million airport covered in crap. Good job Prince Charles wasn't doing one of his typical hardhat-wearing site visits; I mean, that wouldn't have been at all funny, would it – the future King of England dripping from head to foot in shit? Course it wouldn't. Not funny at all.

It took a further two weeks to dry the airport out and eliminate the smell of human waste, as well as to fix all the domestic piping, screw all the taps back on and hook the toilet seats down from the light fittings.

But whoever came up with the idea to test the pipes first with water rather than aviation gas deserved a pint or two because otherwise there would have just been a great big smoking hole where the airport and its workers used to be.

One of the things about working with large numbers of the general public is that every so often you encounter one who confirms the crudest comic stereotypes of their nation. And so it was on the day when the passengers disembarked from an Irish flight but they didn't disembark into the old tatty Stansted Airport of before but into the totally brand spanking new airport terminal on the other side of the runway . . . which is why myself and the other officers on duty were astounded to overhear, in all seriousness, a passenger say, 'Jesus, you would hardly recognize the old place . . .'

5. Monkeys, Rats, Jockeys and Other Animals

Each United Kingdom airport has a rating as to what creatures can be landed there: during my time in Customs, Heathrow and Gatwick had full tickets and could take anything; Stansted could accept livestock, pet birds and Chelsea supporters (and I should know, I am one). As we had no quarantine facilities, we could not accept dogs, so we became known for our horse and cattle flights.

It's not really widely known among the public but every single day horses fly in and out of the country. How do these animals even *get* a pilot's licence? I hear you ask. Well, actually they're being transported – no, not to the French as burger meat – but mostly as the incredibly expensive, highly strung and unpredictable freight we call racehorses. They're moved all over the world from meet to meet and they travel so often that, believe it or not, they even have their own passports. (I know, again I hear you ask, how on earth do they get them in a passport booth for the photo? Damned if I know, but the buggers are never smiling . . .)

It has even been known for unscrupulous owners to try to move a horse from country to country on a forged horse passport. Which is a bit like people smuggling but with two people involved and one playing the backside. During these horse flights, we would cover the outbound flights to check the passports – 'Have you always worn your hair that long, sir?' – and to ensure that the correct humane killer was being carried. This was an absolute necessity unless you didn't mind the thought of a very strong half-ton of stupid, smelly animal going berserk on an airplane at 30,000 feet. The slightest thing can spook them, let alone the sound and rumble of jet engines. Personally, I'd prefer the lone horse threat to a plane load of drunk Brits coming back from Benidorm, but each to his own flying hell.

It was during these outbound horse-flight checks that I witnessed the unpredictable, brutal side of horses. An eight-year-old chestnut mare had just been loaded on to a Flying Tigers Airways flight to Hong Kong and, as if she knew she was in for a long haul, she was starting to get unhappy. I was starting to get unhappy. Everyone was starting to get unhappy. Luckily for us, the chap who had just sold the horse was still around for us to ask if he could try to calm her down. He'd known the horse from the day she was born, apparently, and they had a very close bond. So, at the request of the aircraft's captain, her former owner and best friend boarded the flight. He certainly looked like he knew what he was doing: he ruffled her mane, stroked her nose, talked softly to her and soon seemed to have her calmed down. He carried on stroking her nose. Then she twisted her head and, taking his right hand in her mouth, she bit down with her chisel teeth and took three of his fingers clean off at the knuckle.

Well, I did say it was lucky for *us* that he was there, not that it was lucky for *him*.

Being so close to the Newmarket racecourse, our airport also catered for the super-rich owners who flew in and out. A few times a year, billionaire oil-rich sheiks would descend in their private luxury Gulfstream jets and we, the lowly uniformed Customs officers (the unclean ones), would board to do a search of the plane. It wasn't so much that we seriously thought these were legitimate targets for drug smuggling – we didn't – but more that we were just a bit nosy. We wanted to see how the other half lived, so we could then report back to the other *other* half and say, 'Blimey, it's even better than we thought! Actually, they *don't* eat kebab-topped pizza like us!'

The bathrooms alone on these jets were small, gaudy palaces in themselves. Never before has so much gold and marble and onyx been employed in the simple task of a man wiping his arse. Or his manservant doing it for him. And there is a strange pleasure to be gained from having hot water running out of a solid gold tap. I guess it's from getting something so ordinary from something so extraordinary. You'd more likely expect it to dispense chilled champagne. Or perhaps Irn Bru. But somehow the water seemed to take on a magical quality. Tap on/tap off . . . smile. Tap on/tap off . . . bigger smile. Yes, little things like this kept us simple people very happy.

I was once on one of these super-luxurious planes of the super-rich when the owner and his entourage arrived back from Newmarket. The sheik invited me to sit down for coffee. He was fascinated by the job of Customs and we sat talking for a good hour. Finally, he leaned forward and, with his hand out, offered me a job as a sky marshal (an armed bodyguard on an aircraft). I was really shocked by the offer of this prestigious and literally high-flying job, so what could I say but . . . no. I hadn't been with Customs for long and I felt like I owed the department greater service. Fool!

The other unpredictable, sometimes nasty things we came across other than the horses were the little devils that rode them – the jockeys. Now, Patrick, our own little Irish short-arse Customs officer, had a pathological hatred of jockeys. Especially those from nearby Newmarket. We never did find out why. But, if it was because of anything like the encounter we were to have with a famous jockey, then it was perfectly understandable. Now, I've got nothing against a dwarf who dresses like a jester and spends his working life bouncing up and down on horses, really I haven't (unlike Patrick – and why *was* that?). But if the guy behaves like an evil little twerp then all bets are off and, even though I'm a six-footer, don't throw a ladder against me and send a jockey up it to tell me to pick on someone my own size. Some of these guys punch way above their height.

The worst by far was a famous jockey named Steve (the name has been changed to protect my life savings). He really was – and was well known for being – a total shit. Or, to give him his full title, as we called him, the World's Shortest,

Biggest Bastard. He had his own driver and a very large Mercedes limo that one day we found parked up in our staff-only car park. We approached the driver. He was a really nice bloke and he explained that, if he parked in the expensive short-stay car park, his boss, the millionaire Steve, made him pay all the charges. In fact, he had to pay all the parking charges at all the race grounds and airports, and Mr Little Big Jockey would never recompense him. Over a couple of crafty fags, he told us more.

He said that his boss, Steve, made it a rule that any hitch-hiker had to be picked up. Not bad, I thought, maybe I'd misjudged him. But, the driver went on, the hitch-hiker was made to sit in the front, was not spoken to by Steve and, after driving for a while, the driver would be instructed to head for the next petrol station. The Merc would be filled up and the hitch-hiker then told to pay for the fuel or face the wrath, threats and tantrums of the world-famous jockey – not to mention being kicked out of the car. The driver hated himself for putting up with all this crap and for needing the job, but not as much as we now hated Steve. More stories followed of his appallingly aggressive behaviour to others. He really was a nasty piece of work. The fact that he was an undisputedly great jockey in no way excused him being a total arse. It just allowed him to get away with it. Well, we thought, not on our patch, shorty.

Two weeks later, on his way back from a meet in France, Steve came through Customs. Oh, happy day! With exquisite coincidence, it was Patrick, our own softly spoken, jockey-hating, little Irish bloodhound, who had the pleasure of exacting the revenge. Pat immediately buried himself in Steve's suitcase, burrowing in like a mole and throwing clothes and underwear every which way. With his little legs practically kicking out of the case and his head muffled by clothing, we could just about hear Pat's gentle Irish lilt saying, 'No, no, nooo . . . can't find it . . . nope. . . seems *not* to be here!'

Steve, twitching with outrage and embarrassment, launched into a foul-mouthed tirade at Pat, but our Pat simply carried on with the search, more clothes flying out of the case as though it was being ransacked by a hungry badger. Steve finally snapped, 'Don't you know who the fuck I am?!'

At this, Pat stopped dead, looked down at the bag and the clothes, which were now spread all over the floor and the examination bench, looked back up at Steve and smiled enigmatically. Then he turned, walked over to our office, whose door was open, and shouted in, 'Has anyone here heard of some jockey shithead by der name o' Steve Trimmer?'

He was greeted by howls of laughter from all the staff within the office and cheers and applause from passengers without.

Pat walked calmly back to the bench.

'I'm terribly sorry, Sir, der answer is "No"!' And with that he disappeared back into the suitcase. Then, with a nice piece of sleight of hand, Pat re-emerged from the bag with a loud 'Ah ha!' and held aloft an envelope in his hand. We all now appeared from the office and, with the passengers, made a sizable audience. We genuinely didn't know what ole Pat was planning here. Even Steve stopped in the middle of his stream of verbal abuse.

Pat ripped open the envelope and from inside produced a sheet of folded A4 paper. We all looked at each other. He unfolded the sheet and on it, for all to see, were large letters spelling 'I AM STEVE AND I REALLY AM A SHITHEAD!' That was for all the 'little' guys who had for many years been shat on by one of the world's shortest, biggest bastards.

We left Steve to pack his own bag and scurry away. Not one of his best performances. You could say he fell at the first.

Sometimes animals even attempted to enter the country of their own volition, without human help. An Omega Air flight from Nigeria was a good example. Even though the flight was from Nigeria – one of the number-one target countries in the world because of the amount of illegal seizures – not many officers wanted to enter the hell that was this African aircraft's cargo flight hold. Many of us would quite happily wait until the aircraft had unloaded before going anywhere near it. It was on such an occasion that I sat in the boarding car and watched an Omega aircraft being emptied. But about halfway through the unloading we heard a scream from the interior of the craft and two cargo men came barrelling out the rear of the Hercules aeroplane. I quickly stood up and stopped one of them to ask what was up.

'*Fucking* enormous rat, Jon, is what's up,' he said. 'At first, I swear, I thought it was a small dog.' Apparently, this 'king of rats' had actually attempted to attack them as they searched the hold.

Within minutes, the whole aircraft had been abandoned, even the Nigerian crew quickly bailed out. The airport police were notified, as were a couple of chaps from the

Environmental Agency. They all arrived minutes later in a flurry of flashing blue lights and screaming sirens, which I thought was a bit over the top, but the rat must have been pretty impressed. So here was the situation: we had an abandoned Nigerian cargo Hercules aircraft with one very angry resident rat, six police officers (two of which, believe it or not, were armed with Heckler & Koch MP5 automatic rifles), two environmental health officers (who didn't want to get out of the car) and little ole me. So we had the police with their Kochs out and health officers who wouldn't even *get* out.

There was an emergency runway meeting in which we all put forward potential solutions. The armed police decided on the initial action to take place. Their idea was a simple but effective one, I thought: to blow the rat into kebabs with the aid of their rifles. And it did seem a shame not to make use of them. So they duly cocked their weapons and strode purposefully towards the rear ramp of the plane. But I suddenly realized what the now obvious error was with this plan; so I ran after them and managed to stop them before they entered the plane's hold. I explained that firing live ammunition within the confines of a high-altitude aircraft was perhaps not the smartest idea that had ever been had – the chance of an unlucky ricochet, for one thing, was too great, as was the possibility of causing some unknown damage to the aircraft. This seemed to piss them off somewhat. 'OK, smart arse,' one of them said, 'you come up with a better idea!'

I thought for a second and then walked over to the police Land Rover, reached in and took a large spade from inside. Trying not to look too afraid – which would have been easier carrying one of their guns rather than a police-issue garden implement – I disappeared into the rear of the Hercules. Everything got very dark, very quickly. I waited for my eyes to adjust. By following the sound of it, I quite quickly found it – it was what the African crew would have called a 'bush cutter' but what one of us had already quite accurately described as a fucking enormous rat. It was hiding behind two large cargo pallets. I took a deep breath, tried not to gag on the disgusting stench in there, and luckily managed to hit it with the first swing of the spade. I don't know if rats can get into heaven but this one would've had to knock twice because the spade had split it in two.

It was with a feeling of small victory that I walked back down the ramp into the sunlight and out to the tarmac and passed the shovel, with the last remains of The Beast of Flight OA-172 on the scoop, back to the police officers. They turned a little green at the sight of it, which, I have to admit, was understandable. The officers looked at each other, then the spade, then me. One of them said I was a mad dog for going in the plane like that – and the nickname stuck: Mad Dog was what I had to live with for quite a while.

Animals (and their riders) weren't always there just to give us trouble. Sometimes we actually used them in our duty. Drugs dogs, for example, were a vital tool. The two we had at the airport were both legendary – Finn and the afore-mentioned Arthur. Finn looked like a giant, mean poodle but was actually an Irish water spaniel and was as tough as a gypsy bare-knuckle fighter. He also had a smell that could KO you in the first round; true to his breed's name, he loved water, any water, no matter how filthy, and took to flinging himself in it whenever he could. And, if it wasn't water, then it would be shit that he was rolling himself around in or the rotting carcass of a dead animal. What made it more unbearable was that over the years his handler, John, had become immune to the smell, so he'd appear for duty with slavering, stinking Finn and wonder why we all jumped out the windows.

Arthur, on the other hand, was . . . worse. He was a German short-haired pointer with a large snout and a docked tail that, for some reason, was bald and pink, so it just looked like an erect, waggling penis. He also had his breed's trait for 'scenting', meaning that every night Arthur would take a dump in his kennel, then take his beanbag bed in his mouth and wipe it around all the walls, before falling contentedly to sleep. His poor handler had to hose it out very day, with Arthur sat behind him with a kind of dopey, doggy smile on his face.

Arthur had a great nose attached to very large jaws full of very large and sharp teeth. He'd started his life as an RAF explosives dog until they discovered that he had Jaws of Death and would rip open a suitcase with one bite, snap up the offending target item and then shake the crap out of it – not good in an explosive-seeking situation as both dog and handler could quickly end up as a mixed kebab. So he was put on the doggy transfer list – or, as we liked to think of it, a promotion – and moved to HM Customs, where I had the pleasure of watching him rip open suitcases with a single, savage bite. I even got to see those big teeth closer than I ever would have really liked.

One summer afternoon, I was behind the baggage hall waiting for the Jamaica flight bags to arrive. Arthur and his handler Mickey soon appeared as this flight was a good hit for cocaine and cannabis. Mick pointed to some Paris bags that had just arrived. 'Do you mind if I warm Arthur up on those bags before the Jamaica flight arrives?'

'Go ahead,' I said – watching a drugs dog do its stuff is amazing, and they didn't come any better or bigger than Arthur.

'OK. And can you pop this in your pocket while I go get the beast out of the van?' he said and handed me one of the dog's training aids, a small plastic tube containing a rag scented with cannabis. I put it into my pocket and wandered over to the belt as the Jamaica bags started to trundle through. As I watched all the bags being lined up for Arthur's sniff test, I saw Mickey walking over with a strange smile on his face. 'Whatever you do,' he said, 'don't make any fast movements.'

I looked down and saw Arthur, jaws open, inches away from my crotch. Mickey grabbed him just as the dog was about to lunge at my lunchbox and make a messy meal out of it. Even from the other side of the loading bay, he had caught a whiff of the training aid and he was determined to get to it whether my balls were in the way or not.

In the end, it was not Arthur who got them both into trouble but Mickey. One day, he boarded a Korean Airlines jumbo jet with the dog and jokingly announced that the take-away they'd ordered had arrived. Oops.

* * *

We had more than a few good officers at the airport. Mark was a cracking officer. He seemed naturally to have as strong a nose for smuggled gear as either Finn or Arthur. He had been in uniform for twenty years and he took me under his gold-braided wing. He was a real officer's officer with more airport drugs seizures than he could remember and a stack of commendations up to his chin.

Once when a flight from Ghana arrived, Mark decided to give it his once-over. Many people think that we have radar for smugglers, and in some cases it's true (and it serves us well to have people think that), but Mark genuinely did have sensitively twitching and very accurate antennae. So, while most of us had pulled passengers aside who looked good for carrying drugs, I noticed that Mark had pulled a Ghanaian businessman in a suit with an attaché case and Crombie overcoat. Mark had a short chat with him and the passenger placed his case on the examination bench. I was right next to them, so I could hear the exchange.

'So, Mr Apeezy,' Mark smiled, 'you have nothing to declare today? You're not smuggling anything?'

Mr Apeezy was quite loud, but friendly, in his denial. 'No, no, no, sir. I *never* smuggle. It is against my God.'

I saw Mark smile his lopsided smile and his brows draw-bridge in sympathy, as if to say, 'I *see*.' We all knew what this meant: another Mark seizure about to be made. But what could it be? He hadn't even opened the suitcase yet. Mark sighed with the kind of weary resignation that comes from over twenty years of having to politely listen to people lying through their teeth to you.

'Mr Apeezy, I am arresting you for the attempted importation of what I assume is . . .' Mark raised an eyebrow and cocked his head '. . . a *monkey* of some kind?'

Mr Apeezy's demeanour changed rapidly and he suddenly screamed, 'But how do you know this?'

'It's really quite simple, sir,' said Mark levelly. 'For the last thirty seconds, your Crombie has been making its own way to the exit door. I'm afraid you're nicked.'

We all swivelled our heads as one and saw that Mark was right – one Crombie going walkabout. It turned out that Mr Apeezy was a monkey smuggler. He had drugged the monkey and then sewn it into the lining of his overcoat for the duration of the flight. Unluckily for him, it had awoken in the airport and – the inside of an overcoat not being its natural habitat – it had very understandably made a bid for freedom.

When we later congratulated Mark on a good job, he just shrugged. 'It was easy really: as he was coming from the baggage belt, I couldn't help but notice that his Crombie was having a piss . . .'

6. *Beware the Boys in the Black and Gold*

I hate you, you hate me – let's get this over with.

You could sometimes get the idea that the line above summed up the Customs officer and the passenger attitude towards each other. There's a natural antipathy between the two that goes both ways, bred from the demands of the job. But, when you approach the dreaded blue/red/green declare/nothing-to-declare channels, it's not so much a gauntlet of hate that you have to run, but a gauntlet of immense suspicion. And if there's an 'Us and Them' situation it is only between Customs as the Us and smugglers as the Them. Officers don't want to waste their time or yours by stopping and searching someone who is bringing nothing more into the country than the tan-lines from their flip-flops. That just helps the ones that should be searched to get through.

In the 1,500 years of Customs' existence many strange items of interest have passed into the sphere of Customs' control. One of the major times for new smuggling legislation was during the Napoleonic Wars. The catalyst behind this golden age of smuggling was ole shorty himself – Napoleon. He identified that, as an island nation, Britain's economy leaned heavily on import and export tax because of our reliance on tax from a huge list of goods such as booze and tobacco but also such things as playing cards, cloth, lace and anything else you could think of. So, Napoleon cleverly reasoned, if he could flood certain markets with untaxed goods, he could damage the English treasury. I could almost suggest that this was one of the first occasions of direct economic warfare.

The French set up warehouses in their Channel ports to supply the 'free traders' with everything they needed, from barrels of booze to playing cards. At the start of the war, the drink issued on British naval ships was brandy (a French-produced spirit). The British government identified the potential supply problems and so replaced the 'brandy tot' with rum, which became the sailors' tipple. It was unpopular to start with but tastes soon changed. Another advantage of switching to rum was that it was produced within the grow-ing British Empire. Kipling, the author and not the cake maker, penned a whole poem on the subject called 'A Smuggler's Song': 'Five and twenty ponies/Trotting through the dark –/Brandy for the Parson, 'Baccy for the Clerk/Them that asks no questions isn't told a lie –/Watch the wall my darling while the Gentlemen go by!'

Since then, it's been the job of Customs officers to *not* watch the wall as the smugglers go by. And in one of those strange historical eccentricities of British law, ten-oared boats are still illegal in this country, believe it or not. It's because Napoleon's shipwrights invented smuggler cutter ships that could turn into the wind and use their ten oars to make their escape. And, at this time in history, Customs and Excise officers were heavily armed and also operated armed revenue cutters. In fact, it was the Excise men that ran the press gangs on behalf of the Navy.

Until recently, many of the prohibitions from these days still existed, such as bringing in foreign prison-made goods, badger-haired shaving brushes or Napoleonic coinage – not that there was really any need for them still to be banned; we weren't exactly overrun with badger-haired shaving-brush smuggling operations. As far as concealments went, sailors used to weave tobacco into ships' ropes and bottles of brandy would be hidden in barrels of the ship's tar. And just to prove that some things never go out of fashion – in both crime and detection – almost 200 years later I would be finding 10 kg of cocaine within 200 yards of climbing rope, and packs of drugs hidden in barrels of bitumen. Funny how the modern smugglers think they are up to something new!

One strange Customs law that still exists is one that I came across on duty when I stopped and searched a perfectly respectable-looking gentleman for no reason other than I had a feeling and, as it happened, the feeling turned out to be right. Though I wasn't at all expecting to find what I did: when I opened his suitcase I saw that it was completely full of human hair, long strands of it bundled together. Now he wasn't some kind of strange hair fetishist that was sneaking up behind women and snipping off bits of their hair: he was actually a wig maker. His trade, he said, was with the Jewish community in north London. His problem, though, was that he had attempted to avoid paying tax on the stuff and had tried to make it through the 'nothing-to-declare' green channel. But we now had him by a different kind of hair – the short and curlies. The duty and tax on hair is higher than that on gold.

Between Stansted, Gatwick and Heathrow airports, I'd see a wide selection of passengers from all walks of life – and some of those walks were pretty funny (you try walking normally with half a kilo of drugs up your jacksy) – and I also worked with fellow Customs officers who were just as varied. Most of them were perfectly normal, ordinary fellas. But don't panic, I'll tell you about the other ones instead.

Terry was a strange one, and how he ever got into the uniform branch I shall never know. Because Terry's particular affliction was that he couldn't talk to strangers. Now that's a little bit of a drawback when your job, essentially, is spending all day long stopping, searching and talking to strangers. I suppose if Terry could have just searched passengers that he *knew* then he would have been OK – but then he wouldn't have had any friends left!

It wasn't that he didn't want to talk to people: it was that he really couldn't do it. So the ideal position was found for him as the keeper at the airport's Queen's Warehouse, which, contrary to popular opinion, was not a storage facility for Elton John's wardrobe. He did the job very well because all he had to talk to all day was himself, the warehouse boxes and the officers he knew. I liked him for the fact that he made the senior officers see red as he always looked like a complete and utter bag of shit. His uniform was always clean but he flatly refused to iron it . . . flat. His excuse was that he didn't get paid to iron his uniform, though he did get a tax allowance for cleaning it.

Another officer, jockey-hating Patrick from the south of Ireland, was usually an absolute gentleman in every way. He was only about five foot four yet had nerves of steel. He didn't panic or back away from danger at all. One day, a massive Swedish bodybuilder threw a steroid strop in the airport over some minor inconvenience and physically lifted his whole baggage trolley – complete with suitcases – up over his head and threatened to drop it on Patrick. It would have tonked little Pat into the ground like a tent peg. But, before we could get around the benches and rugby tackle the big Swede, Patrick had gone into his sweetly smiling routine.

'Now stop it, yer big focker. If you pulled out your ole fella and it was bigger than mine then I may get a bit worried. *OK*?'

The Swede stopped, cracked up laughing and slowly lowered the trolley down. (We later heard that he went on to become a top contender in the World's Strongest Man. The Swede, that is, not Patrick. Patrick just went on to *eat* a swede . . . in the canteen.)

During his allocated annual break, Patrick decided to take his wife to Rhodes on a surprise holiday. It was a surprise to us as well as we didn't even realize that he was married. So we decided to pull a prank on his return. Two weeks later, his flight touched down back in England – and at our airport. Bit of a mistake. Pat had forgotten our golden rule – never fly into the airport at which you also work.

Three of us uniformed officers identified Patrick's large suitcase behind the scenes of the baggage belt. I picked the lock and the other two emptied all of Pat and his wife's clothes into a large bag. The clothes were then replaced with a large concrete paving slab, so big that it took all three of us, grunting, to heave the bag back on to the baggage carousel. Then we rushed round and stood at the end of the channels. We could see Patrick and his wife, and he gave us a courteous nod as we attempted to do the professional thing and ignore him. Pat then started doing the Baggage Carousel Unlucky Fucker Look – that is, like everyone else, standing there like a lemon, peering at the belt, wondering why on earth your bag always comes out bloody last. But, when the bags started to appear, it was only then that we noticed there was a problem – another bag, *identical* to Patrick's, was also on the belt. A senior officer, in on the whole thing, sidled up to me and the eight other uniformed officers who were lined up for the floor show and, without taking his eyes off the belt, he whispered, '*Please* tell me that you got the right bag . . .'

Luckily, we had identified it not just by how it looked but also by the name and baggage tag number. Pat looked at the tag of the first one and let it pass; it disappeared around the belt and he waited for the one that he now knew was his to reach him. But, as he started to move to grab it, he was suddenly brushed aside by a very annoyed old lady.

'Excuse *me*, young man, that's *mine*!' She had obviously missed the appearance of the first suitcase and was convinced that this one was hers – and, with the determination and sharp elbows of a jumble-sale veteran (and former rugby player, from the looks of things), she made a grab for it with one hand while fending off Pat with the other. Her vice-like grip on the handle was impressive but the staying power of an eighty-pound slab of concrete meant it was not for moving. So, in quick succession: the lady pulled – the bag stood still – the lady heaved – the bag stood still – the belt moved around – the lady clung on, fell over, gave a little yelp and then got dragged along the shiny floor on her backside, knocking over passengers like bowling pins as she held on tightly for dear life. Pat slowly turned to look at us, eyes wide, smiling, with that *you-cheeky-cheeky-fockers* look on his face. But all he saw was the retreating backs and shaking shoulders of ten black uniforms as we all fled back to the channels, crying with laughter. We could still hear the little yelps and cries for help as we slid away.

Why she didn't let go of the bag, I'll never know, but that part of the airport floor around the baggage carousel got a bloody good polish.

An officer whom, unfortunately, we didn't get to play that trick on was Richard. Even we, his fellow Customs officers, hated him, so God knows what everyone else thought of him. He was the world's most perfect example of why 'Richard' should sometimes be shortened to 'Dick'. And he was another one that we were surprised to find had a wife, but simply because we couldn't fathom how he'd got another human being to stand him long enough to make it up the aisle. We thought a stun gun must have been involved.

He arrived at the airport as an experienced senior officer but, from day one, he started making enemies. One of his first official acts was the implementation of the red line in our duty-log signing-in book. The two day shifts started at seven and eight o'clock. At seven o'clock, Richard appeared with a ruler and red pen and proceeded to draw a red line in the book, meaning that any one arriving a minute late would have to sign in under the line. He did the same for the eight o'clock shift. Not a good way to make friends with new colleagues.

He carried on not making friends as if it was a sport. Patrick pulled over a young lad who had arrived from Amsterdam. A baggage search revealed that cigarettes weren't the only thing that he'd been smoking in the Netherlands. Patrick needed the agreement of a senior officer to carry out a further search. Unfortunately, the senior officer was Richard. Pat explained to him why he wanted the search, and, without a moment's hesitation, Richard replied, 'Well, search him!' Now, that wasn't the type of people we were: we didn't distrust anyone, we distrusted *everyone* – equally. So Patrick immediately turned on his heel, returned to the young lad and said, 'Right. Don't do drugs! Now bugger off!' He didn't even search him; it was his way of trying to redress the balance. It didn't take long for word to get around about Richard's little outburst. His hate rating increased but he seemed to enjoy it even more.

We did some research and found out that he had a history of being about as popular as a turd in a swimming pool (on his good days, he moved up to being as popular as a fart in a spacesuit). He had attempted to join the Investigation Division. The ID was strict when it came to your first six months' service. If you didn't shine, you were returned to your original post. Richard started rubbing people up the wrong way from the beginning. But they had their own ways of dealing with his type. He was sent on a solo mission to Dover. His instructions: to identify a white Mini (registration not known) that belonged to a known criminal (name not given) arriving on a ferry (which one not known) from France. Richard's job was to follow it to its final destination in the UK. Easy job, but what Richard didn't know was that the operation didn't exist.

His first white Mini took him into Wales, but when he contacted the senior officer with the address he was told, 'No, that's not our man. Back to Dover!' So he returned. The next white Mini took him to Manchester, and he received the same answer from the senior officer. The third white Mini took him to Newcastle, the fourth to Birmingham and the fifth to Cornwall. He was on the road for a total of six days before it dawned on him that this operation was a 'sickener' – a job invented to crack him. It worked; he drove back to London and requested a transfer. Good for ID, bad for us.

After three months, we'd had enough of him. We could do nothing right in his eyes. He would tear up official paperwork if it was written in blue ink rather than black and banned officers from bringing in any food that smelled too much. We knew he had to go when we realized he was so bad that he'd even give Customs officers a bad name.

Our get-rid offensive started simply but effectively. We'd had brand-new lockers delivered. Richard had spent quite a lot of departmental money on them. Compared to what we'd had before – which were like school gym lockers – these were state of the art. But within a few days, as is always the way, officers started individualizing their own lockers with name tags, pictures and small stickers. Richard went ballistic. He got the poor old office manager to remove all the stickers and tags while he himself pinned up an official notice that contained enough exclamation marks to crucify Christ: 'PLEASE NOTE!! – The placing of name tags or stickers on the official lockers is banned!! It will be seen as defacing official government property!! The perpetrators will be reprimanded!!'

All through the day and night, officers made themselves busy bringing stuff from home, scrounging stuff from the airlines and airport shops, etc. The following morning, Richard arrived to witness the handiwork of myself and all my colleagues: every single locker had disappeared – hidden under thousands of tags, stickers, pictures, photos and signs of every kind. Two lockers were even fully wrapped in Christmas paper with giant ribbons and bows. It was the first of many pranks. Richard was on his way within the month but he did have the final say. He gave all the officers that worked under him the lowest possible ratings on their annual reports (black marks that could never be removed, affected your promotion chances and prevented a pay rise). Thanks, Dick.

I'd become justly proud of the officers of HM Customs. It was as rare as rocking-horse doo to find a genuine 'bad un'. But we had one at the airport called Chaz. He was my reporting officer for a short while and I knew that the senior officers hoped that I'd lose my temper and wipe his clock clean. He was also, among others things, a meat burglar.

We were very hot on the importation of all food types, especially meat, with its potential for disease. Ireland was a major source country for the bulk of meat seizures. The Irish were very proud of their produce and rightly so, but the meat ban covered all countries and all meats from dried chimpanzee in a Nigerian suitcase (not an unusual find) to a pound of sausages in a carrier bag from the Emerald Isle. And to stop us seizing their purchases, passengers sometimes even ate their meat, raw, right in front of us. Which wasn't too bad for the passenger if it was a fillet steak but it was quite a sight if it was three pounds of black pudding. We tended to just stand back out of curiosity and see what would happen. You haven't lived until you've seen a Scotsman so desperate to get his money's worth that he tries to stuff a whole haggis in his gob at once.

Having seized the offending food, we would place it in a giant chest freezer that would be cleared out by a little man from the Ministry of Agriculture, Fisheries and Food (MAFF). The white MAFF van arrived at the same time, same day, every week, so it wasn't too difficult for Chaz to time his pilfering. Nobody really checked the weights as we passed the food over to the MAFF man so Chaz had it made. A pound of steak here and a couple of kilos of sausages there. Until, that is, he got a touch too greedy and spotted a huge great ham that had been seized from a Spanish passenger. Now these hams were very popular in Spain (you may have seen them hanging in bars) and are very expensive. But Christmas was two weeks away and Chaz decided to add the ham to his meaty Christmas list.

He hung on until his late shift, which occurred the day before the arrival of the MAFF van. He then waited until there was a flight in and we were busy screening passengers. He grabbed the ham and a few kilos of assorted meaty treats and snuck out of the office into the airside car that we had parked out the back. He then drove the short distance to the edge of airside area, near to where his own car was parked the other side of a wall. His next job was to throw the stolen booty over the wall – only his meat heaving was met by a thump and a loud scream. Spooked, Chaz jumped into the car and sped back to the office. An hour later, we were visited by the local police. It appeared that a member of the public was returning to their car when they were badly assaulted by a large flying ham joint and lassoed by several strings of pork sausages. It was so lucky for Chaz that he had taken the meat out of the Customs seizure bags and put it into plain carriers. Still, it did prove that pigs really could fly . . . but also that they came down to earth pretty sharpish, too.

The police never made the link to our office, but the person who did notice something was the MAFF chap. After Chaz stopped his antics, he commented to our senior officer that our meat seizures must have shot through the roof as he seemed to be picking up more food than ever from our seizure freezer!

So Chaz could not go unpunished for our silence. He was an old revenue officer of the type that we would refer to as a Waterguard man ('Waterguard' being the term used for preventive Customs officers from the mid-1800s until 1970). Whenever he was duty officer, he always kept an eye on the TV monitor that covered the baggage area, and the second he spotted a single passenger he would start shouting at us to get in the channels as he dashed out of the office with his little pigeon-toed run. So, knowing this, during the week we had the opportunity to video the passengers arriving on a Toronto flight. This was a jumbo-jet load and, as such, completely filled our baggage hall. We then waited a few days until Chaz was the duty officer on a late shift and one night we put the video of the incoming flood of Toronto passengers through the CCTV system just five minutes before his clocking-off time. We had no flights due until 6 a.m. the following day. Chaz looked up at the monitors, saw the apparent crowds piling through, did a quick double-take at the sight, and was then off shouting and running for the channels. Two minutes later, once he was inside, we made sure the channels were locked up nice and secure until the next flight at 6 a.m. As we headed home, we could just hear a little voice crying out, 'Hello? Is anybody there? I seem to be locked in.'

Almost every port or airport had one officer that the rest of the staff would regard as a mascot. They were often the officer that had the Midas touch with smugglers. At our airport the mascot was Harry. He was originally from the West Indies and was built like a weightlifter, although he was only about five foot two – so, stood next to me at over six foot, we did look a bit comical, like Danny DeVito and Arnold Schwarzenegger in *Twins*. Some of the height disparity was made up for by Harry's one-foot-high Jackson 5 afro hairstyle. One morning, though, when he returned from a two-week holiday, we were all really shocked to see that Harry was totally bald: he'd gone mad with the hair clippers and reduced his height by about 20 per cent.

Harry was such a well-liked feature that regular travellers

often stopped to say hello to him; he was as much a part of the airport as the duty-free shops. But his personable nature hid his speciality – sweet-talking the truth out of unsuspecting passengers. One day a woman swept brazenly through the green channel wearing what was obviously a very expensive fur coat – difficult to prove it was a purchase if we didn't find a receipt. But, before we could say anything, Harry ran after the woman and as he neared her he started saying what a beautiful coat it was and how it really suited her and that it must have cost a fortune. The woman turned, smiling, saying that it had cost nearly £3,000 and that she'd bought it on holiday in the States. Harry's smile didn't drop, but hers did when he put his hand on her shoulder.

One day, Harry had gathered all the new officers around a baggage bench in the green channel. His morning lecture, between flights, was the identification of real and fake Rolex watches. We were all ears – this was a popular subject as there had been a number of seizures over the previous month of fake Rolexes, which because of their value were always a popular target.

Harry started his demo by first producing a Rolex and passing it around so that we could all have a good look. Unless you had seen a real Rolex, you would be hard pushed to tell the difference. Next, he produced a brown paper bag into which he placed the watch. The bag was then placed on the baggage bench and we were instructed to stand back. Harry now reached under the bench and produced a club hammer, with which he enthusiastically went to work on the bag and the watch inside. A few seconds of vigorous hammering later and the only thing in one piece was the hammer. Harry emptied what was left of the watch out of what was left of the bag. The bench was sprinkled with little cogs and wheels, tiny screws and glass. We all stood open-mouthed. Harry smiled and said, 'And if by now the passenger is in tears . . . then, gentlemen, it was definitely a real Rolex.' And with that he turned and walked back into the office.

It was easily the best demonstration I had ever seen.

On the basis that even a broken clock is right twice a day, an officer of ours called Alan was allowed to carry on working. Though he had got too out of control to continue working in the channels; he was just too mad to be let loose on the general public anymore: his temper had become clingfilm thin and he didn't really bother about his appearance. Something had to be done about him so our surveyor (the head of airport Customs) took the bold step and made him a Queen's Warehouse officer. This was a very responsible job, looking after all the seized goods such as money, drugs, etc. The question remained as to whether he was the right man for it.

Our question was answered a fortnight later when I found him slumped in the corner of the Queen's Warehouse. He was on the floor, out cold and with a stun gun in his hand. He came round slowly, peered at me and Pat through his thick bottle-bottom glasses and stammered, 'I . . . I don't know what all the trouble's about . . . I only . . .' and then fainted again. It turned out that out of idle curiosity he had shocked himself with the stun gun, just to see what it felt like, y'know, to piss and shit his pants. As you do. When you're not well.

On top of trying to destroy his own nervous system, one

of Alan's actual official duties was to destroy certain seized items such as fake watches, plants and booze when he was given permission to do so by the London Queen's Warehouse. So, one afternoon, he was doing just that when he suddenly ran from the warehouse screaming loudly and clutching his face. He had been ordered to destroy a number of red-pepper gas canisters. The standard operating procedure (SOP) on these was to incinerate them but Alan had a better idea. He decided to empty all the gas bottles underwater. Bad idea. The gas, like any gas, is somewhat lighter than water and so tends to bubble up and enter the air. Alan was on his third cylinder before the gas hit. It enveloped poor Alan and he had to be rushed straight to hospital. It took three days to clear the gas out of the contaminated warehouse. I suppose we should have just been thankful he hadn't decided to jolt himself in the naked arse with the stun gun at the same time or the whole bloody place could have gone up. Picture the headline: 'QUEEN'S WAREHOUSE BURNS IN CUSTOMS OFFICER ARSE SHOCKER!'

The one thing that surprised me most of all when I joined the uniformed service was the amount of drinking that went on. For some reason, rum was a favourite with preventers – perhaps in historical homage to the British consumption of rum during the Napoleonic Wars – but the rum was taken only after copious amounts of beer had already been ingested. We couldn't claim we were drinking for medicinal purposes because no one has ever been *that* ill. There were lunchtime drinking clubs and evening drinking clubs, depending which shift you were on. The worst of the lot was the night shift.

With few flights after nine o'clock, the team would start the proceedings with a takeaway curry and then the booze would flow. Sleep for a few hours followed, before the arrival of the first flights at six in the morning.

Simon was one of our hardened drinkers. He drove a bloody enormous Jag (courtesy of his rich wife) and, because he lived only a few miles from the airport, drink-driving was nothing new to him. His route home was a well-known 'rat run' that the police seldom, if ever, patrolled. One October afternoon, the airport became fog-bound. Checks with the Met Office revealed that the fog was due to stay with us for the next twelve hours. So, for Simon, there was nothing for it but to hit the airport bar for a few starters followed by the airport staff club for main course followed by a short trip back to our office for a few Scotches as dessert. A three-course extended liquid lunch during which no food was consumed at all.

By the end of his shift, he was ratted but still walking. One officer did remonstrate with him about driving home but Simon flicked him the V-sign and headed off to his Jag. All was fine on the drive home until he reached a little village halfway there. In his later explanation to us, he said that he hit a right-hand bend just a touch too fast, left the road, skidded on the wet grass and slammed into a telephone box, which had jumped out at him from the thick fog. The car was working fine and he got home without further incident. The phone box, on the other hand, was severely wounded and later died of injuries received. Simon got into his bed and reflected on how lucky he had been.

Seven o'clock the following morning saw him being rudely

awoken by a hammering on his front door. On opening the door, Simon was faced with two very serious police officers asking if he knew anything about the severe damage to a local telephone box. Simon stated clearly that he had finished his shift at the airport late that night and had driven home very carefully because of the thick fog. As far as he was aware, the phone box was in one piece when he passed it. The older of the two officers said, 'Well, sir, can you explain this?' and produced Simon's front number plate, which had been found embedded in the carcass of the phone box. As this was before the high-tech drink-driving kit with its ability to do a 'count back' and calculate earlier inebriation levels, Simon escaped with 'driving without due care' and 'leaving the site of an accident'. But the repairs to the Jag cost three grand and it was another two to replace the telephone box.

At the end of the year, Christmas was always another good time for officers to let their hair down. Although the drinking culture was very strong among Customs officers – even putting the Army to shame – it wasn't often during the year that we would have the opportunity to all have a drink together because of different shifts. But at Christmas there were numerous parties around the airport courtesy of the airlines, police, Immigration, etc. And all these parties were very heavy-drinking affairs: you were either an alcoholic, a trainee alcoholic or a teetotaller – there was no middle ground. And if there had been a middle ground it would have all been covered in empty bottles anyway . . .

This one Christmas, we had five new officers and they all believed that they were good, hard drinkers. The trouble was that we already had a lot more barrels of experience over them. At about 4 a.m., we were woken from our drunken slumber by the sound of the baggage alarm going off and the baggage carousel belt being started. Two of us donned our uniforms and wandered out to see if an unexpected, unannounced flight had arrived. The scene that awaited us was peculiar in the extreme. Three of the new officers were lying drunkenly comatose on the baggage belt and the other two were attempting to start it. Having got it running, their next idea was to open the baggage-belt security doors. I have to admit we found it quite funny to see the three sleeping officers slowly making their way around the baggage hall, then disappearing on the belt outside into the rain and reappearing some seconds later still on the carousel and soaked to the skin. It was like a little human car wash. The two joker officers then thought that it was a good idea to use the belt's security doors like a guillotine and try to bring them down on one of the sleeping beauties. I realized that once the mechanism was started it had to carry out a full closure and so would decapitate anyone underneath it.

We were about to put a stop to it when we heard a cough behind us and there stood the duty senior officer. Now this, I knew, could put a lot of painful flames up Santa's chimney. But he looked at the scene with a sage eye, shrugged and said, 'Bloody idiots.' And then he escorted myself and Pat back into his office, where we helped him demolish the best part of a litre of rum.

Outside, the carousel of comatose Customs officers kept on turning, as did the rest of the world.

7. *Shooting the Queen's Corgis*

Death by rabies is a nasty way to go: inflammation of the brain, hallucinations, high fever and frothing at the mouth – it's not a good look. There's no known cure and it has the highest death rate of any viral infection; to date, there has only ever been one reported case of someone surviving an infection. Only Ebola rivals it as a nasty way to go, and that's only because that might lead to you exploding blood out of every orifice. Take your pick. But, either way, keep away from me and my sandwiches.

Rabies is spread mostly by dogs and vermin (and also known to be carried by bats). But the UK is one of the few safe, rabies-free European countries. We've been safe here for many years and we have stood as one of the only countries in Europe not to have this terrible killer. Thanks to Customs. Despite years of animal lovers having a go at us for the quarantine rules, we are Dickensian-strict about rabies law. Little frothy-mouthed, potentially rabies-infected Fluffy was not getting in on my watch or that of any other officer.

I was airport duty officer for the night and it was very quiet. You could hear a fruit fly fart on cotton. My senior officer was off sick and I was the only one left to guard the country – or at least the Stansted entry to the country. It was due to be a quiet night shift with only a couple of freight flights and no passenger jets. Time for me to put my feet up, pour a lovely cup of tea, unwrap a pasty and tackle the *Telegraph* crossword. By 1 a.m., very little was stirring. The cleaners had done their stuff and buffed the floor with those weird-looking machines, and even the airport police were grabbing forty blue winks.

I always liked it when it was quiet. But this night I conveniently forgot about exactly what the expression says the quiet is *before*. . . and I was about be reminded by an encounter with the storm. I suddenly got a call: it was one of the airport's airline handling agents.

'Sorry to interrupt you at this late hour but we have a private jet landing, due in at about 1.30 a.m.'

Bollocks. Tea down, pasty going cold, newspaper away. I asked the agent to come to my office with the advance paperwork. The papers showed that the jet was inbound from Milan and on its way to Aberdeen with four passengers and three crew. It was stopping here to refuel and clear Immigration and Customs. Nothing unusual in that, just a pain in the arse in the middle of the night. The agent asked me if I wanted to clear the passengers on board the plane or for them to get off and walk through the channels. The little devil in me said to get them off their fat, rich arses and make them walk, they could probably do with the exercise.

'I'll clear them in the channels, hand baggage only and a full crew declaration. Also,' I said to the airline agent, 'I think that we should watch the aircraft taxi on to the stand. I'll pick you up from your office.'

One last bite of pasty and swig of warm tea and I set off to pick up the agent in one of our little boarding cars. I parked us up near a stand on the runway as the gleaming white Learjet taxied to a halt. As the roar of the jets began to subside, the agent told me that on board was a billionaire Italian industrialist and his family who were on their way up to Balmoral to go grouse shooting with the royal family. Nice. Very similar to the evening I was planning with some fellow officers next week to go out and get hammered blind on cider with whisky chasers and round off the night with a kebab-topped pizza, quite probably leading to some synchronized projectile vomiting behind a wheelie bin. So you see, they're no different from us, the other half . . .

The passengers disembarked and were led to the terminal. Next came the pilot, the co-pilot and the stewardess with . . . what the hell is that? The handling agent had seen it, too, and his head was already in his hands as he knew this quiet night was about to get an awful lot less quiet.

'Ah, it looks like a dog, sir,' he said, reaching for the boarding-car door handle. It was, in fact, a bloody great golden retriever, tripping merrily down the steps with the stewardess who then stopped and paused while the animal cocked its leg and took a slash against the plane's landing gear. I decided to make my feelings broadly known.

'GET! THAT! BLOODY! DOG! OFF MY BLOODY RUNWAY!'

The stewardess jumped and the dog looked up from its

activity against the wheel. Still carried on pissing, though (like they do). Cheeky swine.

My shout must have wakened most of the night staff. I turned to the handling agent. 'Not happy!'

He ran off and quickly ushered the stewardess and the animal back on board the plane. I spun the boarding car around and headed back to the terminal. Not happy, indeed. Tea, pasty and crossword interrupted and now a non-quarantine animal. These breaches were actually regarded as extremely serious situations and have, on occasion, been career-ending ones for officers involved. I wasn't about to let that happen to me. Italy's border controls have never been as strict as ours – and the borders of a connected country as opposed to an island one are always going to be more porous (even as recently as 2010 there was a rabies outbreak in northern Italy).

Within the next hour, the billionaire, his wife, their two best friends and the three aircraft crew members were also not happy. They all sat in the green channel, unable to go anywhere, as I had detained them. The head of the family, in particular, was not best pleased. He was clearly used to being obeyed and getting his own way. Did I not realize, he said at the top of his voice, that they were attending a grouse shoot with the royal family? And that the golden retriever had been a gift from the Queen? And that the dog, as such, was *British*? We must call the Foreign Office! And the Italian Embassy!

The guy was frothing at the mouth and he hadn't even *got* rabies yet. Well, as far as I could tell. I told him that the answer to all his questions was 'Yes' and that it didn't make a blind bit of difference. This didn't go down well at all. Italy is a country where, how shall we say it . . . power and wealth more readily influences and smoothes over certain situations. I'm not saying that doesn't sometimes happen in Britain, but it doesn't happen as often, it doesn't happen with Customs and, I thought, it certainly ain't happening tonight, sunshine.

I wandered over to the captain and asked him what the hell he thought he was doing landing an unchecked dog in a quarantined country. He looked so sheepish that I almost quarantined him as well for that (no unchecked farm stock!), but he just said he didn't speak much English. Which was crap.

'OK, you're under arrest.'

The airline agent overheard this and rushed over in a panic. I explained that the captain of an aircraft is responsible for the plane and crew, and also for landing the dog in the UK, and that all international pilots had to speak good English to get their licence. At this point, the captain suddenly rediscovered his ability to understand English.

So I've got one shouting and wildly gesticulating Italian billionaire, one sobbing wife, two pissed-off friends, three crew members playing dumb, one grounded jet and a dog pissing on the runway. Within an hour, the night has gone from being *All Quiet on the Stansted Front* to *Carry On Airport*.

In the office I called the London Airports Customs Control duty senior officer and explained the case. He didn't know what to do either but said he'd get back to me. Outside the racket was getting louder, the Italians getting even more shouty and . . . well, Italian. I love Italy but, boy, they sure know how to create a fuss. From outside I could again hear the words

'Embassy', 'Foreign Office' and 'diplomatic incident' being bandied about. I thought, ho hum.

Ten minutes later I received the first of many calls. I answered my phone to find I was speaking to Buckingham Palace's private office and a very stern-sounding lady. (*Not* the Queen, I hasten to add.) I explained the case for the ump-teenth time and she took great care to make me aware that the royal family was in no way involved in this; she said they had issued the Italian party an invitation but it certainly did not include a PS saying 'Please bring own gundog'. I said that I had at no time imagined Her Majesty was in any way remotely complicit. At this, the lady from Buckingham Palace grew a little less stern. But not much. I was told to hold fast.

The cavalry arrived in the shape of a very tall, very distinguished-looking older gentleman in a tweed sports jacket. He offered his official ID but I'd already recognized him from his appearances on the news. He was a knight of the realm and the head of the Civil Service. He smiled. We shook hands. He had the bearing of someone who had been through an extremely expensive education and a very success-ful career, probably had a father who had almost ousted Churchill and – not always also present, this one – was very charming. Which was nice, and frighteningly disarming.

'Officer Frost, I believe we have a little problem. I'm sure we can come to an accommodation. Got any decent tea?' And with that he breezed into my office and made himself at home. We chatted and I explained the laws regard-ing the importation of dogs, quarantine and aircraft pilot responsibility. The latter was of some relief to Sir because, as he said, 'We can't have the Queen's guest to blame.'

Sir sat back and arched his fingers. 'What would happen, for instance, if we just let them merrily go on their way to Balmoral?' He looked at me expectantly and smiled.

'I'm afraid that's just not going to happen,' I said.

'No. But let's just say it *did*. Hypothetically, what would happen?'

I could now see that our charming Sir Tweed was looking for a face-saving way out of this problem that kept everyone happy. I thought for a few seconds.

'Well, if they should continue to the shoot, with the dog, and the dog comes into contact with the royal family's animals there, then they'll all have to be put in quarantine for six months or, if infected, something much worse; and I would hazard a guess, sir, that you don't really want to be the one who starts shooting the Queen's corgis . . .'

He started laughing, slapped his thigh and got up. 'That's it, my lad, that's what I wanted to know.' And with that he strode out of the office and went off to tackle the Italians, armoured with his reason for refusing them entry.

It was sorted in minutes. I agreed to release the pilot and they were all soon on their way back to Italy. And in the near future Buckingham Palace would receive a letter of apology from Milan stating that the industrialist had come down with a cold and was very sorry that he could not attend the shoot.

So, the billionaires plus the dog are sent home. The Queen is informed. I make a cup of tea.

Job done. Now where was that bloody crossword . . .

This story reveals a little-known truth behind the myth of the Customs officer only picking on the little guy. We don't. We pick on the *right* guy. Whoever that is. Customs officers are sometimes disliked by a public who are used to coming back from holiday and running the old blue/red/green channel gauntlet, and that's kind of understandable. But we actually distrust everyone equally, both high society and so-called low, and treat everyone the same. We are equal opportunity *suspectors*. In fact, we'd much rather land a big fish than a small one. We'd sooner nab some knob on a private plane who thinks it allows him to sneak in a suitcase of cocaine than some kid back from the Netherlands with a spliff in his sock.

Now the boys in blue may not like this, but it is true that it's far easier to find a bent copper to bribe than a Customs officer. In fact, in Customs it is very rare. Which is something to be proud of.

So I like to think the British public would be cheered up considerably to know that, when it comes to stopping people trying to bring things into the UK that shouldn't be here, it all rests on the shoulders of the officers in black and gold braid that line our borders, and those officers (to put it impolitely) don't give a badger's arse who you are.

If we can make the Queen of England wait, do you think we'd bat an eye over inconveniencing, say, the now deceased King of Pop? Never mind the Queen's corgis, there came a time later on when I would shoot Michael Jackson.

8. *You Strip Search the Vicar – I'll Question the Nuns*

Who to search and who not to search? – that is the question. And, as I stood in my gold-braided uniform on airport duty, I realised that *how I decide* is something that every smuggler would give at least one big consignment of stash and cash to know. As would every tourist facing the old blue, red or green channel dilemma.

So how would I know to stop six nuns that have just stepped off the plane? I think I'll put it down to instinct and curiosity, just to keep all future nuns on their toes. Now, I like nuns; I think that they are great fun. I'm not a Catholic so they don't worry me or give me sleepless nights. And anyone who can spend their working life dressed as an immaculate penguin of Jesus gets my vote every time. And as I'd been warned early in my career to trust no one – and fortunately, or unfortunately, it mostly paid off – I decided to put this advice to the ultimate test.

The six sisters were returning from a pilgrimage to Lourdes. I beckoned them over for a chat and they all looked slightly surprised, but amused. I introduced myself and explained what I was going to do and then I did a quick baggage search. The only thing I could find that got a twitch of suspicion from me were the large two-litre bottles of holy water that each was carrying. I checked each one in turn and found that the first three were, indeed, water. There wasn't even a flicker of a reaction from them so they were either wholly innocent or unholy good actresses. So – and this might be a lesson in perseverance in the face of sweetly smiling nuns – I carried on and checked the last three bottles and found that they were full to the brim with . . . gin!

I put my findings to the sisters and they were all suitably embarrassed, while still smiling sweetly (it suddenly occurred to me they actually might all be stewed from drinking the other three bottles on the flight!). The chief nun – is that an official rank? – spoke for the group.

'Well, officer, would you believe me if I told you that it was a miracle?'

I thought that was a pretty good effort so I smiled and replied, 'Well, Sister, actually I don't need to. You see, there are six of you and you don't have any other alcohol so these three two-litre bottles of gin are the same as your legal entitlement. So feel free to carry on . . .'

The poor ladies had wasted their time rebottling their gin. Perhaps it was some power from above that had protected them from becoming known smugglers. But then, I thought, how on earth do I tell my mother that part of my job now is making nuns blush?

I could never really suss why people would try to smuggle large amounts of booze when they were a foot passenger. Did they really think that an officer would search their bag of clothes and *not* find ten bottles of Scotch? My favourite booze chancer was a very short chap called Percy. He arrived from Tenerife with his wife and three suitcases, and they all headed for the green channel. I pulled them over for a chat. One case contained both of their clothes and the other two were completely full of bottles of wine. Percy was very apologetic. He said he'd forgotten about the wine and that he knew he should have gone in the red channel to declare it. He started to reload his trolley and reverse his route, so to enter the red channel. I stopped him and told him that I was more than happy to work out the duty for him as I knew that it wouldn't take long. I told him the amount and he asked if he could pay by card. He searched through his wallet and pockets but couldn't seem to find his card. Then Mrs Percy remembered that they had put it in the suitcase with the clothes for safe keeping.

Percy banged the clothes suitcase on to the bench and scrambled to open it. As he flung open the lid the whole case slid off the bench and emptied its contents on to the floor – Speedos, bathing costumes and Hawaiian shirts flew everywhere – but there was one T-shirt that didn't fly like the others. This T-shirt hit the ground with a loud clang. They were either using a hell of a lot of starch at the laundry or there was something hidden inside. Percy shot forward to retrieve it but I got my foot on it. I unfolded the T-shirt and inside was a well-used, twin-handled corking machine. So now we had reason to uncork the two suitcases full of (apparently) red wine.

After I had opened all thirty bottles, I couldn't find one with red wine in it. There contained instead every spirit under the sun – whisky, gin, rum, vodka, etc. – and it took me over an hour to work out the duty and the fine. It came to such a high amount that Percy and his wife abandoned it all to the Crown, and its final destination was down the drain. Shame, but that's where it went. The airport drains probably had the only alcoholic rats in the country.

I couldn't help but think of the two of them – little Percy and little Mrs Percy – night after night after night, uncorking, refilling, rebottling and corking again all those bottles. What a holiday. No wonder they didn't have a tan.

Part of the job that made me go more red than Percy's wine – mostly through holding my breath too long – was having to search such things as the dead body that had recently arrived back on an unexpectedly early return from a holiday in the Costas – unexpectedly early because the deceased had back-flipped off a fourth-storey balcony into a swimming pool that was actually around the other side of the hotel.

There is something about having to search a corpse in a coffin that, not for the first time, can make you wonder how you got here. We could usually tell how long they'd been on holiday by how tanned the corpse was – faint tan lines, probably died in the first few days; back and shoulders like a lobster's arse, probably died at the end of a two-weeker. Any smuggler who thinks a coffin is less likely to be searched doesn't know UK Customs – we'd unwrap the body of Tutankhamun or machine-wash the Turin Shroud if we thought it held iffy gear. Our old friend 'Jaws of Death' Arthur was a great drugs dog but we had to make sure he was kept on a short leash near any dead bodies we were searching so he couldn't bite off one of the hands and make it his new chew toy. I didn't fancy having to chase him up the runway, shouting, 'Drop the hand, boy! DROP it!'

It's all in a day's work when you don't know what's coming out of the blue above. Such as a potentially drugs-laden shit bowser full of excrement off a jumbo jet. Happy days.

After that type of thing, it was a blessed relief to get back to searching members of the clergy. I pulled aside a mild-looking Church of England vicar who seemed very nervous. Maybe he'd been given a heads-up by the nuns I'd searched. Whatever it was, he looked rattled. He pleaded that he needed the toilet, which just aroused more suspicion, and I soon discovered why when, in an attempt to hide his contraband, we found him stuffing into his underpants a stash of what turned out to be child pornography. Heavenly wings weren't much in evidence, even though his feet didn't touch the ground as he was whisked off to the nearest police station. No one was off limits, not even a pilot of God.

And not even the real pilots, aircraft cabin crews and, at the ports, the ship captains and seamen – they are always kept under a wary eye. For obvious reasons: as you can easily guess, with their frequent trips abroad, smuggling is always a possibility. It's not that the people who work for airlines are likely to smuggle but that it is what you would class as a temptingly opportunistic crime: their privileged position provides the opportunity and therefore the temptation. Another potential strength of the aircraft-staff-as-smugglers (and, therefore, a weakness of ours) is that they always know the workings of ports and airports as well as the workings of the Customs staff, security and the police.

As far as normal allowances go, the aircrew have reduced fag and booze allowances due to the amount of times they can travel in a day (short hauls over to Europe, for example). But you might well think, well, that pretty looking trolley-dolly or that snappily dressed captain would never smuggle, would they? To which myself and every other Customs officer in the country would reply – *my arse*.

So, at the larger airports, the aircraft crew have to clear Customs at a different location to that of the passengers. For example, Gatwick Airport puts the aircrew through a totally different building called Concord House; there is no need for a full Customs mob to attend so it can all be handled by a couple of officers. 'Crew Clearance', as it is called, was often referred to by us all as the Penal Colony because it was such an unattractive and unwanted duty. Mess up big time in the channels or piss off your senior officer and you would be reassigned to the Colony.

At smaller airports like the old Stansted, the crew would clear through the 'Declare' red channel and so they were as vulnerable for a check as much as any other passenger. I'd seen half bottles of Scotch hidden in pilots' underwear, body-packed hand-rolling tobacco wrapped around a stewardess and cigarette packets concealing cannabis on co-pilots.

Sometimes the evidence trail we found led to things that were completely unexpected – and unwanted. One day late on in the channels, I stopped one of the incoming male cabin crew members who seemed ill at ease. When he was undressed for the strip search and obligingly bent over, he revealed a string dangling down from his bum. Now that threw up two possible explanations: he was either smuggling drugs and the string was part of the packaging; or he was smuggling a very expensive firework and it was the fuse. I strongly hoped it wouldn't be a firework – the last thing you want is an arse exploding in your face; I'd always prided myself on never being shitfaced at work. So, I thought, sonny Jim here is obviously smuggling drugs – I was certain of it. And I was wrong. It turned out that the dangling string was actually the string of a tampon that was currently *in situ* because of this crew member's anal syphilis. Which is a nice thought for everyone to take with them on their next flight when the meals come around.

There were actually stranger things that could be found on, and in, people walking through airports. In the days before pornography was so readily available on the internet, we were, you might say, very hot on pornography. The UK pornography laws are very strange as no MP has ever really wanted to get involved in sorting them out. I don't think there's much career mileage in handling the nation's porn. So in our situation we used the Customs Consolidation Act 1876. Even though the law-makers had no idea what technology was to come, there was a section of the Act that is in constant use, right up to today. It states that we can seize any goods that are likely to deprave a youngster's mind. We were in a position to use the Act on a daily basis as we would get six to eight Amsterdam flights a day. The porn capital of Europe never let us down.

Mr Raven looked to be a well-dressed businessman. He was actually a fairly senior politician. I was having a slow day so pulled him over for a chat in the green channel. The initial questioning was fine and he stated that he had been to a business meeting with the car giants Ford in Amsterdam. Big mistake. The trouble with giving too much detail to a lie is that the detail, unless it's perfect, can give you away. What the passenger didn't know was that, as well as all the Amsterdam flights, we also had the Ford motor company's own private air-line flying out to Cologne three times a day. So Mr Raven's story didn't quite hold water.

Not knowing what I might be in store to find, I asked him to pop his bags on to the exam desk and he instantly trans-formed into a loud and very accomplished verbal abuser. He started swearing and I was called every name under the sun and a few from the dark side of the moon. I was told that I had no right to go through his bags. It's not just that Customs officers, like everyone else, have an aversion to being sworn at; it was that Mr Raven's behaviour was what they call a 'tell' in poker – something that inadvertently reveals what you are thinking. Once he had lost his temper, I knew that I was going to find something in his bag and I had a feeling it would be drugs. But I was wrong. His bag carried not drugs but porn films, and loads of them, wrapped up in his socks, pants and shirts. Right at the bottom of his case there was, much to my surprise, a monster fifteen-inch-long bright-pink rubber dildo. Now whatever my personal view on this – and whether I couldn't give a chuff or not – Customs officers are like the police in that, once they become alerted to something, they have a professional duty to act upon it.

Mr Raven was still going mad as I seized and bagged the evidence and he was still swearing at me as he repacked his suitcase. In the interview room, the direction of his future depended on one of two answers: whether or not they were for his own use or to give to other people, which would have been the more serious charge of intent to supply. Luckily, he chose the right answer, and Patrick and I escorted him to his awaiting car and, inside, his waiting wife. As he climbed into the driving seat of his brand-new BMW, I had a quiet word with his wife just to say that her husband had been helping us with a few matters. I noticed Patrick was standing by the driver's door and I couldn't quite see what he was up to. As the BMW drove off, all became clear: on the car's roof aerial Patrick had stuck something, and there it was, pointing proudly upward, the monster fifteen-inch bright-pink rubber dildo wobbling in the wind. Our upstanding Member in the car now also had one on top of it.

We were having a problem with porn. It wasn't that we weren't getting enough of it – we were making seizures every few days. The quandary we had was that, when the cases hit the magistrates' court, they were giving out minimal fines regardless of the different types of material. So we set up a meeting with the local magistrates to see what the problem was.

Now, the local magistrates were rather aged and that was the first problem. Their experience of the varied content of pornography was rather limited. Just like the myth that the reason there was no law against lesbianism was because Queen

Victoria refused to believe that there was such a thing so the law was limited to male homosexuality in order to get royal assent, so it was with our local bench: they believed that the only pornography available was the standard male/female vanilla missionary kind. We had to think of a way to open their eyes – preferably without stopping their hearts.

The second problem that we had was the chap who was one of the local magistrates. He was the squire of some large estate and when sitting in court he would, believe it or not, always wear a white suit and monocle. He looked like a cross between the Man from Del Monte and a Nazi scientist. Which must have been bloody terrifying for those that were up in front of him. That terrifying effect didn't last long for pornography-smuggling offences, as sometimes he would hand out only a £50 fine and a slap on the wrist.

But should you appear for an offence that involved illegal activity in something in which he took an interest – such as hunting, shooting or fishing (or knobbing the downstairs staff, probably) – then he would reach for his black cap and try to bring back hanging. If he had been on the bench 200 years ago, he would have been transporting people to Australia for not doffing their cap to him. So that was what we were up against when we had to bring the magistrates into the present day, and fast.

What we urgently needed to do was list all the offences involving pornographic material, plus explain about the trusty old Customs Consolidation Act 1876 (the law that enabled us to seize the goods). So we got together and invented what we called the porno tick sheet. This required a Customs officer to sit through a whole film and tick off each sexual act as it happened. The poor bastard. You can imagine the stampede for this duty.

This form, the porno tick sheet, would then make up the prosecution package and the magistrates could compare the tick sheet to the detailed description of the act that we provided to all the local magistrates. We wrote it in our best and most detached medical language so as not to excite the old magistrates too much and push too many of them into an early grave – the risk of the male members having to be buried sideways in their coffins because of rigor mortis issues leading to difficulties in closing the lid was a very tempting outcome to aim for, but we managed to resist going for it.

Our final push for the modernization of the magistrates' porno education was to invite one of them to the airport to view a sample of the videos we often seized; this would hopefully make them the local court expert on pornography. This offer of ours, they gladly accepted. I thought how much I would have loved to have been at the meeting when they decided who they were going to send to us to become the font of all perverted sexual knowledge.

The chosen magistrate arrived at our offices the following week. She was Lady Simmons-something-or-other, and was definitely from the established 'country set'. She was – you could immediately see – quite stern, very prim, terribly serious, probably quietly insane, and the type of woman who would whip her staff with a crop and for sport set the dogs on slow-moving local villagers. She had a stare that could stop a nun smiling at fifty paces. She was wearing the classic combo of brown tweed suit and matching hat, and also, quite ominously, carrying a Margaret Thatcher-style handbag (which could clearly also be used as an offensive weapon). I suspected that inside it there was a full house brick. And I also suspected that, before the end of the day, I would find that out for sure.

We led Lady S. into our viewing room, which housed our video machines and a large-screen TV. She settled down into the comfortable viewing chair with her handbag clenched in her lap and said, 'Right, let's get on with it!'

We had prepared a collection of all kinds of pornographic material for our magistrate's speedy education; a kind of crash course in smashing genitals. Or what someone revising for exams at university would call 'cramming' – which was an oddly appropriate word, considering. Myself and three of the boys – Pat, Mark and Harry – stood behind her, ready to answer any questions that she may have. I started the video.

We'd laid on a proper platter of porn, a fulsome feast of filth, all the better to make our case. First up was what we'd term a normal, standard fuck film – 'Awful. Just awful!' Lady S. said – then followed by an S & M film with a novel use of a broom handle and a spatula – 'Oh, my lord!' – which led to our grand, frothing finale: a bestiality film that ended with a very pleasant young woman wanking off a donkey. Not something you see every day.

'Turn it off!' she cried. 'That animal is NOT happy!' But as we could all see to a man that the donkey was clearly ecstatic, we all burst out laughing. At which point Lady S.

jumped up, shouting, 'You . . . beasts!', and started swiping at us with her handbag.

All in all, we decided, it was a pretty good day. And, after that, we never had any bad sentencing again.

So, as you see, we'd stop and search anyone – nuns, vicars, pilots, friends of the Queen, MPs, cute children holding fluffy bunnies ('That rabbit, princess, is going *straight* into quarantine!') and even the recently dead.

If nothing else, I hope this proves, once and for all, that we didn't play favourites and that we didn't mistrust just anyone. We mistrusted *everyone*. That might make you feel a little better about being stopped yourself – knowing that you are in very good (and very bad) company.

9. Hide and Seek . . . and We Shall Find

When it came to concealments – both in baggage and in the body – we got to see the big and small, the bold and the beautiful, and the foolish and the painful. Early on, all the concealments were for hiding drugs but later, due to the government's tobacco policy, cigarettes and tobacco became a valuable thing to smuggle. I know that it sounds strange but the smugglers soon discovered that there was just the same amount of profits to be made running baccy as running cannabis, and if caught the prison sentence was shorter. I looked forward to a government policy that sent the price of chilli peppers sky high and caused smugglers to turn to bringing those in; it certainly would have been easier to spot a chilli mule with contraband peppers up his arse – the smoke from the ears would have been a dead giveaway.

Smuggling organizations are very much the same as small businesses in that they have overheads and profit margins, they lose stock and even lose employees, and their aim is to make as much money as they can and with as little disruption as possible. And what they are very adept at doing is changing with the fashion. Not only will they move between different kinds of drug – as different drugs go in and out of fashion or become easy or difficult to get – but they will also change their methods of concealment.

For the chancers – or 'personal usage' smugglers – there were plenty of readymade concealments available to buy or get information about via the internet. But, of course, if Customs knows about them already, then you're going to get caught in the long run. Potential smugglers never seem to think that Customs officers might be looking at the same concealment advice on the same internet sites as them. Some of the commercially available stashes that we had come across included: hollowed-out disposable lighters (that still worked) with a removable bottle in the base; AA batteries (that worked when tested and could even be recharged) that unscrewed to reveal a small drug stash inside; beer cans that were labelled correctly and even weighed the same as a full beer can but unscrewed at the top to reveal a large storage space; and even shaving-cream aerosols that unscrewed at the bottom and were filled with drugs but were cleverly made to still squirt real foam out of the top. Come to think of it, if we hadn't been a big bunch of highly suspicious bastards, we'd have never found anything!

Then there was the items that were not always what they seemed to be, such as mobile phones that – in the early days when mobiles were bigger – were in perfect working order and could be used to make calls but inside they hid a small .22 pistol; or phones that had two small aerials and were actually 50,000-volt stun guns. And just think, there were people walking around in the UK with these items because of the ones we missed. So, if you ever see someone on their mobile who suddenly starts glowing bright red with sparks coming off their head, then chances are that they have hit the wrong button on their stun phone.

One noteworthy concealment was found behind the canvases on some national treasures from Eastern Europe. The paintings involved were all over six foot high and the smugglers were convinced that, due to their national treasure designation, we would never touch them. Lucky for us, our drugs dogs had no idea what was a work of art and what wasn't – in fact, they would sniff and cock their leg over a Picasso. But, after our drugs hounds had run their twitching noses over the canvas, we found that each painting had concealments of five kilos of heroin hidden between the painting and the backing, which increased the value of each painting by about £1 million.

Our problems started after the smugglers were convicted. The government of the country in question was furious at us for not releasing all the works of art after the trial. The matter would drag through court for some time due to the fact that any item discovered concealing contraband immediately becomes the property of the Crown. Whether they ever got them back or whether the Queen just got a few new works of art to hang in her toilet, I don't really know. It was one for the lawyers to spend a lot of time (and a lot of chargeable hours) working out.

Footwear has always been a popular source of concealments. All that has changed is that the advent of big trainers created more space for concealments: you can get much more hidden in the thick soles of a pair of Adidas than a pair of brogues. Drugs runners (and terrorists) may be convinced that smelly footwear is a no-go area for law enforcement, but it was usually one of the first things that we looked at during a strip search: the shoes came off straight away and then every area from the tongue to the laces was checked as in the past we had found drugs in each part. Trainer manufacturers may as well have their own smugglers on their design teams because modern training shoes have such huge air spaces in the soles that it's almost as if they were designed with smuggling in mind. What was meant to be an ergonomic design for the sportsman was both a Trojan horse and a gift horse for the smuggler.

Quite often, personal-user amounts of drugs were found in smugglers' washbags. Every single item that could possibly be adapted *was* adapted to carry drugs: toothpaste tubes, soap, deodorants, the aforementioned shaving foam, contact lens cleaners, tampons, etc. One item that also seemed almost purpose-built for concealment were tubs of face cream such as Oil of Olay, formerly Ulay (other face creams for smuggling drugs are available). The tubs were quite large in comparison to the area in which the cream was held, a bit like Dr Who's Tardis in reverse, but with a few tugs and a bang on the table, we found we could get the two parts to separate, revealing a large space that was often full of something else that was used to 'powder the nose'.

Lipsticks are also very popular because it is easy to cut off the end of the lipstick, insert the drugs into the lipstick tube, and then place the cut-off lipstick top back into place. The

ultimate lipstick concealment I found was a personal importation from Colombia. There was a pack of twelve brightly
coloured lipsticks where every lipstick was actually moulded
from cocaine paste. Very clever. They looked perfect, until you
realized that no colour came off the lipstick. (At this point I'll
make it clear that we tried them out on the back of our hands;
I wouldn't want to leave you with the awful image of a six-
foot, fifteen-stone hairy-arsed Customs officer pursing his lips
and trying on different shades of lipstick. I always saved that
for the Christmas party . . .)

Of course, the very best concealments are the ones that
have never been discovered by any Customs officer and are
still in use today. In fact, some concealments are so good that
they have probably survived for centuries – going back to the
old Napoleonic Wars – and will be passed on down through
the generations. I could tell you what they are . . . and I will
do when I find out!

I was mostly in the green channel but I knew that it got
very boring in the red channel at times, although it shouldn't
have, as many smugglers mistakenly thought that doing the
apparently honest thing of entering the red channel and
declaring something legal would negate them from a detailed
scrutiny that might discover something illegal. It took more
than a bit of fake sincerity to fool us. Though I have to admit
that there were some officers who were quite happy to sit in
the red channel and do nothing but take VAT and Excise fines
on over-allowances of booze and fags instead of exercising the
rummage gene, that is, the instinct that makes you want to
search. Every good Customs officer is a natural bloodhound.

I didn't need to be Sherlock Holmes to know that, when a Turkish flight was in the baggage hall, there were going to be long lines of waiting passengers in the red channel with carpets to declare. A pretty dull assignment, and against my better wishes, I was sent over to the red to help out. My first customer was definitely a potential strip-down merchant. He looked like a bag of shit that hadn't been packed properly and one that hadn't slept for a week. He slapped down 600 fags in front of me on the bench and mumbled, 'I wanna pay for these.' I totted up the VAT that he owed and took the payment. Then I thought, bugger it all, I know this is going to piss off the senior officer but I can't resist: 'Whip your bag up here, sir, and let's have a quick look in it.' He looked a little taken aback, mumbled something about my parentage and then heaved up his bag.

The officer next to me leaned over. 'What the hell do you think you are up to, Jon? Look at the bloody queue we've got here.'

I made a nice neat pile of the disgusting, stinking clothes that were inside the bag and then I came across four brand-new, A4-size hardback books, all wrapped up in cellophane. Nothing out of the ordinary there, except that they were all the same book: *The Bird Life of Asia Minor*. This guy looked no more like a birdwatcher than my granny did a pole dancer; I doubted that he could recognize anything more than a fried chicken leg in a bucket. And wherever in the world there is a suspicious little Herbert in an airport mumbling insults under his breath there will be a Customs officer ready to flash the blade of justice from its scabbard . . . or, in my case, my trusty little lock-knife (not quite the same as a sword of justice, I know, but I've always found it difficult to get a sword under my jacket without snagging my shirt).

So the cellophane wrapping on the books was soon off, and then two different smells hit me: first, I was pretty sure that they didn't use woodwork PVA glue in book production; second, there was a slight fish-and-chip-shop whiff (and one I would later get very used to in my Investigation years) – the scent of heroin. I flicked through the books' pages but nothing there, so I examined the hardback covers. They felt OK and looked fine apart from the fact that they just seemed a millimetre or two too thick. I started running the blade along the edge of one of the covers. The hardback separated quite easily, revealing inside a very thin, flat package of heroin. My passenger mumbled, 'Fuck that!' and was off on his toes. The shout went up from the officer next to me, 'Runner in the red!' and I vaulted straight over the examination desk and was after him. The red and green channels converged at sliding exit doors and as two officers were legging it from the green channel and I was barrelling in from the red . . . guess who got to him first? Well, none of us.

As our runner reached the channel convergence, a grey-haired old lady who had just arrived from Jersey was wheeling her overloaded trolley to the exit and straight into the path of our fugitive. Moving too fast to take evasive action, he slammed into the trolley at high speed and there was an audible bone-snapping sound that made us all wince – and then in slow motion he took off, wheeling through the air over the trolley like a dropkicked scarecrow. It was almost majestic, like a gymnast . . . a pissed and really crap gymnast. Fortunately, when he came down, he landed on his softest part – his head – and knocked himself out cold. We dragged his limp and newly broken body to the interview room and watched the hero of the day – the little old lady – obliviously disappear into the waiting throng of families in arrivals. Just like the woman in *The Ladykillers*, I very much doubted that she even noticed what had happened.

The result of my appearance in the red channel was one very broken-legged smuggler and 750 grams of 80 per cent pure heroin. That should have been the end of it. But two months after his trial (at which he was found guilty), our hop-along smuggler decided to take out a civil action against Customs for compensation, stating that we had caused his broken limb. The case was dropped when we pointed out to his legal team that CCTV footage clearly showed that the break was not in fact caused by officers of HMCE but by an unknown little grey-haired lady assassin who had just arrived from Jersey. We helpfully pointed out how she wasn't one of ours (more's the pity).

During my early years at the airport, computers were pretty few and far between, but Customs had one advantage over the police when it came to intelligence gathering. The police only had one national computer system, which was the Police National Computer (PNC), and was what we would refer to as a positive intelligence system. This was due to the fact that it only recorded persons who had been caught and charged with a crime. Her Majesty's Customs and Excise, on the other hand, had an active computer system, CEDRIC. This meant we were able to put people on to the system who were just suspected of being smugglers or even just associated with persons who were known smugglers. There was no need for people to be caught smuggling to be ensconced on our system.

A dodgy character called Billy Cree was one of these suspects who, even though he had previous form, as yet had never been caught by us. He had his fingers in many criminal pies. Essex police knew him very well but, as far as they were concerned, he was always clean, although he was constantly in the company of high-ranking criminals and drug dealers and appeared to be in their employ. He also appeared to be the King of Concealments, with an array of ways of getting past us without being detected.

One day when I was on duty, Cree just happened to be due in on the next Amsterdam flight. We would always get flight passenger manifests from the airlines just before the planes left their foreign airports. This gave us a good chance to run all the passenger names through CEDRIC before the aircraft touched down. It's an arse of a job when you have a suspect called Smith or Jones but, in Cree's case, his surname stuck out. We had stopped him five times in two years and he was always clean or, to put it more correctly in our minds, we never managed to find anything on him. Where *was* he hiding his stuff?

My colleague, Big Martin, sidled up next to me as I was checking the Amsterdam passenger list. 'Anything on the flight, Jon?'

It was a slow morning and most of the officers were busy concerning themselves with the ever-present devil of the Civil Service – paperwork.

'Looks like we have Billy Cree inbound again,' I told him.

Now, Big Martin had a particular dislike for characters like Billy. He was a highly respected officer who had seen it all at Heathrow and now wanted a nice easy life out in the country. The only fly in this ointment was that you cannot just relax and sit back in this job: the fun of the chase, the thrill of the find and the joy of catching a smuggler never really leave your system.

'I don't think that you have ever had the pleasure of Mr Cree, have you, Martin?'

Martin, who was now busying himself with Cree's intelligence record, said, 'No, but looking at this intel log, it seems to me that this chap needs a proper fingertip job. Fancy giving me a hand when he lands?'

A 'fingertip job' was a deep and thorough search of every single thing that the passenger had that could be searched or taken to pieces.

Cree was first off the plane and first into the terminal. With only a largish sports bag, he went straight through the baggage hall and into the green channel. If Martin and I hadn't been so keen to observe if he was mingling with some other passenger, we would have missed him. As he quickly passed us, Martin's voice boomed, 'Yes, thank you, sir, over here please,' and he pointed to a nearby exam bench.

Cree's mouth immediately slipped into overdrive. 'Oh fuck me, here we go again, always the bloody same with you fucking VAT men: every time I come through I get stopped and searched. Got nothing better to do, wankers? Fucking bastards!'

You'd think someone smart enough to have discovered how to stroll through Customs undetected might be smart enough not to verbally abuse the boys in the black and gold – but no.

The usual body and bag search produced, as usual in his case, nothing. But I noticed for the first time that Billy paid a little bit too much close attention to the actual bag itself as we were searching it. Martin had noticed this, too. Telltale sign no. 1. So as a test Martin placed the bag to one side and started asking why our passenger was travelling from Amsterdam. And, bingo, with the bag now apparently discounted, Cree perceptibly relaxed. 'Tell' no. 2. Martin passed the bag to me to be X-rayed.

Once again, in the early days for technology, Customs didn't have the money to supply all airports with X-ray machines, but luckily I was on good terms with airport security and they had two of the machines in the outbound lounge search area.

I X-rayed the bag upwards, downwards, sideways and on its ends but nothing showed. Defeated, I walked back and plopped the bag back on to the table. Billy Cree gave the smallest of smiles. 'Let me guess: nothing. You found bugger all! See, I've been telling you, I'm fucking clean and you lot are picking on me. My lawyer will have your plastic sheriff's badges for this!'

Nothing new there – we were used to threats on an hourly basis and some days would have felt something was missing, and that we weren't doing our jobs properly, if we didn't get any.

But it was the victorious smile that was his undoing, as Martin was on the very edge of letting Billy go when that annoying little grin appeared on his face. So Big Martin reached into his pocket and retrieved a knife, pressed the button on the handle, and the blade swung out. Knives were a personal type of thing among officers. Some liked the Swiss Army penknife, some liked a pruning knife, while I personally carried a lock-knife and Martin had a flick-knife – illegal outside of our working environment. But it suited him down to the ground. And, as Martin was a good six foot five and eighteen stone with huge shoulders that you could have a picnic on, no one was going to tell him that he couldn't have a flick-knife.

With a couple of swift cuts, he had split the stitching on the handles of the bag. Suddenly Mr Cree got jumpy, so jumpy in fact that he tried to grab the sports bag away from Martin. A quick growl from Martin made him back off. Next for the search was the bag's base hardener, usually a sheet of plastic-sealed thick cardboard. In some sports bags you could remove it and that was the case here. Martin examined it closely, nothing unusual in the sealing or the thickness, but as we were doing a full turnout . . . the flick-knife appeared again and slashed the plastic open. At this, Billy's head dropped into his hands. He didn't even bother to show any interest in what we would find because, of course, he knew what was there. Martin reached for his latex gloves and removed all the plastic covering from the cardboard, only it wasn't cardboard, it was twenty compressed sheets of LSD tabs. Twenty sheets, 100 tabs per sheet, £5 per tab, a nice total of £10,000. One very expensive sports bag and one suddenly very quiet passenger.

God only knows how many trips he had made through various airports back and forth from Amsterdam; and God knows how many others had used the same kind of concealment. We had once again come face-to-face with the next level of smuggling: the commercially prepared concealment from specialist gangs who catered for smugglers and supplied them with very high-quality concealments. The only weapon against that was good old-fashioned distrust, Customs-officer tenacity and a sharp knife.

As for Billy, well, let's just say that we didn't see him again for at least six years.

10. The World's a Stage . . . and We Are the Trapdoor

As your mum would say, it's all fun and games until someone loses an eye. And you might want to be struck blind by some of the things Customs officers have to see. There was a Lufthansa jet inbound from Berlin that was having trouble with its landing gear after take-off – the front wheels had to be lowered and raised a few times before they locked into place. So the airport was already on standby for a crash landing. All emergency services were ready and raring to go, and all security was on high alert. And so were we. You might wonder why. Well, a quirk of the law is that Customs officers have to attend all air crashes to protect the Queen's revenue by salvaging the duty frees. I know: how sick is that? Even we thought it was mad.

So I drove to the runway with a flashing-lights convoy of police cars, ambulances and multiple fire engines. As the plane came into view, dropping in altitude to beam in on the correct flight path, we were all in a state of suspense – it's difficult to imagine a way for a large commercial jet to land without wheels that leads to a good outcome. As the jet roared over the runway, its wheels started to drop . . . and the plane's tyres hit the tarmac with a puff of smoke. It taxied to its terminal and we followed, but, just before it arrived at its stand, a large lump of something fell out of the front-wheel housing. All the emergency vehicles stopped except the fire trucks, which followed the plane. We got out and walked to where the mystery bundle was now lying. We found one of the saddest things it had ever been my misfortune to see: the body of a teenage boy, a stowaway in the undercarriage, crushed to death by the retracting wheels on take-off, his body then frozen solid by the sub-zero icy air of high altitude. Listed: Stowaway DOA.

Airports and their officers see not only some of the wonders of the world but many of its fatal blunders, too.

The pay-scale for uniformed Customs officers at ports and airports was much lower than those of comparative ranks in the police. So overtime and shift allowances were always sought-after commodities. One area for guaranteeing increased numbers of beer tokens was babysitting duty, or doom watch as we called it. This tedious job had to be done night and day, and consisted of sitting and watching a prisoner at the open door of their cell. But we didn't do this for everyone – oh no, you had to be special. The three categories requiring a twenty-four-hour-a-day babysitter included the two categories of drug smuggler I've already mentioned – stuffers and swallowers – and a third: the doomers. The doomers were those who had threatened to hurt or kill themselves, and there were far more of these than you may think.

One doom watch I was glad to just miss occurred when my colleague Pat, who had just finished his eight-hour shift and was due off the following day, was collared by the senior officer who offered him another eight hours at overtime rate for a spot of babysitting. We had a Ghanaian swallower in custody and, as yet, he had not produced what we suspected he had inside him. Pat jumped at the chance of extra beer money and joined Kevin, who was already stationed at the door to the cell. Kev had been with the smuggler all day and explained to Pat that the chap was constantly complaining of being ill. Apparently he had been sick a few times and Kevin had needed to clear it up. Another lovely perk of the job. Then, just as they were talking, the bloke vomited again. This time poor Pat had to clear it up – the overtime was suddenly not smelling too good.

As per the protocol, the on-call doctor arrived to examine our smuggler from Africa. Kevin decided to stay around for a few minutes to see if the doctor thought that the chap was faking it. But, after examining the patient, the doctor moved suddenly out of the cell and into the corridor and, just as quickly, he got hold of Kev and Pat, pushed them back into the room and slammed the door shut! Pat and Kev, too surprised and overwhelmed by the doc's unexpected actions to have resisted him, stood there agog. The doctor then suddenly slid back the metal plate in the door and shouted, 'Stay there! You are all under quarantine! Lassa fever!' Pat and Kev went a little white at that point.

Lassa fever is known as (you'll like this) 'an acute viral haemorrhagic illness', similar to Ebola. Lovely. It first originated in West Africa – where, indeed, our smuggler was from – and is caught from rat shit. In humans, it can lead to organ infection, eye pus, facial swelling and nasal bleeding. Which is a really great look for a zombie party but not such a hit if you have to pick up the kids from school. The virus is also excreted in urine for three to nine weeks and in semen for three months. Fancy breaking that good news to your missus.

So there Pat and Kev were – locked in a small cell with their own version of the Exorcist who, at any given minute, was liable to start bouncing ropes of infected puke off the walls or squirting hot shit down his trouser legs like twin sewage pipes from hell. Some overtime!

All three of them were rushed off to the nearest hospital with a specialist contagious diseases ward. On the basis of in for a penny/in for a pound, the lads decided to still keep up their watch on our smuggler; and it amused the nurses that our boys had to regularly check his shit with a stick. When the surveyor paid them a visit, he was shocked to find that Pat and Kev were having the time of their lives. The reason? Well, they realized that they were going to get a three-week stay in hospital with food and rest and attentive nurses and, best of all, they would be paid full whack, twenty-four hours a day. For three weeks they'd be on triple money, which to me was still not enough for the risk of becoming a Customs Officer of the Living Dead with a ball sack full of rat germs.

This was one of the dangers of working in airport

Customs – your workplace could become a big meeting place for a house party for the world's exotic diseases.

But sometimes the smugglers hit back with more than what they might infect us with. The Lassa fever incident was a pure accident but it did take two well-trained officers away from the front line for a few weeks. But at least they would recover. That wasn't always the case regarding what was aimed at Customs officers. A few years ago, Canadian Customs was having great success against cannabis smuggling from the West Indies. Over three weeks, they were finding a lot of toasted breadfruit wrapped up in silver foil and containing cannabis. On the fourth week, the smugglers hit back. They had reeled the officers in nicely with the breadfruit consignments and then, instead of cannabis within the foil, it was suddenly magnesium and black powder plus a few sharp metal objects. Two officers at different airports suffered the same injury – they had all their fingers blown off, the result of a real homemade grenade that exploded its deadly contents when the packages were opened to the air.

We were targets here, too, but not for the breadfruit bombs. We sometimes found hypodermic needles hidden along the inside of suitcases to make a mess of your hands when you touch-searched the interior. If you found one with your fingertips, you just hoped the needle wasn't a used one that was infected with something. Hidden razor blades were another nasty little trick just waiting to lop off a few finger-tips. These little hideaway horrors were sometimes put in bags that were from a drug-source country but were not picked up by a passenger. The bad guys knew that we were immediately suspicious of these bags because it looked like a smuggler had lost their bottle and left a case full of drugs behind – we would be into this unclaimed luggage like a ferret down a hole. It only takes one dirty needle or a row of very fine blades to ruin your piano playing for life.

There was one incident where breadfruits and finger damage came together in an unusual and unexpected way. Tracey, an Essex girl and proud of it, had just been promoted from the local VAT office to the airport. She was a lovely person but it was quickly evident that her mind was not always fully on the job. As the boarding officer, when a jet landed from Kingston, Jamaica, Tracey bagged the first examination bench and pulled over a passenger. Inside his case she found one of the infamous breadfruits wrapped in foil and, never having seen one before, she quick as a flash whipped out her brand-new search knife, flicked open the sharp blade . . . and promptly lopped off the end of her index finger. Blood everywhere. Cue very quick dash to hospital with a fingertip in a bag of ice cubes.

There are certain flights from source countries that Customs drools over. These are the flights where you know that at least 10 per cent of the passengers are smuggling drugs. A combination of social deprivation and available local 'produce' leads to the high figures. One of our 'drool factor' flights was an inbound route from the Montego Bay in the West Indies. It was only a question of what you stumbled over first, cocaine or cannabis. Even the poor old drugs dogs were overworked when Montego Bay flights touched down. The dogs signalled on so many bags that we had to run two hounds on any one flight. And they were given so many reward snacks for good finds that they were in danger of getting overweight! And that was just the dog-handlers.

We were so successful at finding gear that the Jamaican ambassador eventually wrote a snotty letter to our surveyor, complaining that we were stopping too many innocent visitors. With tongue firmly in cheek, our surveyor wrote back that, if the passengers on those particular flights would kindly stop smuggling, we would be happy to stop stopping them.

Flights from China were generally uneventful, but I thought I had broken my duck with this Chinese Army basketball player. This chap was big. I'm six foot but he towered over me at about six foot ten or eleven. I pulled him over with his bag for something to do (we did get bored sometimes and, in those situations, a near-seven-foot-tall passenger was bound to stand out). He was calm and polite as I rummaged through his bag's contents until, that is, I grasped a smallish package wrapped in red velvet. It had been carefully sealed with some very fine stitching. As I examined it, the passenger started to get very upset, which is usually a good sign that you've found more than a few sugar lumps. This could, I thought, be a real slam dunk. I flicked out my trusty lock-knife to do the honours of cutting open the package, and my passenger started going absolutely ballistic. Such was the commotion that three other officers had moved over to the scene. As I cut away the last couple of stitches, I was convinced that I had another smuggler bang to rights . . . and then a human index finger fell from the velvet package on to my exam bench. Well, I wasn't expecting that. It turned out that it was the preserved remains of his great-great-grandfather's finger. Why he was carrying it, I've no idea – maybe as a good luck charm.

In another case, a Mr Black was visibly shaking and stuttering his answers to my questions. Immigration had stopped him as he arrived and they weren't too happy with his reason for travel to the UK. To find more documents, Immigration then did the usual thing of bringing their detained passengers to us for a 'turnout', that is, a further search. Immigration could do it themselves but then they would be buggered if they found something like a kilo of coke. So it was easier for both departments if we did the turnout.

In this case, Mr Black was starting to snap, crackle and pop, and I don't think it was because of his breakfast cereal. He was hopping from foot to foot as if on a hot tin roof and was soaking in sweat. There was definitely something up here. He was almost vibrating as I examined his baggage. Right at the bottom of his suitcase I found a number of envelopes containing lots of tablets. But, surprisingly, they were all Valium. Although Valium is a prescription-only medicine (POM), we were not interested in it; but it did explain his nervousness. Or did it?

The Immigration officer had found stamps in our passenger's passport that showed that he had travelled between Poland, Thailand and the UK a number of times over the last few months. Was this some new drugs route that we had no idea about? I knew that Thailand was well known for heroin and cannabis but where on earth did Poland fit in?

I decided to probe a little bit deeper and took Black in for a body search. He stripped down and there he stood, naked as the day he was born, but with a large body belt around his waist. At first he refused to remove it but myself and a fellow officer approached him, so off the belt came and Mr Black collapsed into tears. Only one thing for it now – we sat him down for a cup of tea. (Well, we weren't savages!)

As yet, I hadn't opened the body belt. But neither Mr Black nor his belt was going anywhere fast. He soon stopped his crying and started his pleading: 'I'm so sorry, it's not my fault, I just wanted to sell them.' I had arrested him and cautioned him so that now we had to write down everything he said. I calmed him down again and undid the body belt, looking for the drugs. I found nothing but lots of paper wraps. I would expect to find drug wraps on a street dealer but never on a smuggler, there was just no need. Then I undid one of the wraps and four large diamonds fell on to the table, bounced a little and then lay there, sparkling in the lights. We all stared, equally amazed. Even Mr Black seemed shocked – but that was at being caught. I emptied the other wraps and found four diamonds in each of the thirty wraps: 120 large diamonds, undeclared and hidden in a body belt. I did a quick calculation on the huge amounts of VAT and duty that would be owed. No wonder our diamond geezer had been vibrating at the baggage desk.

My senior officer was over the moon as his monthly revenue figures for seizures were just about to shoot through the roof. We dispatched two officers with the diamonds to a local jeweller that we used for valuations. The value he gave us was double the amount that I had estimated. And it was about to get better . . . and stranger. During my interview with Mr Black, he stated that he had purchased the diamonds in the Far East and brought them to the UK to sell to a dealer in London's Hatton Garden with whom he had some kind of arrangement. But apparently the dealer didn't want them; they were just a little too flawed. So Mr Black then went to Poland where, he said, he found a well-known priest who was also known to the UK dealer and the priest wrote a letter telling the dealer to buy the stones from Black. So back he came to London and back to the dealer again with his letter in hand. On seeing Black and the same stones, and then reading the priest's letter, the dealer had a heart attack and collapsed. Poor old Black flew back to Poland with the stones and waited for news of the dealer's improved health. When at last he heard through a friend that the dealer was back in his shop and looking chipper, Black boarded the next plane to the UK and . . . promptly got nabbed by Immigration and Customs, and here he now was, in a cell with me.

I was slightly speechless at this confession. I thought at first it might be all invented for sympathy but then realized it was just mad enough to be true. But what Mr Black didn't realize was that there was a hidden consequence to his bouncing in and out of the UK like he was flying on Pinball Airways or as if his braces had got caught in the doors at Heathrow. We knew that there is a strange but nasty little twist in the laws concerning smuggling – every time he entered the UK without declaring and paying the tax on the diamonds counted as a fresh offence. So not only did I have him for one smuggling attempt and all the tax that was due, but for a total of three smuggling runs, which was three times the tax and duty.

Mr Black burst into tears, and I didn't blame him. I think in his position I would have done the same thing. He said he had no money, that it was all tied up in the stones. Oh dear. How sad. Never mind. I knew it was going to take one hell of a special cup of tea to make this better.

And so, in the end, a woman with probably more diamonds than anyone else on earth – Her Majesty the Queen – became the official owner of 120 brand-new ones. It was like throwing pork pies to a fat man.

One disgusting item that we would come across regularly, when searching passengers from certain African countries, was bush meat. It is a generic term for meat from, guess where, the bush. That may sound innocent enough but in reality it meant it may be zebra, lion, gorilla or chimpanzee flesh. In the early days, we were lucky enough to have a blanket ban on meat imports by passengers, and today the bush-meat trade is banned under CITES (Convention on International Trade in Endangered Species).

When you examine the business of bush meat, you realize that the ban is partly in place because of the way we feel about the animals from which the meat comes. We should perhaps look at ourselves first before we criticize Africans for eating their local resource. We eat pork, which is abhorrent to the Jewish community; we eat beef, which disgusts the Hindu community. So I sometimes wondered if we were really in a position to tell off the African nations for eating something that had wandered into their back garden. Sometimes it really is a matter of context . . . and what tasty animal happens to be easiest to catch. For that reason, I imagined a quarter-pound lion burger with chips was bloody expensive.

Food came into the UK from every country and in every shape and form. One day I stopped a chap from the West Indies in the green channel and opened his large suitcase. There were three T-shirts, two pairs of pants, a pair of socks and twenty-five kilos of large, still wet red snapper fish. The fish weren't even wrapped in anything or prepared. It was as if the bloke had just caught them, threw them straight into his suitcase, put his clothes on top almost as an afterthought, and then thought, right, let's go to England for some chips! The trouble was that this was so mad and so blatant a smuggle that it occurred to me it could have been a double-bluff for a drugs run. It did indeed smell very fishy. Which meant that I knew I had to gut and check every single fish.

At the end of a very messy and unsuccessful dead-fish cavity search, I stood there with my bloodied knife in hand, looking and smelling like I'd been savaged by a gang of angry haddock. It turned out the fish were clean . . . well, not clean, but drug-free anyway.

There were two African countries that were not regarded as specific drug-manufacturing source countries but were still number one and two on our hit parade because of the frequency of smugglers originating from there. These were the West African countries of Nigeria and Ghana. The problem with smugglers from these two places got so bad that the

Ghanaian government passed a law that, if any Ghanaian national was arrested carrying drugs and subsequently imprisoned, they would also receive the same prison sentence again when they returned to Ghana. Which is a pretty extreme measure in anyone's book. Did it slow down the smuggling trade? In a word: no. It's a sad state of affairs but unfortunately some people do desperate things for money. And, on top of this, the Customs controls in their own country are very basic, so that it is quite easy to get the gear in. But, as there is little or no market for heroin or cocaine inside these countries, the gear is then quickly shipped out to countries like ours where the market has always been lucrative and there is the money to pay for it. In the UK, as well as an appetite for tea, we also have a very unhealthily healthy taste for Class A drugs. Funny how little old plant leaves can produce such different substances. Then again, if tea was illegal almost all of us would be doing life.

Now, if we look at the smuggling routes from a smuggler's point of view, what would we find? Well, at one point in Bali airport you would see a sign before Customs that said 'Death Penalty for those who carry drugs to Bali'; at Jakarta airport, Indonesia, there was a huge sign in bright orange that said 'Death Penalty for drugs traffickers'; in Singapore airport, a sign read 'Warning! DEATH for drugs traffickers under Singapore law'; and in the UK we had 'Drugs are illegal, talking about them isn't. So talk to Frank'. I'm not saying we should have a return to capital punishment, but it isn't difficult to see which countries you would avoid and which you would favour if you were a smuggler. For that reason, British Customs is a lot busier than Bali's.

The African countries that served as starting points for smugglers did, however, have one apparent power that was lacking in most of the rest of the world – as I was about to find out. I stood and watched as a colleague opened the suitcase of a gentleman from Ghana. Inside there was a single unwashed and unironed shirt spread over the contents of the case. That was it. The officer removed the shirt and revealed that the whole bag was packed solid with herbal cannabis. It was one of the most blatant and badly disguised attempted smuggles we'd ever seen. The gentleman just stood there, smiling.

'Well?' asked the officer. 'What's all this here?'

He smiled back. 'Nothing!'

The officer looked down at the big blocks of dope. 'It doesn't look like nothing.'

'It is *nothing*. There is nothing there.'

'Really?'

'Yes, really. *Nothing*.'

'Well, sunshine, I hate to burst your bubble but it certainly doesn't look like nothing to me. What do *you* think it is?'

The gentleman's smile didn't waver. 'Oh, you see nothing.'

'I think I *do* see something.'

'No. It is the juju!'

'Right, that's it, son!' said the officer, his patience snapping. And with that the gentleman was promptly marched straight into a nice cold cell (tea optional).

It was my first encounter with the 'juju', but it wasn't to be the last. And some of the cover stories that were concocted were also stunning. I stopped a Nigerian man who was very sure of himself. Which is another telltale sign – over-compensating confidence. He had a cash-paid ticket (telltale sign no. 2) and his name had popped up on our computer system as worthy of a closer look. As we talked at my search bench, he told me that he was coming to see the big football match. I was all ears as it happened to be mid-July and off season.

'So, tell me, who have you come to watch then?'

'I am here to see the famous Manchester Town . . .'

'Oh, them.'

'. . . play at Old Trafalgar stadium.'

'I see. Interesting.'

Before he could tell me the team manager was Sir Alex Fungal-bum and his favourite player was David Pecker, I started searching his baggage. It was clean, but he also had a video camera with three extra batteries. They were all carrying a charge but two of them were strikingly lighter than the other. I whipped out my faithful lock-knife and started cutting into one of the lighter batteries. At this, the passenger started swearing at me and cursing me with what was clearly the fiercest language in his arsenal (before they moved from Highbury).

The battery case popped open and there inside was the heroin, neatly packed and quite solid. Once this was removed you could see that a smaller battery had been wired in, to give the appearance that it carried a charge. Very clever. Very sly. Very silly.

We soon learned, as officers, what this 'juju' actually was. Or what it purported to be. Apparently, at least in our experience of it, juju was a terrible spell that was purchased from the tribal witch doctor and that was supposed to make suspicious officials like me unable to see whatever contraband was being smuggled in the case.

We learned that a whole trade, over many parts of Africa, had set itself up to feed the drug smugglers the lie that the magic spells – which, of course, had to be paid for – would protect them from the evil powers of the Customs officer. At the bottom of the scale was the spell that would see them safely through the green channel without being stopped. Or, for a bit more money, you could have your drugs blessed so that they were supposedly invisible to a European's eyes. There were hundreds of these juju spells. The traffickers that got caught ended up in prison for fifteen years so perhaps word never got back that the spell didn't work. Or, on the other hand, those that successfully got through spread the word back at home that the spells were effective and that, indeed, juju made us blind.

We decided, between ourselves, that if the large quantities of beer, cider, whisky and absinthe that Customs officers consumed out-of-hours hadn't yet made us blind then no voodoo spell on earth would do it either.

11. Mickey Mouse Goods (Including the Ears)

Brits can be a very strange bunch when it comes to travelling abroad. We love our cups of tea and warm beer. If things aren't the same as they are at home (which we've come on holiday to get away from), then we talk about complaining . . . but never do. I'm sure that there is a written rule somewhere that says, 'When two or more Brits are in a foreign country, they shall gather together.' And one strange thing that was also common and that we used to see on a regular basis was the crap that British holidaymakers returned home with. I think it was partly a desire to spend their last euros on whatever could be found at the nearest souvenir shop and partly the result of sun-stroked brains still waterlogged with cheap beer.

A popular item at one time was the large stuffed souvenir camel from North Africa, often from Egypt. Nothing says you've had a good holiday like a stuffed straw animal. And they were as popular with drug smugglers as with travellers. They were also great for the kids – until, that is, you happened to open one. I'll never forget the first one I opened in order to search it in case it was being used as a miniature Trojan . . . camel. With my trusty old lock-knife, I turned into a HMRC veterinary surgeon and split the camel's belly open with one slice. I was certainly surprised by what I found, but not in the way I'd expected: the insides of the camel were padded out with what looked like dirty, bloodied, used hospital bandages. And that's exactly what they were. Apparently, for years these items had been filled with the cheapest things the makers could get their hands on, and this was often local waste. Every camel that I dissected from then on was stuffed with the same thing, bandages, usually from the local hospital and mainly used and unwashed.

From the same area of the holiday globe would come the Fez hat. Tommy Cooper had a lot to answer for. But it did make our job very easy when it came to officers playing a diverting game of Spot the Twat in the incoming holiday parties. The bright-red upstanding fez did show up very well in the white environment of the baggage hall.

Carpets, of course, were very popular from Turkey. But unless you were a carpet expert (and Customs had to be) chances were that as a holidaying punter you would be flogged a third-rate bit of rag for a nice large amount of money. If you did happen to know what you were looking for you could haggle the seller down to a good price. But still the carpet would have to be declared, in the red channel, because it would always be way over the 'other goods' allowance. The best Turkish businessmen, though, recognized that the Brits and their money are easily parted if they can avoid paying tax, so the carpet salesmen would offer holidaymakers a second or even third receipt proving that they had only spent a few quid on a double knotted silk carpet instead of the £800 that it really did cost.

We could spot a real, kosher Turkish piece in an instant and the traveller would be pulled over for 'the chat' and invited to land their flying carpet on our inspection bench. Some of the faked credit card receipts produced were so good that they were almost believable, as were the travellers' stories of how they had beaten the trader down in price. Now, because we, as officers, had to learn about anything and everything that might pass before us, we knew that the only way to get a top-notch piece of weaving like that so cheaply wasn't to beat the seller down on price but to beat him up with a cricket bat. Which, come to think of it, is a pretty good way of bartering . . . and also of getting yourself buried in a Turkish prison for a few years. And anyone who's seen the film *Midnight Express* knows that is not a good idea. Their prisons make our prisons look like Sunday school missions.

Another thing not in the Brit travellers' favour is that we will never be able to out-haggle the haggle masters; just as we are not natural complainers (even though we're bloody good moaners), Brits abroad are also not very good hagglers. Another strange British habit – but one that goes in Customs' favour – is that we appear to never, ever destroy the original receipt. I don't know if that's a consequence of everyone shopping at Marks & Spencer for most of their lives and getting used to the idea that it's OK to take something back after five years *as long as they've got the receipt*. But for us Customs officers, it was just a matter of finding it. Usually a simple baggage search would suffice but, in some situations, a full body search had to be carried out.

My favourite technique was pure mental torture backed up by mean authority. With experience, I could usually estimate a carpet price to the nearest £100 but in this I was just an amateur: some officers could get it within £5. So I would have a punter standing in front of me, swearing blue murder that he only paid £50 for a £800 carpet. Bring forth the guillotine: 'The estimation of price for revenue purposes.' I would explain that I disagreed with the proffered receipt and that the carpet was to be detained and would undergo professional, trade pricing, from which I would calculate the evaded duty and VAT. After letting the idea of professional pricing and having the carpet locked away for three months sink in, you would hit them with the 'Or I can . . .' option. I would say those three words and pause, and the passenger's eyes would widen slightly . . . 'Or I can estimate it myself and work out the duty and tax from what I believe it's worth.' This was the clincher. You could almost feel the sigh of relief exhaled at you. Until, that is, I estimated the carpet's true worth of £800 for tax purposes – and then a sharp intake of breath from the punter would suck the sigh of relief right back out of your face. Ten seconds of quiet swearing later and the correct receipt would magically appear like a genie from a rubbed bottle. Well, come on, we had to have *some* twisted fun when we were working the channels all day!

And this technique worked every time, and not just on Turkish flying carpets but also on imported golf clubs, designer watches, clothes and jewellery of every metal and gem.

The most regrettable things that people brought back always fell under the heading that covered a multitude of holiday sins, namely 'I Was Drunk at the Time' (see also: misspelt tattoos on arse; cracked skull from moped crash; sex with travel rep; chlamydia). But my favourite article import was by a young man who appeared in the red channel and honestly declared a very old and tatty copy of *Great Expectations* by Charles Dickens. He said he'd been pissed when he paid £550 for it in an antique book shop in Boston but it was, he said, a very special item as it had been signed by the author himself. I opened up the cover and there was the very valuable signature in all its glory – 'Charles Dickens'. I had a closer look at it and then passed it over to my senior officer who also studied it carefully before he passed it back to the passenger.

'On your way, lad,' I said, and the young man looked surprised and bemused.

'But what about the VAT?' he asked.

I thought the news might best be delivered with a straight face. 'Well, if I were you, mate, I'd try to stay sober the next time you buy an antique book. Because I don't think Charles Dickens ever signed his name in ballpoint pen.'

An inbound Orlando flight also attracted another buyer whose judgement may well have been clouded by the fog of inebriation. In his travel bag I found a large stuffed cobra coiled up in the folded shirts (it would have been one hell of a surprise to bag thieves if it had been alive). At least, the passenger *thought* it was a cobra. It was, in fact, the worst stuffed snake that any of us had ever seen. It had one eye (the other having fallen off in the bag), one fang (the other one never found) and a large fist-sized lump halfway down its body. On top of this the snake's corpse was sloughing, that is, shedding its skin. The guy had basically just bought himself a very expensive and tatty draught excluder. That smelled.

Then there were the Mickey Mouse goods – literally. The American tourist version of the Egyptian fez was the Walt Disney store Mickey Mouse ears. These were like a beacon to a baggage officer. And they were very helpfully worn by passengers as they came off the plane. Officers knew how much they cost and knew that the families' 'other goods' allowance would be taken up by the cost of the ears so anything else that they had purchased would be fully taxable. It was like wearing a numbered pound sign on your head.

It was, of course, at the discretion of individual officers whether or not they pursued this matter of adults wearing big black plastic cartoon mouse ears, dependent, often, on how bored or how crappy a day the officer had endured. Contributing circumstances might apply, as they say. So, if, for example, a Customs officer had just found out his wife was shagging someone called Donald, then a Mickey Mouse-eared passenger was also likely to get fucked.

The other goods that everyone else more commonly referred to as 'Mickey Mouse' were, of course, all the fake, counterfeit or 'hooky' items that we used to find and process. For many years, the UK had very stringent rules on these goods and absolutely tons of counterfeit clothes, watches, perfumes, handbags, designer goods and so on would be destroyed every few months. I was always a bit fifty-fifty on the reasons for detention or seizure of the goods. Sometimes the counterfeit items would be a serious risk to the public, such as – from the lower end of the scale – whisky made from industrial alcohol that may blind people or give them irreparable liver damage, right up to the completely insane knock-off items such as aircraft spares – which may, if they failed, wipe out a few hundred people.

While at the airport one day, I assisted the local investigation team in searching the hangars of a well-known UK-based aircraft repair company (I won't name them in case you're flying this week . . . or reading this on one of their planes!). This company ran fleets of enormous long-haul passenger airliners. And in their service bays at the airport we found millions of pounds' worth of counterfeit, non-authentic aircraft parts. We checked each part on a serial number database against the purchasing company and, surprise surprise, none of the parts existed.

What didn't come as a surprise was that we didn't put out any form of press release. The job was hushed up, with the company being fined millions behind the scenes. Why was it hushed up? you might reasonably ask. Well, we had no idea which aircraft had which dodgy parts. And, on top of that, the company had also been supplying these parts to other airline repair companies. It was decided that for the 'public's own good' the job was to be kept secret, which made the company in question very happy.

You could see all type of counterfeit goods being brought into the country from watches to skateboards, from cigarettes to cheese. But the only home market counterfeiting seemed to be pirating DVDs. And sometimes we didn't even have to be on duty to see this stuff. On many days off-duty, while sitting in a pub in north London with a Customs colleague, I'd been approached by blokes offering every type of DVD from porn films to Disney films to 'Disney' porn films (*Snow White Does the Seven Dwarfs*, for example, and, in this version, I think they were all Happy).

It seemed that the high-speed world of home computing was inhibiting the multimillion-pound film industry and its companies from ripping us off for themselves, which was a shame for them.

Another area of Mickey Mouse goods where I felt a little sorry for the smuggler was that of hooky watches. Major companies spend millions of pounds hunting down the makers and distributors of these fake designer watches. It was only the fashion companies that did this, though, as the normal watch companies don't seem to be that worried about it. So a luxury brand, for a purely hypothetical example, might bring out some black and gold watch for £10,000; but the brand is not a watchmaker, so it's just possible, if you are a cynical old bastard, to believe that all they have done is buy some middle-market £100 watch, glued a logo on to it and then added an extra two '0's to the price. Now that would seem to me to be more criminal than somebody copying the watch and selling it for a price much nearer to what it was actually worth. Yet the designer companies go berserk at a cheap copy being sold to someone who would never have the money to buy the original anyway. As I said, I was sort of fifty-fifty on the issue of counterfeiting.

The strangest thing was when we discovered people being

ripped off and conned not by strangers but by the people closest to them.

Mr and Mrs Robinson looked like an upstanding couple. Both were well dressed and with expensive luggage. They had arrived on a flight from Las Vegas and appeared to be very much in love. The couple had been married for ten years and owned a number of successful shops in north London. However, a year before I met them, they had split up when Mr Robinson's gambling addiction had started to eat away at the businesses profits. Mrs Robinson had thrown him out and had taken control of all their bank accounts. Mr Robinson managed to shake the gambling habit and the two had got back together three weeks before their tenth wedding anniversary. To mark the event, the couple had decided on a second honeymoon in the States and off they went. And now they were back.

I stopped the Robinsons in the green channel as they looked quite affluent – it was our experience that it was the big spenders who would buy lots of nice goodies and not declare them. So I asked the standard questions as I started to search their baggage. A little polite conversation followed and then the couple told me the whole marriage story. It didn't take long before I found a small washbag full of luxury watches. I could see straight away that they were counterfeit: they looked and felt cheap. They were gold and white with scissors for hands.

'They're for the assistants in our shop. Just a little gift from us,' said Mrs Robinson.

I informed the couple that the watches would have to be

seized. Mr Robinson took it badly. He started to shout about how he knew that they were fake and they weren't even trying to be the real thing. I had to agree with him on that, and I would have turned a blind eye and let him through with them, but the trouble was that, while I'd been checking the watches, a senior officer had walked passed and mouthed 'good job'. So, that was that, the fate of the fake watches was sealed. But just then I spotted Mrs Robinson's brand-new luxury watch on her wrist.

'Do you mind if I have a look at your watch, madam?' I asked Mrs Robinson.

She looked a little embarrassed as she removed it.

'Oh dear,' she said in a not very convincing way. 'I forgot all about this one. I think we should have gone in the red channel to declare it.'

'Well . . . actually . . . I don't think the red channel officer would have been too worried by this one,' I said as I examined the watch and then slid it into the seizure bag with the other fake watches. There were a few seconds of surprise while this information sank in, then a few seconds more while it was processed, then a look of dawning realization on Mrs Robinson's face as she suddenly sussed what had happened – and then turned to her husband and she released one of the greatest right hooks I have ever seen. Mr Robinson flew backwards with a small cry and met the floor, unconscious with a cracked jaw. Mrs Robinson followed up her punch with an equally perfectly timed cry of 'Bastard!' But by then Mr Robinson was already in the land of nod. So what had changed Mrs Robinson into Sugar Ray Robinson?

Apparently, Mr Robinson, with a nice piece of persuasive pillow talk, had convinced his wife to give him £2,000 from their account so that he could, he said, buy Mrs Robinson a nice present, e.g. a real luxury watch. Which he had apparently done in LA. But, when I'd slipped it into the bag with the other fakes, the penny had dropped and she realized that her dear husband's addiction had returned. He had clearly gambled away the two grand and then bought her a Mickey Mouse watch.

By the time I had finished the paperwork with his wife, Mr Robinson had been whisked away to hospital for treatment to his socked jaw. Here's to you, Mrs Robinson, indeed.

It wasn't only wives that could do for you – kids could be a self-inflicted lethal weapon, too. Most people have had the experience of travelling with young children and all the joy and fun that brings – the moaning, the crying, the constant toilet breaks and the annoying kicking of the back of the seat in front. And that's just the behaviour of the parents. But as Customs officers we could be extra evil and use the children as willing intelligence sources against their parents. It's one of the dangers of travelling with a little mobile truth-telling machine.

One day, I was working the green channel at Gatwick when a flight came in from Jamaica. The Jamaica flights were always a good shot for cannabis, coke and bottles of Wray & Nephew rum, which, at 62.8 per cent alcohol, was like flavoured rocket fuel (normal whisky being 40 per cent). I stopped a large woman and her nine-year-old son who came through the channels. Coming from outside of the European Union, the lady was allowed one litre of the W&N firewater but, on examination of her large quantity of baggage, I discovered she was carrying another fifteen litres. It was the sound of sloshing that gave her away. This kind of rum running was a never-ending conveyor belt; and everybody seemed to try their hand at it. But once a 'find' is discovered it has to be acted on. During the interview, the lady said she had never done this before and she was very sorry and she'd never do it again; to calm her down, I asked her how she was planning on getting home. She said she was really afraid that her husband, who was due to pick her up, would think that he'd missed them and go home.

It took me another twenty minutes to process the case but I tried to do it as quickly as I could so at least she and her son could get their lift home. In the end, she coughed up about £600 in duty tax and the fine. During all this time, the young lad had not said a word, just watched and taken everything in.

As she was leaving the channels, I asked where her husband might be waiting for her. 'I've no idea,' she said, 'but I'm sure he's been waiting too long and has gone home.'

Then, perfectly on cue, the young lad looked up and very clearly and loudly said, 'Won't Daddy be waiting in the same place that he waited last time you were arrested here?'

Bollocks. I'd forgotten to check if she had previous. Feeling a bit embarrassed that I'd not done a background check, I let her and her son on their way. When I thought about it, I really should have questioned the brains of the operation – the nine-year-old.

12. Machine v. Man/Customs Officer v. Pilot

Is machine better than the man? Well, in my experience in the airports, I would have to say a definite 'no' to that one. Over the years, Customs has tried many ways of doing the smuggler-spotting job better than its best trained officers, and every time the machine or the alternative method has seemed to come off second best.

The first form of the ANPR (automatic number plate reader) was deployed at Dover ferry port. The idea was that the number plate reader would scan the plate and send the data to good old CEDRIC, and this in turn would alert the officers in the car hall that a suspect vehicle was approaching. It was a great idea and one that later went on to work well all over the country. The problem was that in the beginning it only worked 50 per cent of the time and this was down to mud and muck on the registration plates. There was a way to solve that but it was one that rather gave the game away: an officer with a mop and bucket standing by the reader, ready to swab down any dirty plates as cars came through. You didn't exactly need to be a master criminal to realize what that meant.

The next great leap forward into the future was something called the Sniffer Arch that was installed at Heathrow. The manufacturers claimed that, as passengers walked through it, the arch could easily identify the smell of any major drug. So, at last – we thought a little dubiously – the ultimate smuggler spotter had been found. Unfortunately, and unsurprisingly, it didn't work out that way. The arch was more easily aroused than a nymphomaniac on a pogo stick bouncing over cobbles. Every few minutes it started going off, screaming with alarms and whistles and bells and flashing lights; it made the airport terminal look as if a permanent conference of the world's drug dealers was passing through. Instead of drugs, the machine was registering perfume and aftershave. After a few days of shrieking madness – mostly from us at having to listen to it – the arch was relegated to a back wall, never to be heard of again. And how many people did it catch? Precisely none. (It did later raise a few quid at the local car-boot sale, though.)

The concept of the Sniffer Arch was later revived with more success when it was reconfigured as a detection device for explosives, using lasers to scan for the relevant materials. And anything that stopped passengers from having to undress in the airport had to be a good thing.

Next came a competition not between man and machine but man and fly. The fruit fly, to be exact. A number of European scientists had found that fruit flies could be trained to identify the odour of controlled drugs. In experiments they discovered that the insects would swarm to the specific site location of certain chosen illegal substances. Whether or not they had to turn these little buggers into junkies in order to get them to search out their drug of choice, I don't know. But, if so, it must have been hell trying to tap up a vein in a fruit fly. And I couldn't see how a doped-up, cannabis-sensitized fly could be bothered to get up off its tiny, lackadaisical arse and do *anything*. The last thing we wanted in the airport was a swarm of smacked-out insects, dopey bugs and amphetamine-hopped flies turning the Butterflies Ball into an acid house rave.

Flies, apparently, use their highly developed sense of smell to determine their flight patterns and they can detect red wine from three-quarters of a mile away, but in practical terms how could that really help us in drug detection in an airport? Well, the scientists explained that it was all a work in progress. But, as yet, Customs has still not adopted it – much appreciated, I'm sure, by the detection dog officers who didn't have to retrain as fly handlers! Which is a good job, because I'd be damned if I'd have walked around an airport with another officer with a fruit fly on a tiny leash.

But this was not a new thing; if you look back in history, we have always strived to find something that would take away the guesswork or the reliance on the law enforcer's intuition. A hundred or so years ago, we believed that criminals could be classified by the bumps on their head, the length of their nose or the distance between their eyes. We laugh at this now, but then it was cutting-edge science that took years to dismiss. Even today, not many people realize that handwriting/graphology readers have now been discredited. It's rubbish, but, once again, for years we believed in it. Big companies spent hundreds of thousands of pounds using graphologists to hire the best person for the job. They would have been just as successful counting potatoes on the applicant's hands. Or, indeed, the bumps on their head.

The same is true of voice-stress analysis and even MRI (magnetic resonance imaging) as ways of supposedly detecting the truth from the lies. But the great-granddaddy of them all, and the last great myth of techno-detection, was the lie-detector test. The trouble is that it is unreliable and can easily give false positives – meaning it can make an innocent man look guilty. How many millions have been spent on this piece of unreliable kit? Luckily, we have always been wise enough to know that the machine can be fooled and, in fact, you can train yourself to deceive the technology. The polygraph is more widely used in the United States – despite there being ample cases that show its failure to detect, for example, things like double agents working for the Soviet Union during the Cold War – but the evidence that is produced from the polygraph has never and, I think, will never be acceptable in a British court.

So, back to the original question: is machine better than the man? The answer, at this present time, is that, like it or not, the ever-twitching antennae of that uniformed human radar – the Customs officer – beats all the technology, hands down.

There are also a couple of very important things that machines can't do but a human being can (Customs officers, you may be surprised to hear, also being human) and that is to show some discretion and display some empathy. And, funnily enough, after years on the job, a search on my last ever day as a uniformed HMRC preventive officer fell into this category.

It concerned a young male steward who had been on a long-haul British Airways flight. He was visibly shaking as he entered the clearance area for crew, so that was immediately a strange thing for an employee that travelled through Customs controls every day. But as we've already established, and as you may be glad to hear (unless you are an aircraft employee), the aircraft crews were no more trusted than ordinary passengers.

I decided it wasn't really worth going through the palaver of the normal passenger questions with this young chap as he'd know the procedure off by heart, so I just got down to a search. It didn't take too long to discover why the nerves were taking hold of the lad. Inside his washbag was a soap container and inside that there were twenty neatly rolled joints. Even as I opened the container, the steward was starting to cry, which I was a little shocked by. I guessed that in his mind he was quickly running through all the possible consequences and seeing that very few of them were good. Aware that a member of his crew was in distress, the captain, who was walking past, strode over and demanded to know why I had his crew member in tears.

Now, this was a fifty-fifty type of situation. Rules and regs stated that I had to do something with the lad and, whatever was going on, that was just between me and him. Also, if this captain found out, then British Airways would have to be told and the lad could kiss his job goodbye. On top of that, American law regarding drug possession (even minor incidents) would prevent him from ever working the Atlantic route again – aircraft crew being expected, understandably, to lead by example. How could they expect the best behaviour from passengers if they themselves decided to cross the line?

So there was an awful lot riding on what I would decide to do, and all of the possible consequences, I had to admit, would be a result of what was a pretty minor infraction. As well as some natural sympathy for his situation, he had one more thing in his favour – the fact that his captain was being a bit of a twat. He was standing in front of me, hands on hips, loudly demanding to know what was going on. I had been in the job too long by now to be flustered by someone that Customs officers generally considered to be little more than posh, jumped-up bus drivers. And, on top of that, I thought he should have known full well that his own staff member would not have been upset without a reason, and that the reason may well have been that he was carrying something he shouldn't have – as was the case here.

As this was my last day on the job, I decided to get as much fun out of this as I could. All the other aircraft crew members had now stopped and were watching on, so I pointed to the exit from the channels and loudly said, 'Take a hike, Biggles. Your crew member is just helping me out with a misunderstanding. If we need you, we'll send up a flare.'

Crestfallen, but knowing better than to tackle a Customs officer on his home patch, the captain's hands dropped off his hips and he turned and departed.

Once he'd gone, I escorted the steward into an interview room, grabbed a passing officer, quietly whispered what I had in mind and got down to one very fast interview. The poor lad was all tears and it was obvious from the state of him that this was the first time he'd done anything like this. I had to admit that this must have been the easiest interview that I had ever conducted as all it took was one question from me and the accused blabbed the lot. He explained that he had purchased the joints in Amsterdam and they were for his boyfriend. Apparently, it was the old 'you would do it for me if you loved me' threat. It is amazing how many people will put so much on the line because of a demand from a girl-friend or boyfriend. He knew as well as I did that this would be the end of his career. My fellow officer, Ben, and myself stepped out of the room for a second and decided what to do. Ben did what we called 'testing the drugs to destruction' – which was our way of saying that he flushed them down the bog. Then I gave the steward a strong enough bollocking to ensure he didn't ever try it again. I said that neither his cap-tain nor British Airways would be informed of the situation as long as he kept his nose clean. As we had to show some reason for the detainment and interview, we took a £40 fine from him, which we later wrote up as fine for 400 fags, and placed the money straight in the cash register so that no one was the wiser about the cannabis. He dried his tears and looked happier than I think I'd seen anyone look the whole year. We then shook hands and I escorted him from the channels.

So, even though my last job as a uniformed preventive officer was actually letting someone off rather than catching them, it felt bloody good.

13. Uniformed Intel

From the first person I had ever stopped onwards, I had done quite well as an airport preventive officer. But I never quite believed that I had the Customs officer's sixth sense, if in fact that sixth sense ever existed. So, after my years of working 'on the bench', I was now looking at making the move to something to give me a new challenge. The opportunity for that arose during the holiday we hold to celebrate the birth of a man executed by being nailed to a cross, though the holiday more often than not revolves around an Argos catalogue, the supermarket wine aisle and a fat man with a beard in a red suit.

During a Christmas party, held by Special Branch, I got into conversation with Gary, the only Intelligence officer at our airport. The poor bloke was working his legs down to the knees with the demands of the job. Though he was still in uniform, as all airport Intelligence officers were, his job was to gather the 'intel' (intelligence information) that might help the preventive Customs officers, like me, do our job better. It was the Intel officers' duty to provide local intelligence for their own airports or ports. The Intel officers would use any means or route possible, such as airline computers, FedEx and

UPS delivery info, and liaising with Special Branch or the Immigration Department.

One thing we uniforms didn't need any help in doing better was drinking; the drinking culture in Customs was well established and ingrained. So take it as a measure of my Christmas party intake that, when, the following day, Gary came over to me and said that he agreed with my idea, I had no idea what he was talking about. I couldn't remember any idea that I had suggested or even talking to Gary the night before. I just hoped that, if the idea was for me to have gender reassignment surgery and change my name to Barbara, Gary hadn't already bought me a dress, a wig and high heels. That would be just silly. I was obviously more of a Margaret.

Apparently, I had suggested that the Intelligence team – i.e. Gary – should grow by 100 per cent by adding me to the line-up. I'd always fancied the hush-hush world of Intelligence and I knew I had to start somewhere. Gary said he was going to have a word with the surveyor about it and see how it went.

A week later, I was in my new Intelligence officer uniform (which was the same as the old uniform but minus the badges of rank). I arrived in the Intel office for training. As this was what we would now classify as the early days for Customs preventive intelligence, the training was basically officers such as Gary making it up as they went along. Intel work was still viewed with some suspicion by a lot of senior officers.

So, no training as such then, just Gary trying to explain what he got up to and what was expected of us. And this is where the first hurdle appeared. We were preventive Intelligence officers and, as far as our local management were concerned, our job was to find smugglers for our local staff to stop and arrest. But intelligence information is strange stuff and is rarely what you want it to be. During our duties, I found that much of the intel we came across had nothing to do with our airport, and the other intel we discovered had little to do with Customs. We would come across police targets, Europol suspects and Interpol's most wanted, etc. All interesting stuff – and stuff I filed away as something I could move on to later – but of no use to the airport officers. And our management were unimpressed with the amount of non-local intelligence that we processed as it didn't improve their stats and, as such, to them was a waste of time.

At this time, we had one computer and that was for CEDRIC (i.e. Customs database) and PNC (police database) use only. We had no other forms of intelligence storage except a card index for suspects that we had come across or smugglers that we had caught. It sometimes felt like our intelligence methods were no better than sticking a pin into a list of names. But we stuck with it and gradually our methods improved and we actually started to talk to other ports and airports. One method that we used was simplicity itself: we would stand behind the Immigration officers in the airport at outbound (departures) and we would memorize the passport details of anyone we thought looked a bit iffy. That meant looking over a shoulder and remembering the full name, date and place of birth, plus what the suspect looked like. You soon started to improve your memory with practice; I could manage four of these clumps of details before I had to write them all down. Gary, with more practice, could do six, and the details would be perfectly correct. These details were then checked on CEDRIC and PNC as well as our index system. If we managed to get a hit, that passenger would be pulled for a search on their return. It was basic but it worked for us. The art of these early days of intel gathering was to be covert enough so that the smuggler never guessed that we were checking up on them. Our Intel team even became successful enough to add a couple more officers.

There were a limited number of people that I genuinely disliked but a character I kept running into fell easily into that category. We called him Benny the Dip, for the rather obvious reason that he was a notorious pickpocket. He'd been in more purses than a ten-year-old pound coin and in more pockets than pocket fluff. But Benny's chief problem with his chosen career was that he was crap at it. If he'd tried to nick a kid's pocket money out of a piggy bank – which he would've happily done – he'd have got his finger stuck in the slot. He was so inept that anyone who wanted to write a letter to him – such as a parole officer, a bailiff, a debt collector, the taxman, the DVLA, etc. – could send it directly to Benny at his local police station. And, as with many rubbish and habitual criminals, his crimes were directly linked to his drug habit. Benny would smoke, snort, sniff, chew, chomp, inject or lick anything that he thought could get him high. Personally, I wouldn't have trusted him to babysit my goldfish, on the basis that he'd probably see if he could inhale it. It's very hard to trust a man that you can easily imagine with bright-orange tailfins waggling out of one of his nostrils.

Not only did Benny make appearances at the local police station on a regular basis – matinees too – but he would also show up with distressing regularity at the airport. We began to think that he must have advertised himself as a drugs mule in the local paper:

> Experienced smuggler available. Travels extensively.
> Own bag.
> Good swallower. Will work for drugs (preferably not goldfish).

The trouble was that Benny was only ever caught on the occasions when he just had enough on him to be done for possession, not supply, but we were sure that we knew what his MO was, which was to purchase the gear in the Netherlands for a third party, and then post the drugs back to the UK. Our problem was that we had no idea who he was sending them to. Chances were that he would use a different address every time. We never seemed to get the intel at the right time or place to nail him. And this had gone on for a few years, with Benny ducking and diving through both UK and Dutch Customs. But then he finally ran into trouble. It seemed that the Dutch police had got as fed up with him as we were as he was constantly being arrested for drugs offences, being drunk and fighting. Benny the Dip was one of the only people I knew that actually got banned from entering the Netherlands.

So, Benny had to come up with a new system – and this was to fly to Belgium and then drive or use the train to cross the land border. He was still being picked up and deported by the Dutch and he still kept turning up on their doorstep like a dangerous boomerang. But all good things must come to an end, and his face was now so well known at our airport that he decided to change his travelling arrangements and fly back to Luton. The trouble on this occasion was that Luton was at a standstill because of fog, so on his day of travel Benny yet again arrived in our airport's green channel. With this info, we tipped off the uniformed airport search boys that he was inbound and, as luck would have it, they were very quiet so we decided to give Benny the full treatment. He was put into the paper suit which is given out to those who have had their clothes removed for testing, and then he was given a nice holding cell. We never really expected much of the urine test as we all knew that he had a little bit of blood in his drugs stream, but, as it turned out, this time we were wrong.

The procedure was that, if drugs were discovered in the urine on the first test, then we would carry out a second test some time later to see if the reading had increased or decreased. Benny's second test shot off the scale for amphetamine. This was a positive indication that he had gear concealed inside him as drugs were released into his bloodstream. With the good news of this new finding, Benny clammed up. He wouldn't speak except to ask for a solicitor. Most of our cells were full that day so we were holding him in an overnight cell with bed and blanket and a babysitting watch waiting for the drugs to emerge. The on-call solicitor phoned the office and demanded that he talk to Benny without any officers within hearing range. Although this was against standard operating procedures, the senior officer said that this could happen as long as we could see Benny's head. So the officers were pulled out of the cell and a phone was attached to the socket next to Benny's bed. The officers did as they were told and waited for the call to end before returning to the cell.

As they approached, Benny stood in the doorway and stated that he was ready for nature to take its course, which meant that the drugs would finally make an appearance. On their way to the toilet, one of the officers noticed a smallish, brown-rimmed hole in the backside of the paper suit. Grabbing Benny, they rushed back to the cell where they were almost overcome by the smell of human waste. They lifted the blanket and there, in the middle of a steaming pile, were six golf-ball-sized packages of drugs. Benny smiled. 'Well, don't look at me, I never done that. It's a plant.'

Our dear friend Benny was given three years and new nickname that sort of rhymed with 'dip'. And our paths never crossed again.

As Intel officers at the airport, we were always on the lookout for new ways of catching a potential drugs run. Bob, my manager, came up with a corker. He knew that in my skills armoury I had the ability of a pretty good lock-picker. When likely-looking smugglers were spotted going outbound through passport control, he would pass their details to me, down in the bowels of the airport. I would then pull out their checked-in luggage, pick the locks and see if I could find any evidence that might link them to drug smuggling. Now that might sound a bit hit and miss but it worked really well. The hit rate was high.

You would never have sussed that passengers Mr and Mrs Whitehead were husband and wife as she was a good twenty-five years older than him. But there they were, snogging each other in the passport queue, so they were clearly a couple. For some reason, Bob's antennae identified them as 'possible' so he passed down their details. Ten minutes later, I had their bags off the belt for a search. Inside there were hypodermic needles, lots of condoms, dental floss and clingfilm – the perfect kit for both personal drug use and an internal drug-smuggling attempt. The two of them were booked out for a two-week stay in Thailand, a drug-supply source country, so they looked a good bet for coming back into the country with more than tan lines and cheap flip-flops.

So, two weeks later, a four-officer team waited for their arrival. Bob and I watched the couple on CCTV. 'I see the love is still there,' Bob said, as the Whiteheads once again came through the airport with their lips latched together, but this time with the addition of the husband's hand up his wife's skirt. In fact, this ostentatious display of affection was what had first caused suspicion, as Bob, with all his wisdom and experience, knew that smugglers sometimes fell into the psychological trap of thinking that behaviour that attracted attention would somehow make them look above suspicion. It was the kind of double bluff that Customs rarely fell for because we saw it for what it was: a diversionary ploy that also acted as an inadvertent reveal. In other words, if you give yourself a fake 'alibi' and that alibi looks false, then it's worse than not having one in the first place.

The couple were both pulled over and their baggage searched, and this time the entire drug-smuggling paraphernalia had disappeared. As the two of them were taken to different interview rooms for body searches, etc., I got a better chance to run their passports and other details through all our computer systems. The result that I got was very surprising, and unpleasant: Mr and Mrs Whitehead were not husband and wife but were, in fact, mother and son.

In the following hours, both of them showed a positive reaction to heroin on the urine test but neither of them was going to admit to smuggling. After forty-eight hours, Mr Whitehead's urine reading was going sky high as more drugs were being released internally into his system but his mother's reading had dropped by a few points. Now this wasn't unusual with smugglers who were carrying their consignments inside their bodies but the local magistrate didn't seem to understand the technicalities of the urine test and thought that the slight drop in Mrs Whitehead's test meant she wasn't carrying – and so the magistrate refused us an extension on her detention. So, with a huge grin on her face, she was set free.

Early morning on the third day of detention, Mr Whitehead was as unhelpful as ever, but he did receive his breakfast very eagerly. The officer on babysitting duties, waiting for Whitehead to inevitably pass the drugs out of his body, reported another no show. But, unknown to the officer, just before breakfast had arrived, Whitehouse had shat out the package of heroin into his hand. When the meal did arrive, and before the officer could stop him, Whitehead grabbed the cup of orange juice, slammed the package (still covered in crap) into his mouth and washed it all down with a gulp. This changed the game completely. A well-wrapped package of heroin may make it, intact, through the human body once, but put it back in there for a second time and it's likely to rupture and kill the carrier. So we got him to hospital ASAP and within two hours he was secured in the contagious diseases ward and handcuffed so that he couldn't do a repeat performance of his heroin/crap-eating act. The duty hospital doctor was angry with us for the handcuffs and demanded that we remove them. He soon changed his mind when it was explained to him what had happened in the cell. Within the next two days, Whitehead produced fourteen packages of heroin. He later pleaded guilty in court (he had no defence) and was given seven years. He later admitted that his mother had also been carrying the same amount of drugs. We never got to the bottom of why they thought it would be better to pretend to be travelling as a romantically involved couple than as mother and son. But then we'd already learned that the desperation – and eating habits – of people in the grip of drug addiction should not be underestimated.

Sometimes good things attract bad people. For example, the American delivery company FedEx could get a package from point A to point B almost anywhere in the world within twenty-four hours, which is quite a feat. Now to us, at Customs, that meant one thing: FedEx would be viewed, by smugglers, as the smuggling carrier of choice. Their belief was that the speed of the package's movement would prevent us from finding any intelligence linking it to either the sender or the recipient. And that was quite true (it still is a problem). False names for the two parties – sender and recipient – left us little to go on. So we had to rethink our whole approach towards identifying naughtiness. The first giveaway was the recipient's address, such as a hotel room, which perhaps suggested trying to avoid a home detection. This method led me to arrest the secretary of a very famous rock singer.

I had identified the suspect package as going to a Hilton hotel room in London. The package was then removed when the plane arrived from Memphis (FedEx's main international hub). A quick examination revealed a package of very pure cocaine. We knew that the consignment would likely be shared between the secretary and her boss as it's always in the interests of the celebrity to get their lackey to take the risk.

As I was repackaging the box with 20 grams of icing sugar, I received a phone call from the FedEx office saying that a Miss Harris had just phoned up to see whether her package had arrived from the States. Now, this was out of the ordinary. I asked them to call her back and say that the package was cleared and that she should receive it at about nine the following morning. This message was relayed, and she then asked if she could come down and pick it up from the Stansted Airport FedEx office. Of course, I immediately said yes to that as it would save me hours of preparation and travel – let the smuggler come to me for once. I thought, I could get used to this.

She turned up at Stansted within the hour, handed over the correct paperwork, identified herself with her passport and received the package. She then headed for her car where I was waiting with my HMCE-issue silver wrist jewellery. While processing the lady at the custody office, a number of the staff there passed round her American passport. None of us could believe that the woman in the photograph was the same as the one I had just arrested. Her passport photo was taken when she was a beauty queen and a stunningly beautiful woman. The same woman at the desk was the result of years and years of cocaine abuse: she was stick thin, her nose was being eaten away by the alkaline drug and her face was all skin and bone. If any of us needed a reason to carry on foiling drug-smuggling operations, there stood the reason.

Funnily enough, my next significant find while working on the Intelligence team also featured a FedEx package, but this time a portion of the drugs in the package ended up in a place they'd never been before – inside my body.

I had identified a package arriving on the evening FedEx flight. It had started its journey in the Colombian capital, Bogotá, and was addressed to a small town in Sussex. Now there was little interest in it other than it was on its way from an obviously drug-saturated country like Colombia. But what had tweaked my extra interest was that the contents were described as a satellite TV box. Nothing strange in that, you may think, but the trouble is that South American stations were working on a different TV system than ours. There was also the fact that the postage cost was more than the box was worth. So I flagged up the FedEx computer and waited for its 9 p.m. flight to arrive. By 10.30 p.m., I had commandeered the box and returned to our workshop, which was located in the main passenger terminal, behind the green channel. I could have passed the job on to the uniform boys but they were too busy with a Montego Bay flight that had just arrived. Unpacked, the box was just an old and battered satellite TV tuner. So out with the screwdriver and off with the back, then stand back and stare. Inside there were no electrical components, just a big chalky, grainy mass of hard-packed powder. A quick field drugs test revealed that it was pure cocaine. And a quick X-ray revealed that it was *all* pure cocaine, right the way through. That amounted to about 3.5 kg of pure cocaine, wrapped up in a battered aluminium satellite box. Quite a haul considering it was the pure stuff, which meant it would be 'stepped on', i.e. weakened by cutting with other powders – until it made many, many more times the weight in wraps and individual deals.

I contacted Investigation control in London and was passed on to the cocaine team's duty officer. I gave him all the details that I had and he asked if I could dummy up the package and his team would be up to us at 8 a.m. the following day. 'Dummying up' is as simple as it sounds: remove all the drugs and replace them with something that on initial glance would appear to be the same thing. It must weigh the same and you can't leave any telltale traces that you have been into the package. Which was easier said than done with the satellite TV tuner box and the way the coke was packed hard into it. Having examined the options, I decided that the only way that the coke was going to come out was with the aid of a hammer and chisel, and I got to work.

Two hours later, and without the protection of a face mask, I was still hammering away like a good-un. An hour after that and it had all been completed, and I had dummied up the package with the substance that we used to calibrate our X-ray machines for drug detection – same weight and density as the real thing. The satellite tuner box was put back together, packed in its FedEx parcel and ready for the Investigation team to carry out a controlled delivery to the destination address where it would arrive just ahead of a gang of large-booted Customs officers who would gently kick the door off its hinges and then ever-so-politely question the occupants about their future career plans before kindly escorting them to the nearest police station for a further cosy chat and some tea and biscuits.

Meanwhile, I was . . . you might say . . . *buzzing*. Even though I'd been at work all day from the early hours and was physically very tired, I got no sleep whatsoever the whole night. Or the next. Because, of course, all my hammering away with a chisel, without wearing a face mask, at a block of solid cocaine meant that I'd snorted enough Class A powder to revive a dead donkey and propel it to a clear win at the Grand National.

Luckily, we didn't yet have staff drugs tests, so it didn't go down on my record that for at least one day I was higher than Keith Richards in a hot air balloon.

14. Plain-clothes Intel

As Customs Intelligence teams improved, we started to get access to airline computer systems, which gave us details of ticket payments and full details of a passenger's travel. This was so successful that we could, and often did, inform overseas Customs agencies of smugglers that were heading for their borders. This in turn became reciprocal and the intel started flowing back to us. Intelligence started to come of age and Customs management realized that they were sitting on a gold mine. So our Intel team grew to six officers. Another change that occurred was that, against the wishes of the Intel team's first officer, Gary, we moved from wearing unranked uniforms to plain clothes. I kind of missed the uniform but, now we were in plain clothes, so to speak, we really did feel like we were part of the genuine undercover mob.

Similarly, as our airport intel grew in importance and effectiveness, all ports and airports started increasing their teams. And this is where an obvious problem occurred. Where does one get one's Intelligence officers from? Well, they were taken from the red/green channels at the airports as there was nowhere else to get them from. So now we had less officers stopping passengers, and those officers that remained tended to act only on intelligence-based information. It became in some ways self-defeating and an ever-tightening circle.

It may be a surprise to all who read this, but Customs does a great deal in times of war. The greatest misunderstanding and misinformation about Customs concerned the so-called 'supergun' parts going to Iraq. Matrix Churchill was a Coventry firm involved in exporting machine tools, which it was said could then be used for making military equipment. The press never understood what happened and the senior Customs officials never really put over the correct information. Yes, Customs did indeed know about the exportations of the gun parts and wanted to stop them but the British secret services wanted to know where they were headed and who was behind the whole project. This can only be done if Customs allowed what we called a 'live run', that is, a free run-through of information or goods in order to flush out further information and intel at the other end. Then, at the end of the exercise, when the secret services had all the information that they needed, we seized the very next exportation.

Of course, as a country heading for war, the last thing we needed was for the enemy to know what we had been looking at and, as such, in the short term, we played the secret-services participation down.

At the same time as the gun-parts affair was going on, we were working with the FBI, CIA and US Customs. The Americans had discovered that a military electrical company was supplying computer chips to the Iraqis for their fighter aircraft. The chips were for the aircrafts' weapons system called the IFF – Identification: Friend or Foe. Basically, plane A sends out an automated signal to plane B. Plane B sends an automated reply to plane A. If the reply is coded correctly, then plane A's weapon system does not deploy because plane B has identified itself as friendly. If the code is incorrect, then plane A deploys its weapons and plane B becomes toast ASAP and there's sweet FA it can do about it. So it was rather obvious why Saddam Hussein's air force (as small as it was) wanted to load up these chips and become untouchable by faking friendly code responses.

The rogue American company was sending the chips to the UK via the old trusty FedEx. Then the package was to be sent to the Isle of Wight. The recipient company there would repackage the chips and send them to Turkey, then on to Cyprus, then Jordan and finally by road to Iraq. The tortuous, roundabout route into Iraq could be made to mean nothing if we could intercept the chips early enough and before they began their long journey. Which British Customs, working with our stateside cousins, was able to do. The major difference between this case and that of the supergun was that all parties involved wanted the Iraq Air Force to get the chips – and to use them. And there was a very good reason for this. The plan was very simple but extremely cunning.

As they came into the country, I intercepted the chips at the FedEx base at Stansted Airport and then passed them on to an American secret service agent. He disappeared for a couple of hours and then returned with the chips, perfectly repackaged as if they had never been opened. I then got them back into the FedEx delivery system, and I did a touch of jiggery-pokery with their computer programs so that even FedEx didn't know that the packages had been removed for a few hours or that I had ever pulled out the chips for examination.

While the chips were away, they were, so the CIA agent later told me, radiated to clear their memory and then re-programmed with a different IFF code. So when the chips finally arrived in Iraq and were installed in the fighter jets, the only good they did was to arm up Hussein's Air Force with IFF chips that would send out the signal for 'I am the enemy – please shoot me down'. It was one of the best examples of Britain and the United States making good bedfellows since Edward winked at Mrs Simpson. And it was a team-up I was proud to be involved in (the fighter plane one, that is). However, international cases didn't always go that well.

Asil Nadir was the head of a company called Polly Peck, which went bust owing millions after an investigation by the Serious Fraud Office (SFO). As the evidence against him mounted, Nadir readied himself to do a runner and escape to his birth-place, the Turkish-occupied north of Cyprus. It was a clever move on his part for two reasons: one, because the UK did not recognize the Turkish Republic of Northern Cyprus so no extradition treaty was in place; and two, his family were involved in an airline called Noble Air that flew to Northern Cyprus.

So alerts were put out to my airport, which is where the airline operated from. We were to arrest Nadir on site. The SFO coppers that wanted him were a group of mainly deskbound number crunchers and, as you can guess, we didn't hold these plods in high esteem. Unfortunately, the SFO had put all their eggs in one leaky basket and Nadir slipped out of the UK via another route. Nadir became front-page news and one of Britain's most famous and most wanted fugitives. He took his exit routine right under the noses of the authorities and headed for freedom. Two days later, the SFO officers turned up at the airport. They were met by comments of 'wankers' from both our officers and Special Branch. Now they had to try to make up for their mistake, or, to put it more clearly, we had to pull a rabbit out of a bag for them to save face.

As it happened, the day that the SFO turned up was one of the days that Noble Air flew out of the UK. Within the hour, I was called to the surveyor's office, as apparently my skills as a bag-cracker and lock-picker were needed. Fourteen bags had been checked in under the name of Nadir, yet there wasn't a Nadir registered with the airline as travelling. The SFO had received intelligence that Nadir's sister was shipping out all of her brother's paperwork before the SFO could get their hands on it as evidence. So we all tramped down to the bowels of the airport and waited for the bags to spin around the automated baggage system before arriving at the Noble Air chute. It was quite obvious who was going to be doing the work here: the SFO officers were all suited and booted and I was in my overalls.

All fourteen bags appeared in a stream and every single one was different from the other. Some were Delsey, some were Samsonite and others were locked up with bloody great padlocks. The SFO weren't choosy, they wanted the lot opened, so I got down to a lot of concentrated lock-picking. The SFO checked every bag that I unlocked and they discovered . . . absolutely sweet FA. Once again, Nadir had out-smarted the police. As if deliberately adding insult to injury, the bags only contained his extensive wardrobe of suits, shirts and shoes. I was only surprised he hadn't left instructions that every bag should contain a note saying 'Fuck You British Customs'.

Among the officers of different law enforcement agencies, it is no secret that the agencies often don't get on. The only people who do think that we get on are the general public, who have seen too many 'reality' TV shows that depict the fiction that we are all best buddies working for the common good. But law enforcement departments are not in love with each other. That's a simple fact. Working relationships were often paper thin even if we were on a joint operation. Customs and Special Branch were thrown together at ports and airports as our prey was the same – but our reasons for being in the hunt were different. In the end, we realized that our final aim was the same and any fallouts could be resolved. Sometimes to everyone's benefit. One way we had of resolving differences was a drink-draughts match. So, for example, one time we had fallen out big time with Special Branch due to one of our junior officers saying something to the wrong SB officer. As a result of this, working relationships broke down quickly and something had to be done. My governor and I walked into the SB office to have a wee chat with their

Detective Sergeant. We sat down for deep, complicated and very long negotiations.

'So, gentlemen,' said the DS, 'draughts match?'

My boss and I looked at each other, nodded and said, 'Yep.' And that was it: negotiation over and done with.

The next night in the airport staff club, the match began: two teams of five officers for the best of three games on the giant draughts board, marked out on the dance floor. The board was 20 x 20 foot and the draught 'pieces' were a mixture of pints of lager, bitter, Guinness and cider placed on the squares. The rules were simple: if you took the opponent's piece, you drank it. If a pint became a king, a double Scotch was poured into the pint. Within an hour, everyone was legless and could barely remember what the original argument was over, and we were the best of mates again. I don't know why politicians and world leaders don't take the example of thrashing things out over a game of drink-draughts. And it would make great TV.

We'd had a BMW 5 series sat on a trailer in our exams shed for at least three days. It wasn't being ignored; it was just that the search team were much too busy on a couple of forty-foot containers that had been discovered to contain a ton of cannabis. I happened to be at the port sharing some intelligence with the ports Intel team and, in turn, they happened to be in the exams shed checking out the car.

The reason that the car had been pulled for examination was that not many cars turned up at the port on a trailer coming off a roll-on/roll-off ferry. It just didn't happen, because the cost alone would make the exercise prohibitive. So it had aroused suspicion. And here we had it, a three-year-old, right-hand-drive BMW with English plates from Rotterdam. The Intel officer was giving it a once-over, collecting details such as the Vehicle Identification Number (the VIN, which could be seen through the windscreen), car tax details and trailer details. Every check that he carried out made this motor look more interesting. No trace on the car's registration – the registration did not exist. No trace of the VIN, so the car didn't really exist either. And on top of all this the car tax disc was fake. Not much going for the car but plenty going for this being a prime tool for a smuggling run.

A new shift arrived at the exams shed and a couple of officers were allocated to the car. Their initial problem was that the car was locked and there were no keys available. Smashing of the driver's side window would be a last resort but, luckily, the team had a car entry kit (there are such things: a complete kitbag of every possible instrument of entry). The locks were sprung on the car and we wandered over to see if there was anything immediately apparent, such as the unmistakable smell of cannabis inside the car instead of the stench of a magic tree hanging from the rear-view mirror. I opened the driver's door and something dropped out on to the ground and rolled under the car. We all looked at each other, and then bent down to look under the car. Cue six pairs of Customs officers' eyes all suddenly opening very, very wide. Cue six Customs officers running for their lives as I shouted out, 'GRENADE!'

Knowing that a live grenade had a detonation time of about six seconds, we all ran out of the shed at full belt, each one trying to beat the current 100-metre world record. We dived for cover and then . . . nothing. Which was a little embarrassing, but then you can't actually die from embarrassment but you can from standing too near to an exploding grenade.

The police were informed and they arrived with sirens blazing, presumably to scare the grenade into submission. The Army bomb disposal boys were also called, and they turned up an hour later, also with sirens blazing. By now, the grenade must have been really worried. Two hours later, the area was cleared and we returned to the shed. We found that, apart from the grenade, the car was somewhat full of other interesting articles, such as machine guns, automatic pistols and even more grenades. This time, the anti-terrorist SWAT team boys were called and they turned up, you've guessed it, with sirens blazing, and took everything away.

And that's the big trouble with being in a profession where your job is to be on the lookout for anything strange. Sometimes you find it.

Another case provides a good example of how one apparently small piece of intelligence information can lead to the unravelling of a much bigger plot. The Drug Trafficking Offences Act (DTOA) 1994 dealt with the financial proceeds of drugs crime, and it was a piece of legislation that was brought into being in rather a hurry. You could tell it was a bit of a rush job by the strange rules that we had to adhere to when we were operating under the DTOA. We could seize any amount of cash over £10,000 as long as the owner had no convincing story for having it. But the flaw in that rule was that as soon as the smugglers and criminals found out about it – which they very quickly did – they started carrying only £9,999 knowing that we couldn't touch them.

But that didn't last long. In fact, it lasted only as long as it took for the first Customs officer to say, 'Right, turn out your pockets, son . . .' They would invariably find that the loose change in the smuggler's pockets was enough to tip the cash amount over the magic £10,000 barrier – and bingo, out come the handcuffs and off goes the money.

Many a smuggler lost the lot because of the bit of loose change in their pockets taking the total amount of money carried on their person over the limit. In for a penny, in for losing ten grand.

One passenger who was searched and fell foul of the DTOA was Martha Degal, a South American from Dutch Suriname, which is bordered by Brazil and Guyana. She was searched at outbound by BAA security and they happened to find £12,000 cash in her sports bag. A Customs officer was called and Martha was questioned under caution. She said she was on her way back to Amsterdam after visiting a friend in London. Unfortunately, she couldn't recall her friend's name, and she didn't even make one up, so the money was seized under the DTOA and she was sent on her way. All her paperwork had been photocopied, including a black address book with almost 150 names in it.

After seizure, the case was split into two parts: the court case and the intelligence case. The second fed the first with the evidence that would suggest or even prove that the money was drugs related. Court was a bit of a pain as we would have to appear almost every month in front of the magistrates to show that the case was progressing and they would then award us another month to continue the investi-gation. Before every court case, I would write to Martha with the court details and it was up to her whether she appealed the case. She never did and a few months later the seizure was confirmed and the money ended up in the Treasury.

But it was the intelligence and investigation side of the case that was of real interest to both me and the department. The initial links to drugs were very weak. A number of UK addresses that I found in the address book came up with drugs links, but that was it. It was the Dutch intelligence that was the real eye-opener. Nearly every Dutch person in Martha's address book either had a drugs record or was already under investigation. I contacted the Dutch police and soon had them onside and they said they would do anything to help further my investigation. They knew I had access to the British Airways computer and via this almost every airline in the world.

The case itself now revolved around the belief that the names in Martha's address book were linked in some way. We currently had the grand total of £12,000 and no drugs, but my senior officer was very keen on my continuing. The major thing to do was to whittle down a long list of 146 targets to a manageable number. The Dutch assisted with this by informing me who was in prison and who was dead, and this brought the target number down to seventy-eight. Next thing was to group together families and those in a relationship. After doing this, I got the target list down to a more manage-able fifty-five. The next task was to get every target registered to me on our CEDRIC system so that, if any of them should pop up at any of our seaports or airports, I would get to know about it and could take appropriate action. The forms that I had to complete to get the targets on the system were a nightmare of tedium as each target would take a couple of hours to do, as well as putting in addresses and companies. What was that I said earlier about the glamour of undercover work?

I managed to get the lot done in a week and Operation Howiff was now up and running. It didn't take too long before the first target appeared on our radar. The guy, called Mac, fitted the standard profile of a smuggler, complete with the one thing that always rings an alarm bell – travelling on a cash-paid one-way ticket. He arrived at Stansted from Amsterdam on the early-morning flight. I had already issued instructions that he should be given the full works but they weren't even needed. The initial search of his bag revealed half a kilo of pure cocaine and the subsequent body search found the other half a kilo. Quite a good way to start an operation. Later in the day, I contacted the Dutch with the news. If they weren't especially interested before, they certainly were now. Then things went quiet with the gang for a couple of weeks; this was a normal thing to happen, as a gang tries to find out exactly why they'd lost a valuable load.

It was becoming increasingly obvious to us that this smuggling organization was large and that it had never been hit before. They had reacted so quickly to our nabbing one of their mules that it was clear they weren't used to it happening – they didn't have a Plan B in place to put into immediate action – and the shockwaves led to a temporary lockdown. It was turning into a cat-and-mouse game between us and them.

I knew they could send out a bait, that is, a small carrier that they wouldn't worry too much about losing, but they could use to gather info on how we were operating, and from that work out how to foil us. So I wanted to be sure that, when we pounced, we got more out of the operation than they did.

As it turned out, the next hit we got didn't even enter the UK. Via the airways computer system, I identified a group travelling from the Netherlands to Suriname – three adults and three children, with the adults all being on my list. I contacted the Surinamese authorities and, despite their being 4,500 miles away, the wonders of technology meant that we received a cracking set of photographs of the group within an hour of their clearing Surinamese Customs. I called a halt to anymore surveillance in Suriname because this was still very early days for the operation. The three adults with children continued on their two-week holiday and we bided our time and waited to pounce.

Twice a day, I checked all the flights leaving the Suriname capital of Paramaribo, just in case the family decided to sneak back to the Netherlands before their planned return date. That was a possibility if they suspected they were being tracked. But they played it straight and, when I was sure they were on their return plane home, I contacted the Dutch authorities again. And so awaiting them when they landed in Amsterdam was a Customs team ready to give them the full monty. We now had to just sit tight and wait to see what transpired.

It was always a nervous time waiting to get a result, positive or negative, back from the uniformed boys on the front line. I'd been there, of course, doing the searches of passengers that we had been tipped off about by our own Intel boys. But working on the other side now in Intel was somehow more nerve racking. The phone finally rang at ten o'clock that night: the whole family had been stopped and searched – even the children, as drugs mules were known to use kids to carry their stash – and the result was 75 kg of top-quality, uncut cocaine. The Dutch were over the moon, as was my senior officer as that was 75 kg to add on to our yearly total of seizures.

After this large find, I was given access to any resources I needed – surveillance teams, undercover officers, etc. – in the hope of pursuing the gang with further success. But in reality I knew that I didn't need any of them. All I required was copies of any address books found in searches or any new names that might crop up in interview. I knew that I could now take the four targets that we had captured off my list, but, with new intelligence coming in all the time, I had to add another seven targets to the total.

Once again, the organization reacted quickly to the seizure and went into a defensive hibernation. You could almost hear the turning of cogs and the clicking of wheels as they set in motion the mechanism to discover the problem. I knew that during this time a gang would start to look at itself to see if it could identify where any information was leaking out, who might be a weak link or who might have been turned by the police to work on the inside – or even if they were being infiltrated by undercover Customs officers or police. We hadn't planted anyone, and I didn't want a Dutch undercover operative to join the gang because, as far as I could work out, all the members were from Suriname or the Netherlands Antilles.

During this downtime in the gang's activities, I was able to study it via the information that I now held. It was obvious that there were four head members, a number of henchmen and moneymen and, last as always (and the most disposable), the mules. The worry for me was that they would start employing unknown mules from their homeland, which would make them more difficult to track – but the Dutch assured me that they were quite confident that they could target newly arrived nationals coming into the Netherlands.

Things finally came alive again when the crew clearly got tired of hibernating and restarted their operations. Our next hit happened closer to home. To get an idea of the pattern of the lifestyle of the gang, our Dutch colleagues had placed one of the gang's four leaders under surveillance. We were all pleased when the chap (with girlfriend in tow) led the surveillance team to Amsterdam airport. As always, he purchased two last-minute, cash-paid, one-way tickets to Heathrow. I was pretty pleased with this as it would give me a chance to update my paperwork and get some photos of them, which I was sadly lacking.

I just managed to get to Heathrow fifteen minutes before the Amsterdam flight arrived and brief the evening shift senior officer (who, it turned out, was an old mate from my uniform days). He asked what the chances were that the passengers were carrying drugs. I told him they were slight as I assumed that, as one of the main men of the gang, he wouldn't be willing to get his hands dirty and risk being nabbed. But then again, I thought, he did have his girlfriend with him so he might think he could easily pass as an ordinary traveller.

176

So the Heathrow team went to work on the couple, targeting the girlfriend as the most likely to be carrying. This annoyed our real target, the boyfriend, who started to get very angry and abusive, but the team ploughed on. The team leader finally left the search and joined me in the office.

'Bad news, Jon, I'm afraid. She's clean. She may have taken some coke this morning but, other than that, nothing. Sorry.'

'Oh well, never mind,' I said. 'I thought it was too good to be true that we'd get them that easily.'

'But,' he continued, 'that boyfriend of hers is being a right twat to my team. Can I have your permission to spin him as well?'

Well, I couldn't see any harm in it, plus I'd always hated (as we all did) passengers who got out of their prams and started throwing rattles around.

'Fill your boots, mate,' I said, 'but I can't see him carrying, unless he's dumber than he looks and thicker than he sounds.'

Fifteen minutes later, the team leader came back to me with a big smile and told me that Mr Big's urine test results were off the scale. That meant that he had it all inside him, there was no doubt about that. And, when we later scanned him, what we found was almost half a kilo of pure cocaine, swallowed in small packages.

Sometimes it only takes one crack to smash a pot. And, in taking out one of the four heads, we fatally weakened the structure of the gang, as well as making it extra paranoid about its operations. And each bust led to our gaining more intel on the gang and its workings. We continued to get some large drug seizures from the rest of the intelligence we gathered and took millions of pounds' worth of gear out of circulation. And all of this – an internationally ranging investigation requiring tri-national cooperation between the British, the Dutch and the Surinamese that severely dented a drugs gang trading between two continents – all of it came about just because of a £12,000 cash seizure and a harmless-looking address book found in a passenger's sports bag. Sometimes a little intel went a long, long way.

Another thing that was on its way was me. After coming out of uniform bench work, moving into uniform Intelligence and then plain-clothes Intel, I'd now got a taste for the real undercover work – I wanted to move on to Investigation.

In a way, for all its successes, Intel had become a bit of a monster, and was seen as a cure-all for instant results, a bit like how drugs dogs had been seen fifteen years before when it was believed that they would completely solve the problem of smuggling. Which, of course, they didn't; every new part of the system was just that – a new part. And no one part could ever replace the team, and the effort and expertise it takes to run a successful team. But everyone was now getting involved in the so-called Intel revolution. Senior officers, who had been sceptical years before, had started to build their own Intel empires. Things had really changed. We were even put on training courses run by officers who had only been in Intel for a couple of years. So I thought that it was time for a change.

I decided to get into heroin.

Part 2: Undercover
(On the Knock)

15. Joining the Fun Factory: Checking in to Charlie Hotel

The Intel team at Stansted had expanded and we all had our own specialist skills: mine were lock-picking, outbound baggage rummage, a nose for drugs runners and, weirdly, seeming to know every Turkish smuggler south of the Humber. I was also training BAA security in concealments – that is, the smugglers' nefarious art of hiding their contraband. This was all well and good but I guess that most people at some point reflect on their work position, and I'd got to that stage. I had an itch that needed a good scratch. I decided that I wanted another challenge in life and that challenge would be the Customs Investigation Division (ID).

The ID had always been a ghost organization to us in uniform. We were aware of their existence and we knew that they were supposed to be the elite investigation unit in UK law enforcement, but other than that we knew very little. Even a couple of months of searching for details about the ID when I was still in Intel revealed very little about them – they tended to keep themselves to themselves.

My big break came with the announcement in the department weekly orders (DWO) of an ID recruitment trawl. These were few and far between: the last one had been eighteen months before and, to my knowledge, very few people got through it. So, with nothing to lose, I sent for the application form. What I received back was more than a form; it looked like very hard work. In fact, it was so comprehensive that it took a good two weeks to complete. I even sat down with a mate (who we called Reverend G.) who was already in the ID and we went through it together. Following his good advice, I ripped it up and started again, checked it with the Revd, and then ripped it up and started yet again. Finally, off went the form with a cheery smile and I instantly forgot about it. My hopes weren't that high.

It took a month for the ID sifting team to go through the applications. They had a few hundred applications and only a limited number of vacancies. I was lucky enough to get selected for an interview. But things in the Civil Service are never simple so it wasn't a case of just turning up for an interview. The next step was an ID recruitment interview course, which would take a couple of days at the Customs Training Unit, Heathrow. There, we were put through mock interviews, taught how to answer questions and what questions to ask back to the panel. London Airports Collection (the overseeing Customs body for the major London airports) wanted to be known as the best region when it came to turning out officers with the right stuff for the 'elite' Investigation Division.

I turned up for the interview with my head near full of questions and answers, standing straight as a guardsman and dapper-suited. Most of the questions asked of me were about my experiences dealing with heroin smugglers and the weapons-of-mass-destruction case. Before I knew it, the interview was soon over and I was sitting in the nearest pub wondering how I'd done.

A month later, I was still in the Intel department and was on an intelligence course being brought up-to-speed on the latest methods. But evenings spent in the bar were actually where most of the learning was really done, chatting with your peers from around the country. Suddenly, the head of the course wandered into the bar and asked for our attention: apparently someone was in the class who had no right to be there. We all looked at each other, wondering who it was.

'Jon Frost, if you would make your way to the bar and purchase everyone a drink,' said the course leader. 'It appears that this course is for Intelligence officers only, and I have just heard from your surveyor that you are now an investigator! Well done and mine's a Scotch!'

An investigator who was on a different course walked over and put his arm around my shoulder. 'Well, brother investigator, welcome to the fun factory. One thing to remember: when the shit hits the fan and everything is going wrong . . . *you* volunteered for the ID. And mine's a pint, by the way.'

'Charlie Hotel' was the call sign for Custom House, London, which was the home of the Customs Investigation Division. The building, on Lower Thames Street, just past Tower Bridge and opposite HMS *Belfast*, was a vast, imposing Grade-I listed Portland stone building that was almost 200 years old and was originally purpose-built for HM Customs after the growth of trade, the opening of the docks and the increases in duties during the Napoleonic Wars. The interior was a rabbit warren on a number of floors and contained warehouses, cellars, over 150 offices and the famous 'Long Room', measuring 190 feet, hence the name. On the ground floor was the central Queen's Warehouse, and underneath were the dark and dingy cellars (which would later house the Queen's Warehouse), which were fireproof and were originally used to store wine and spirits seized by Customs. The building itself was like some great architectural version of a hard Customs officer rendered in stone. One look at it told you that it was built to represent a profession that didn't muck about when it came to the carrying out of its duties.

At any one time, the Queen's Warehouse part of Custom House would hold more Class A and B drugs than anywhere else in London. It was lucky that the building was such a fortress as any drugs gang brave enough to carry out a smash-and-grab there would have set themselves up for life. As a new Investigation officer, I was hoping to add to that impressive haul in the Queen's Warehouse rooms.

The offices above there held the best officers that Customs Investigations had to offer. The teams were grouped into branches. These covered heroin, cocaine, cannabis, weapons of mass destruction and warfare, VAT, Excise, gold, drugs finance and all the intelligence back-up required for each one of these commodities. The south side of Custom House facing the River Thames was decorative but the north-facing roadside of the building looked relatively nondescript for something that protected society so very well. During the day, and sometimes under cover of night, there was a constant coming and going of surveillance cars and officers, and a steady hum of work being done in the offices that was essential to keeping Britain as free of drugs as it could reasonably be made. Charlie Hotel even had its own custody suite with cells and interview rooms as well as some of the best custody officers that I was to ever work with.

My first day as a trainee investigator was just like the first day at big school. You watched and listened to everything and kept your mouth shut. You may have thought you were the greatest Customs officer that the country had ever known but it meant nothing at all now, because to the ID you were just a pleb who got in the way and took up good breathing space. No new entrant could possibly know the complex makeup of the Investigation Division. I learned it would take the six months of probation just to get an idea of your own branch. Then it would take another six months before you could call yourself an investigator. If you were lucky.

I was grabbed for the heroin branch because of my prior workings against the Turkish heroin smugglers. Years of intelligence from my duties in uniform and working at Intel were stored in my mind and someone in Investigation thought that the heroin branch would profit from it. I knew the training was not going to be a walk in the park, and the initial training lasted for most of the probation period; we then moved on to specialist training such as a police surveillance driving course, followed by the general surveillance course, which would mark your ascendancy into the division. But, at all times, you had the vulture of potential failure sitting on your shoulder. Do the wrong thing and I knew you were RTU (returned to unit), which was a bit of a bugger if, like me, you'd had a large leaving party. It would be quite a humiliation to go back to the airport and say that you didn't make the grade. But that did happen to people, and other officers just decided that the life of an investigator was not for them. In fact, if I'd known what lay ahead, I might have said that those recruits who decided to RTU of their own volition were the bravest and smartest of us all.

So it didn't take too long before you realized what you had let yourself in for. When not on training, you joined your own team and most of the time the team would be out on the ground, somewhere in the UK. I had a rented flat in the East End of London but I didn't see very much of it. That was the life of an investigator; how officers managed their family life on top of surveillance, I never did work out. What I also didn't know was that working in the demanding world of investigation would change my life so much that I became consumed by the job.

Early on, I learned that for all the dedication of the investigative officers they were just like the uniform boys in one important way – any excuse for a drink. So, on the occasional days when we would have the required fire or bomb alarm test at Custom House, you would find that the test would always be carried out in the afternoon. Why? Well, your average investigator is very well educated in the ways of the world, so, once the alarm was sounded, we would grab our coats and phones and head for the exits. The exodus would then continue to the street outside, and then to the street next to that one, and then the one after that, until the distance for the safest possible evacuation was deemed to be *the exact same distance* to the bar of the nearest pub. Which was a huge but very pleasant coincidence. And that would also mean that the day was over. When the alarm bells stopped ringing, there were never any officers left out in the street to go back into the building. Charlie Hotel was, on those days, full of vacancies.

Royal and official visits were a regular occurrence at Custom House, especially after large drugs jobs. It was surprising that lots of MPs wanted their photo taken next to a huge pile of seized drugs when they had actually done bugger all to help us. It was almost like there was something in it for them. One day, following a very big and high-profile heroin job, we had a visit from some high-powered cabinet ministers who wanted the standard photocall. They sat on the bonnet edge of a drug dealer's seized Mercedes, holding some of the packages of heroin and posing for the press. We watched from the offices, hoping for all we were worth that one of the drug bags would burst and cover them in the lot. 'MPs SNORT SMACK IN PUBLIC!' would have made a good headline. And both ministers looked very happy, sitting there in their suits and holding the drugs . . . that is, until the case officer for the heroin seizure suddenly walked out on the balcony, surveyed the scene and then shouted very loudly at the two politicians, 'Take your *fucking* hands off those *fucking* drugs! We haven't had them *fucking* fingerprinted yet!'

A royal visit was something else entirely. Like anywhere else in the rest of the UK, Custom House was freshly painted for the visit but only in the places where royalty would actually see, or might see (so I suppose someone gave a fresh lick of paint to the loo, just in case). Billy Connolly once said that the Queen thinks the whole world smells of paint because wherever she goes there's always some guy about twenty feet in front of her frantically painting away. After the announcement of the royal visit came the expected news that those in power thought it better if the royal personage didn't bump into any of us unkempt investigators. Senior Investigation officers were told in no uncertain terms to get their teams out of Custom House, and it didn't matter where they went. Charming: nice to be appreciated! So we were either put on unneeded exercises or pointless surveillance gigs. And those teams that were already operational on jobs suddenly got unexpected troops added to their numbers, while nice towns like Bath were flooded by surveillance cars on exercise. Blimey, I thought, you wouldn't think we were *Her Majesty's* Customs and Excise officers, would you? The general consensus was that, if the royal family had put up with Prince Philip for all those years, then we were sure they could have stomached us.

Living in London and working all hours meant that I didn't get to see my parents as often as they were used to. Mothers worry about their kids, no matter how old, ugly or nasty you are. Mine was no different. It's just that the phone calls of a mother to her son can be a little, shall we say, inconvenient when the son is working surveillance duty.

I had just finished training but still had another four months to go before I was a fully operational investigator. Prior to getting my police driving certificate and my surveillance ticket, I knew I was destined to spend a lot of time on my feet. There is nothing wrong in being on foot surveillance – it's the most important part of surveillance and the aspect that requires the fastest thinking; it was our tradecraft. And after years in uniform in the airports, and also the months of investigative training, it was great to be out on the streets and finally putting theory into practice.

On this particular day, the team I'd been assigned to were in the King's Cross area of London. We had the railway station 'plotted up' – that is, covered and observed – which is no mean feat considering there are so many exits and so many people using them. We were there because we had learned that there was a moneyman coming down from the north with a bag full of drugs cash that would, of course, be classed as proceeds from crime. He was going to launder his cash in a nearby money exchange then head straight back home. I knew it should be a dead simple job for us that should not take up too much time, but the problem was that it was now heading towards rush hour. Our one help was that there was a local officer on the train of the target (codename: Tango 16) so he could give us the heads-up when his train pulled into King's Cross.

I drew the short straw and had a plot position on the main front doors. Still being quite new to central London, I didn't know the area very well and had my mini *London A–Z* in my pocket. For about the next half-an-hour, I was quite happy with my surveillance position as all these local women kept coming up and chatting to me in a very friendly manner. Must be my good looks, charm and charisma, I thought. That was until the voice of Mick, our senior officer, came down our radio earpieces:

'All footmen, listen up. New update: Tango 16 due to arrive in ten minutes, so we're on standby. Oh, and one more thing – Jon, please stop chatting to the local prostitutes!'

Ten minutes later, we had identified our target, Tango 16. He was in no hurry and decided to stretch his legs with a nice walk, or maybe he was more canny than he appeared and was trying to shake any possible surveillance. But this was great for us as the surveillance system we used was made for this form of pursuit; we used a rolling system of interchangeable pursuers who would take over from each other, like baton runners in a relay race.

Tango 16 headed west on the Euston Road and I found a good position on the other side of the street. There was no need for me to make a 91-call (meaning 'heading in the direction of') on the target as he was covered from behind, but I was in a good position to take over the second anyone lost sight of him or he turned a corner. We had officers to the side of him and more officers being placed ahead of him. This was excellent tradecraft according to the surveillance handbook: keep at a distance safe enough to be invisible, but within close enough proximity to act.

Eventually, we tracked him to a bureau de change. We

plotted up on the money shop and Mick went in to cover whatever might happen inside. Thirty minutes later, nothing had happened; no one had come out. Mick obviously couldn't alert us to anything using his radio for fear of being overheard. We were getting increasingly tense outside, wondering why things were taking so long. Finally, our target emerged with £500,000 exchanged – or, more accurately, laundered – and stuffed into a shabby old sports bag. He headed back to the Euston Road towards Euston Station. If any mugger or bag thief had at that moment chosen to rob him, they would have had the most unexpected pay-day of their lives. (And they would have been rich for about ten seconds – which is how long it would have taken an angry scrum of investigative Customs officers to jump out of hiding and rugby-tackle the bag thief to the ground.)

Once again, we picked up Tango 16 and from there it was an easy follow to the station. Once inside, he purchased a ticket back up north and then made himself comfortable in the station bar, which was perfect for me as I had already chosen the bar for my surveillance position. On the basis of 'when in Rome', I grabbed a pint of cider. Sitting directly across the room from the target, I was able to give the team a full update; they were happy that I had him fully covered and they all moved back away from the pub.

Still being relatively new to all this, I was a touch nervous about now being the only one of the team that was closely observing our target. Everyone else was now relying on my information and decisions. I was very conscious of trying to keep that perfect balance between observation and vigilance and anonymity and distance. One look too many in his direction and he might notice and get spooked; too few looks and he might slip out into the crowds before I had a chance to follow. Keeping all this in mind and at the same time trying to relax and seem to be just another disinterested, bored passenger wasn't made any easier when suddenly my mobile phone rang loudly. I nearly jumped out of my skin. I answered the phone quickly and said sharply, 'What?' There was a pause at the other end. And then I heard, 'Excuse me, that's *no* way to speak to your mother.'

'It's not really the best time to talk right now, Mother,' I said. I saw Tango 16 raise an eyebrow and look in my direction. I was pretty sure that he couldn't hear me but I wasn't absolutely certain that that was the case. I thought that if I hung up straight away it might look a bit odd, and too much like I was trying *not* to bring attention to myself.

'Oh, that's nice,' she continued. 'I ring you at your flat and you're never in; I ring you on your mobile thing and it's not the right time. At least you could say that it's nice to hear from me.'

'It is lovely to hear from you, Mum, it's just that I'm a touch on the busy side at the moment.'

'Too busy? It's seven o'clock, you can't still be working. Are you going to be home for Sunday lunch? I only ask because I need to know if I need to get a joint in.'

I noticed Tango 16 was still looking at me. 'Yes to all that, Mother. Look, I'm going to have to go now, OK?' My radio earpiece started blaring in my other ear – it was Mick wanting an update. 'Got to go now, Mum, love you.' I hung up just in time as Tango 16 got up and headed towards the toilets, which were directly behind me. As he got closer, I could sense that without a doubt he had noticed me and he was going to react. That's it, I thought, my cover's blown, the job's screwed, my investigative career is over before it's really begun. As he passed, Tango 16 looked at me and smiled. 'Mothers, eh?'

When I met up with my mother on Sunday, I explained what the situation had been when she phoned. She was totally unfazed. 'Well, I'm sorry, love, but how was I supposed to know? But you said you got your Tango Orange chap so it all worked out all right. Anyway, it probably made you look more natural. Cup of tea?'

Now that I was out of the airports, going to work in the mornings was a sheer pleasure. I had rented a studio flat in Tobacco Dock, which was a mile away from Custom House. The walk took me past Wapping Steps, under Tower Bridge and through the Tower of London. I even got on nodding terms with the Yeoman warders. The walk back from work was even better with three good pubs that just happened to be on my route. The worst problem with Custom House was that, as it was sitting on Lower Thames Street, we had the embankment in one direction and the Tower Bridge cross-roads in the other. So, no matter what time of day it was, the traffic on Thames Street was like slow-moving treacle, which was no good when some port or airport Customs had dis-covered a large drugs importation and we had to try to get to them ASAP.

Some jobs involved tracking someone through the city, like the Tango 16 one, which were exciting because of the challenges they posed; these jobs called for a certain kind of surveillance work. First, there was the Underground to contend with. Over the years, there had been lots of films made showing people doing surveillance on the tube, but it was all mostly bollocks. For one thing, underground our radios became totally ineffective when it came to contacting our car team above ground, and so they were always trying to second-guess where you might be heading. One way around this was to sacrifice an officer. They would watch the team and target disappear on to a train then leg it to the surface to radio the cars. The cars would then attempt to race the train to the next station. It was usually utter madness. Then there was the question of radio usage between the officers on the tube. This was next to useless as the electrified lines played merry hell with our earpieces, so it ended up sounding like someone dragging their fingernails down a blackboard, at high volume, right in the middle of your head. The only sure-fire way to keep your team together was to make sure that everybody could see each other, which was just impossible at rush hour.

The next problem was security – both the police and store guards. Places like Harrods had metal detectors at the entrance doors and security officers to do rub downs and searches. This was somewhat of a bugger when you were either wearing your radio in a body rig or, like I did, on your leg; both places being areas where bombers would strap their explosives. None of us wanted to risk being mistakenly shot as a suicide bomber. Getting shot would kind of ruin your day. Especially if you were shot dead. That's always the worst kind. So, to avoid this possibility, if I followed someone into a store, it would usually involve a bit of whispering out of the corner of my mouth and a very brief flash of my badge to the security guards to prevent having my head jumped up and down on for being a suspected terrorist.

The other national security matter that pissed us off was the so-called 'ring of steel' – this was the name for the security and surveillance cordon around the City of London. It was originally installed to deter the IRA's mainland bombing campaign when they started targeting the capital. (In fact, 'ring of steel' was the phrase used in Northern Ireland during the Troubles to describe a fortified circle around the centre of Belfast.) In the British version set up by the Metropolitan Police, roads entering central London were narrowed into small chicanes that made drivers slow down and also enabled them to be filmed by CCTV cameras. The roads also had a concrete median barrier with a sentry box and, to begin with, they were manned by armed police.

Our surveillance cars would spin through the ring of steel without any problems but our observation vans often got stopped. There would then be lots of flashing of badges and bad-tempered police officers demanding that we open up the rear of the van. This always had the same result: the copper would open the back of the van to find a couple of surveillance officers with headsets on, surrounded by technical kit and who, within two seconds of the doors being opened, would start shouting at the police officer, 'Shut the fucking door, you twat!' (Seeing this particular scene played out firsthand was priceless. Especially the looks on the faces of any members of the public passing by who would just see a police officer open the back door of a van and then from the depths of the vehicle immediately hear 'Shut the fucking door, you twat!' I often wondered who they thought must be in there to get away with speaking like that to the police . . . the Duke of Edinburgh, perhaps.)

One day while at Charlie Hotel, I was surprised to get a visit from one of our Queen's Warehouse officers from below stairs. These non-investigators rarely seemed to emerge out from their underground lair and, if they did, it was usually to bollock an officer for getting his paperwork wrong or for having the affront to fill up his nice clean warehouse with dirty drugs. But this time it was different, the Queen's Warehouse officer wanted to be fully briefed on a job that I had been involved in a week before, a nice little job in which 30 kg of heroin had been picked up. It was all now sitting underground with all the other mountains of powders and pills in the cellars of the Queen's Warehouse.

I was curious. 'So why do you want a briefing from me?' I asked.

The officer looked a bit sheepish. 'Well, I need to know everything about the job,' he said, 'so that I can brief a visiting VIP we're expecting.'

What a bloody cheek, I thought: it was my job and yet some Custom House admin cave-dweller was going to try to get the kudos for all my team's hard work. I looked over to my senior officer who had been listening in, and he looked as surprised and disgusted as I was.

'OK,' I said to the Queen's Warehouse officer, 'take this down – G.F.Y.S. That's gee eff why ess.'

The officer grabbed his notepad and pen, thinking that this was the start of the briefing. 'OK,' he said, 'and what does that mean?'

Before I could say anymore, the senior officer leaned over and very slowly and very clearly enunciated, 'Go. Fuck. Your. Self. And, if I were you, sunshine, I'd leave while you can still walk out of here without a boot toecap parked in your arse.'

Welcome to the fun factory, indeed.

16. Spooks and Lumps

If you ever get the feeling that you are being watched or followed, the chances are that . . . you're not. Surveillance is expensive and time consuming and it's usually only employed when the cost of the resources (and the overtime) can be justified by either an achievable result – a conviction – or to avert a serious crime. So it's unlikely any of us are big enough fishes for the authorities to try to land us.

It also comes as a great surprise to most people to find out what the full range of HM Customs work could entail. To the general public, it was just uniformed officers standing at the blue/red/green channels in airports trying to catch students with spliffs in their socks and nuns with gin in their water bottles. Well, as we've seen, that's part of it. But, beyond that, they also cover the areas of intelligence info-gathering on smuggling ops being run through all UK ports. And, even further beyond that, to full-blown undercover investigative work following drugs gangs around the country – and even overseas – and gathering intel on and busting large-scale smuggling operations. I'd been through the first two incarnations of

Customs work – uniform and Intelligence – and was eager to really experience the third.

HM Customs Investigation Division was very accomplished at surveillance (and, in the years that I was involved in surveillance, not once did the target have any idea that they had been under scrutiny, even when sometimes it had been for years). We were even more successful at it than our police colleagues because of the unique system of surveillance that we operated. This was just one of the differences between the two services, and one of the reasons for the love/hate relationship between Customs and the police. They called us the Church (because the initials of Customs and Excise were also the 'C of E' of the Church of England) and we called them the Martians. Each side considered themselves somewhat superior to the other; on our side, we thought that was true because our powers were very draconian and wide ranging, and we also had history on our side – HM Customs being the oldest law enforcement agency in the UK with a history going back over 1,200 years. We were also the world's first law enforcement agency. The heavy powers the service had acquired had been collected over its lifetime and police powers were weak in comparison. For example, up to about 1974, Customs officers had a licence to kill – that is to say (in legal terms), a Customs officer could never be prosecuted for taking a human life in the protection of the Crown revenue. Alongside that, a Customs officer could deputize anyone on the spot, could outrank any military or police officer in the performance of their duties, and could enter any premises in any way we chose. For these reasons, we sometimes seemed to be the target of resentments from other enforcers – like the police and Army – whose public image was of being the ultimate in law enforcement when actually, in truth, their powers were secondary to ours.

And, in terms of historic precedence, Customs officers were armed (and would remain so until prior to the First World War) before the police were even a Robert Peel wet dream. And we could be armed again if necessary at any time today with just a single signature from the Home Office (and this has been done).

So, all in all, though Customs and the police did some great joint jobs together, the prevailing feeling from both sides – and especially ours – was that we were best kept apart.

Unlike the police, our force had changed its surveillance tradecraft in the early 1990s when Army surveillance teams in Northern Ireland discovered that the IRA had worked out how the old system worked. It happened while the British Army specialist surveillance teams – operated by the Intel Corps – were still using the standard form of surveillance that you may now see in TV dramas, with a chain of officers following the target. But, while following a major IRA target, a surveillance team caught the attention of a covert observation position operated by the special forces. The operatives watched the Intel Corps team all wander past in standard surveillance mode. What was earth shattering was that they were followed by an IRA surveillance team using exactly the same surveillance procedures as the Army specialists. So the myth of the surveillance technique had been blown wide open. Consequently, a new method had to be designed as soon as possible, every bit of it from foot to mobile surveillance, from equipment to a new language. And if the game was blown in Ireland then it was bound to carry through to the UK.

What came out of the total surveillance rethink was a new system adopted by the Customs ID called the Enhanced Surveillance Technique (EST). Even if you knew how the system worked, it was still hard to spot it in action. The secret services were impressed, and they decided that they had to know how EST worked so they could change their field officer training to try to counter it when their agents were out on duties and might be followed themselves.

The best form of surveillance kit will always be the most complicated and irreplaceable piece of equipment available – the human eyeball. But there were other aids that were very useful and that we were trained to use.

Covert body set: this was a type of radio system called the Racal Cougar kit used by all good surveillance organizations. Specially designed for the job, it came in three different forms: car kits – big and powerful; field kits – for CROPs operations only (Covert Rural Observation Positions – more on this later); and the everyday body kits that could be worn on most parts of the body, which weighed about half a pound and were a half-inch thick. The body kit was great but limited in the distance that it could transmit. On big operations that used both footmen and cars, the nearest car to a footman would often have to retransmit the footman's radio calls so that everyone knew what was going on. The body kits also had another small drawback, which was that when you transmitted it was the same as turning on a 700-watt microwave.

It may have only been for a few seconds at a time but some long-serving officers ended up with deep vein damage thanks to the radio waves.

Earpieces: fortunately, we didn't have to wear radio-connected earpieces, as some services did, with the giveaway of a visible wire, which was quite a good way to advertise yourself to the bad guys. We used earpieces that were specially and individually made for each officer. These would fit deep into the ear canal and, because of that, were a real bugger to get out.

Tracking systems: the system we used at the time was perfectly operational but also had its limitations because it was the less expensive of the two systems on the market at that point. For example, Europol, the European Union law enforcement agency (and who, believe it or not, chased things like olive oil smugglers), could put a tracker on a target lorry in Italy and watch its progress on a computer screen in Paris. They had the expensive option. We, on the other hand, had the less expensive kit and so had to stay within a certain distance from our targets so that the car tracking system could maintain a signal with the transmitter. (And, after all, we were only following heroin smugglers or gun runners, so why give us the expensive kit?) The tracking screen was like a small laptop and displayed a constantly moving map that could be zoomed in and out. The screen would display the best-estimated position of the target vehicle and your own tracking vehicle. I say 'estimated' because the signal could be affected by anything from power lines to electronic 'noise' in built-up inner-city areas. This tracking system was used to cut down on the chances of our being spotted but it had its limitations. It could not, of course, tell you who was in the car or who got in or out. Which is why, as I say, the best bit of high-tech surveillance kit has always been the human eye.

The UK's secret services – MI5 for domestic security and MI6 for overseas intelligence gathering – are very good. They've been going in one form or another since the reign of Elizabeth I so they should know what's what by now. But, as in any organization, they are only as good as their individual officers and so we had many of the MI5 spooks join us on our training courses and exercises. It is fair to say that you can get rusty, so the exercises got everyone up to speed in both car and foot surveillance. As one would expect, the secret service plays its training very close to its chest. We would only become involved when the prospective field officers were nearly ready for the outside world. It was a sign of how Customs surveillance and undercover work was highly valued that we were used to test and fine-tune the UK's secret service agents. And it wasn't just British officers that the Customs Investigation Division trained: they also taught some overseas agency officers as well. This was a clever ploy as we would learn how these agencies worked abroad, but it didn't go both ways as the foreign officers were never trained alongside British officers – an extra-vigilant way of protecting their anonymity and security – and the full workings of the British service were not revealed to them. The training and testing of secret service surveillance officers helped us to sharpen up our own skills as well, especially when we would run counter-operations against the trainees. And it was also a great way of training recently recruited Investigation officers like myself.

Once the secret service agents had been trained and had played about with their new tradecraft with their instructors, they were placed in the real world with real surveillance officers against them. One at a time, the new officer would be given a number of tasks. These usually started with a meet and handover of intelligence. The officer would then have to make two drops and eventually make it to a railway station. This was bread-and-butter tradecraft. They were to deploy their anti-surveillance skills and if they couldn't do it then they were out. And, remember, this final exercise was at the end of their training so it would be a bloody great shame to fail at this stage. On our side of the exercise, we would pick up the target at the meet and stay with them to identify the two drops and the final destination. We could use whatever equipment and skills that we liked but, mainly, we were there to try to make them fail. Because, when they started doing this for real, their opposition would be out to kill them, not just give them bad feedback on poor performance.

One of our exercises was against three trainees that MI6 were trying to establish as overseas agents. These exercises were enjoyable because most of the work area was in central London so it was easy for us to change vehicles and outfits quickly. All we were told by the MI6 instructors was where the meet was and at what time. On this occasion, the target, Romeo One, was due to have a meet outside a pub near Oxford Street. I was positioned in a phone box opposite and as such would give the agent's full description and the time of 'lift off' – the start of the op. One Middle Eastern-looking chap was sitting at a table reading a newspaper. Surely this couldn't be our target, I thought, as he was wearing a bright-yellow jumper and green trousers. But then these trainees were to be overseas agents so would likely be of foreign extraction and varying ethnicity, depending on where they would be stationed. I broadcasted his description over the net. Seconds later, one of the MI6 trainers appeared on the scene and passed Mr Yellow-Green two packages and his instructions, and then the trainer was off. So he was our man, after all.

The agent then did what most visitors do and whipped out his *London A–Z*. My colleague, Sam, was the closest officer to him other than me, and he decided to start the day with an early victory. He did a quick wander past the target and then sat down next to him. 'Hello, mate,' Sam said. 'You lost?' But the target was totally unfazed and opened up his instructions. Sam had a look at the addresses and started to flick through the guy's *A–Z*. He made sure he kept the 'transmit' button pressed down on his radio as he found each address and slowly read it off the sheet. After five minutes of explaining and pointing, the target shook Sam's hand and was off to his first drop-off totally unaware that we were already there waiting to nab him. One-nil! That was an easy one and showed that surveillance isn't always a matter of complex plans – sometimes the simplest line of attack worked. So, that was one trainee MI6 agent down, two more to go.

The next agent, after his initial meet, was off like a whippet . . . but in the wrong direction. We followed at a distance and ten minutes later he was standing by the side of the road looking at a map. Out of the blue, a private hire car pulled up next to him. 'Hello, mate, want a lift? I'm just packing up for the day.' The agent, not believing his luck, jumped into the back of the car and told the driver his first address. Two drop-offs later, the agent and the driver then went off to Liverpool Street Station. Having dropped the agent off at the station, the driver – who was actually our officer, Paul – parked the car back up at our garage and grabbed a surveillance van to complete the pick-up of the now busted MI6 trainee. The trainee agent had obviously never expected us to be running our own private hire cars as a surveillance vehicle. But really he should have known that a taxi driver would *never* voluntarily offer a free lift to any-one, anywhere! That earth-shattering occurrence would make the first 'bong' on the *News at Ten*.

So, that was two agents down with one to go. Our ground commander for the day said that we should let the next oper-ation run more fully, and he also told us to stop being so bloody clever. So it was back to tradecraft. The 'pick-up', or spotting, of Target No. 3 was easy: he was bald as a coot and wearing a bright-red jacket. MI6 must have been planning an Arab Nations infiltration as this trainee was another Middle Eastern national. His first stop was rather a shock to both us and his trainers. He went against all his instructions and went straight into his hotel – which was an act of professional sui-cide. Five minutes later, he emerged back on the street but this time wearing a bright-orange jacket. He had tried to be clever by changing clothes but had now made himself more visible and also given away his safe house.

Our vehicle-bound officers parked their cars and joined us on the ground. As we now had fourteen officers on foot, our handovers were fast and smooth, each officer taking over the tracking duties from the other, with the covert surveillance baton being passed along from one to the other. In these numbers, there was little chance of being spotted, though there was a slight hiccup on a very busy Oxford Street when we lost him for a few minutes – easily done on one of the busiest streets in the world.

However, Target 3 unknowingly helped us find him quicker than we might have done by the fact that he was constantly munching on a large packet of monkey nuts that he scoffed as he walked, leaving a Hansel and Gretel-like trail of peanut shells everywhere he went. The commander was on the radio: 'Right, no bother, Tango 3's been relocated.' The target then did as he had been instructed and carried out both of his letter drops. On the Edgware Road, he decided to check out some TVs and disappeared into an electrical shop. By now, his MI6 trainers were pulling their hair out at how bad he had been performing so they told us to end the exercise. We agreed, but had our own ideas about how to do it.

Sam and I followed him into the shop and sidled up next to him. 'Hello, son, how you doing?'

This got his attention and, rather worriedly, he looked around between me and Sam and then looked towards the door to make an exit.

'Well, well, Dog,' Sam said, using my old Mad Dog nickname rather than identifying me, 'it looks as if our friend here has never met Mossad officers before.'

At the mention of the Israeli Secret Service agency, our man drew in a sharp intake of breath . . . and fainted on the spot. I looked down at him on the floor. Sam looked down at him on the floor. We both looked up at each other, shrugged and then walked out, leaving failed MI6 agent No. 3 passed out in the middle of the shop with staff and customers slowly forming a ring around his body.

But things weren't always that much fun. There were many trainee agents that had their act together and really made us work for our supper. In one way, it was actually a relief to come up against trainee agents that really pushed us – it meant that we knew our overseas intelligence agency was at last finding some good recruits instead of monkey-nut-munching pass-out merchants. Although, sometimes, even the good recruits let the tension and nerves of surveillance get the better of them.

We were on the south coast, a bit out of our urban comfort zone. This time we were up against a few MI5 British agents, and the first two of the day had succeeded in escaping our surveillance net. The last agent of the day that we were tracking was apparently the star pupil of the group, and right from the off he had us on our toes. He was good. After his initial meet with his handler, he jumped straight on a bus and sat in a position where he could watch who got on and who got off, in doing so 'burning' (negating) our officers. Or so he hoped. But we had played the bus game for real in London and so we had officers on and off at every stop. From the bus, he went into a shopping centre, stopping now and again to watch reflections in shop windows or turn back on himself to catch out anyone tracking him. He actually managed his two drops without any of us knowing where they were and then he headed off to his final rendezvous. By now, his trainers were very impressed with him, and we were very pissed off. We didn't like losing. So we decided to really turn up the heat.

His final meet was to be at a car that was parked on the top level of a multistorey car park. We boxed off the whole area and pumped eight officers into the car park. No one was going in or out without our knowing. Half an hour later, the agent entered, and then, just as fast, we lost him. He remained lost for another two hours. His trainers couldn't contact him and we were sure that he hadn't left in a car. Everyone was puzzled to the extent that a full sweep of the car park was carried out and we eventually found him on the third level, huddled between two cars and crying his eyes out. So what had happened?

He had done everything right; he had entered after doing a sweep of the area, having already identified a few of our officers so he knew that we were about. Once in the car park, he had managed to spot nearly all of the rest of our men but at this point he realized that there was no way that he would ever get to his meeting point. So next he destroyed any ID that he had on him and destroyed his mobile phone (which was never found). Then suddenly he became overwhelmed by the pressure and the expectation and the failure, so he broke down. He had been top student in all disciplines, but not managing to do this task had broken him. Unfortunately, it meant him being thrown off the course.

In the undercover game, theory and practice were two very different things – and sometimes it wasn't until you were put under severe pressure that it was discovered whether or not you had the one thing that training could not create – the nerve.

When it comes to surveillance, people tend to think of agencies such as the CIA or MI6 and expect their surveillance, with satellites and other electric gizmos, to lead the world. But the crux of the matter is that down on the ground, running real-world operations, we have to put people away and that means a court case and concrete evidence. Without solid evidence of the crime, you have wasted time and taxpayers' money and, worse than that, the criminal's back on the street and wiser than ever.

The type of evidence needed are such things as recorded meetings, 'overheards' (listened-in conversations), and observed phone calls and handovers, just to mention a few. On top of this there are very strict rules and regulations covering nearly every avenue of investigation. If we take one example of a job that concerned the use of overheards, it may help illustrate how sometimes the law really is an ass.

On this particular job, we had been targeting a south London organization that was hoping to import 50 kg of heroin from Turkey. We had their cars 'lumped up' – that is, with a magnetic tracking device stuck to the underside of the car – and most of their phones were online. By this stage, there was very little that we didn't know about them and the drugs run: we just needed to know when and where it was going to happen. So for a week we kept close surveillance on the gang's main man, codenamed Zulu 6. After an easy

Thursday of tailing Zulu 6, in which he had gone shopping at the Lakeside Shopping Centre, he pulled up at a pub in Sutton, south London. The surveillance team plotted up around the pub and then we followed him inside. We ordered drinks and managed to get a table just the other side of a low partition next to our target. Within five minutes, the main man was joined by a Turkish guy (who we were already aware of). After a bit of initial light banter describing what they had been up to that day, they got down to business. We managed to radio out most of the details of their discussion via our covert body sets so that the case officer, who was stationed outside, could get all the details recorded – and which would also act as an aid for us later when we had to write up our notebooks.

After about half-an-hour, our two targets changed the subject and started talking about their plan to import five million cigarettes from Latvia over the next five days. This seemed like we had them bang-to-rights with information that was going to lead to a big arrest. But, as we passed on the information, our case officer straight away ordered us out of the pub and back to our car.

The reason? We were only authorized to carry out surveillance on an operation that involved the importation of heroin, not illegal cigarettes. That's the law so our hands were tied. If the cigarette importation had been stopped and a court case followed – as it no doubt would – and information came to light that we had gained evidence of the cig importation at this 'heroin meet', then the evidence would have to be discounted. It was completely mad but that was sometimes how the law seemed to tie the hands of the law enforcers.

Mobile surveillance meant, of course, that we had to be driving around. In Investigation, we used mobile surveillance on almost every target we had. It was either used to move footmen around, put mobile targets under surveillance, to get to a knock (a raid) or arrest someone at lightning speed. So it was to our advantage to be good drivers. Not just good in the normal sense of being safe, but good enough to drive safely at speed and to pursue suspects without imperilling anyone. To that end, myself and my colleague, Pete, were signed up for a specially tailored pursuit driving course at a police driving-school. These courses were three weeks long and concentrated on what the police instructors referred to as 'the method'. Our major disadvantage as Customs officers was that when we drove we carried no blues-and-twos to warn everyone we were coming through.

Pete and I were the only two students in the whole school. This, we found out, was because the course finished on Christmas Eve and any police officer or Customs investigator worth their salt by then would be doing the Christmas party rounds and inhaling large amounts of liquid. Appropriately, our instructor, Clive, looked a bit like Santa Claus. But, even at fifty-nine years of age, he was still one of the best specialist driving instructors in the business. He was, basically, an elderly but extremely friendly speed nutter, and one who could change an ordinary family saloon into a racing car in the flick of the gearstick. He would have scared the bowels empty of any boy-racer one-third of his age.

Even though there was only me and Pete there, Clive delivered his opening announcement to the class as if he was addressing a full conference hall.

'Well, gents, you are here to learn the art of "making ground" – that's what we call it as we don't "speed" in law enforcement! We don't put a single member of the general public at risk; we will drive cars at the limit of their ability and then get 20 per cent more out of them. You, my young learners, will do this without the protection of blue lights or sirens and without the public ever knowing who you are and without the criminals ever seeing you!'

Pete and I resisted the urge – though it was strong – to look behind us and see who he was talking to; it felt as if the room must have filled up. But we knew we were the only ones there, so, impressed, we just looked at each other, and then straight back at Clive.

It's no exaggeration to say that, after three weeks' intensive training, we could shift any car like greased shit off a greased shit shovel. Clive was immense. If it wasn't for the white beard we could have sworn he was the Stig off *Top Gear*. He showed us that most people have no idea what your average family car can really do. Because, on the course, we didn't drive sports cars but just ordinary two-litre Ford Mondeos. People tend to think that police and Customs drive souped-up cars, but it isn't true. They are ordinary vehicles burdened with all the extra kit that a law enforcement car has to carry, such as radios, raid kits, spare kit, etc. So the advantage we had to have could only come from how we drove. We certainly got that advantage courtesy of Clive's skill and weeks of tearing around the track and countryside practising. For once, it was worth missing the Christmas drinks.

So, our surveillance fleet was extremely ordinary. Except for a couple of three-litre cruisers, all our cars were the bog-standard two-litre saloons. But, as our cars carried the radio kit and also our overnight bags, it was possible to leave home on Monday morning and not return for a couple of weeks. Local supermarkets used to do a brisk trade from surveillance officers on the job who had to quickly fill up their bags with new supplies of socks, pants and T-shirts.

Clive's imparted wisdom came in handy when we got the chance to put our driving skills to the test against a professional rally driver who had, you might say, come off the tracks.

Smugglers come from all walks of life, from opportunistic amateur to the hardened professional. But behind the larger smuggling organizations, just the same as with a legal business, there is an entire company of employees keeping the whole operation afloat: packers, cutters, manufacturers, forgers, enforcers, bodyguards, moneymen, gun men and – in the case of those who needed a quick getaway – wheel men. Professional drivers.

One wheel man that we came across was one of the best drivers that I'd ever had to try to keep up with. We already knew from various sources that Peter Butler had been a rally driver when he was younger. This was a bit of a worry, but then we had an officer who was a current amateur rally driver on our team (and who got his kicks by scaring the crap out of us when we were his passengers). The difference was that we knew Peter was in his fifties so we just hoped that he would have slowed down a bit with age. And, soon enough, we'd get to find out.

One lunchtime, the case officer on a current operation wandered over to my team's desks. He explained that he had just got info that Peter was on his way back from Spain with a large amount of cash following a successful drugs run. Apparently, he was driving up to Calais and the case officer wanted us to follow him home when he hit British soil. Although we had an address for Peter in Northampton, we had never actually seen him there, so we thought that either he had moved or that the address was just a cover.

So with six cars in our convoy (all 'two-up', that is, two officers in each) and a high-powered tracker car, we all sped off to Folkestone. We managed to get into place at various spots along the motorway to London by seven o'clock. Peter was due in via the Channel Tunnel at about eight, and bang on time we got a 'ping' on the tracker device attached to his Alfa Romeo. The tracker pinpointed him as having just left the train but it was still in the station area. But, when the signal gave the same position ten minutes later, our ground commander started to worry. There should have been some movement by now. I thought that he could have perhaps switched cars, which would have thrown us completely, but he would only do that if he thought he'd been rumbled. And if he thought he'd been identified, then why come back at all?

The tracker car was still getting a firm ping, but, on a drive-by of his supposed position, there was no one to be seen. We contacted our back-up officers who had another tracker system. They pinged our target car but now it was registering as shifting up the motorway to London and not in the station area at all. It turns out that he had passed us but we hadn't known because the tracking signal was corrupted by the electrified overhead train lines. You could have spotted every single surveillance car in the area at that moment from the loud swearing emanating from them.

Aiming to make up for lost time, our tracker car shot off like a high-velocity missile, followed by the rest of us at quite a steady speed of about 90 mph. Five minutes later, the tracker got a lock on the target and revealed one thing – the target was certainly shifting. So, fifty-year-old former rally driver or not, Peter hadn't lost any of his need for speed.

The ground commander came on the radio: 'The target is doing 90 to 100 mph, so I suggest we all floor it to make up ground.'

As we started to near the M25, all our cars were screaming along at 130 to 150 mph and at last we were starting to close the gap. Then the fog came down.

To add to our woes, our tracker car was spotted speeding and pulled over by a motorway police traffic car. We heard our tracker car driver cursing black and blue over the radio – the words 'give', 'me', 'fucking' and 'strength' were heard, though not necessarily in that order (well, they *were* in that order – it's just that one of those words in particular cropped up several times). Our chap knew he couldn't just plough on because it would have caused even more police cars to join the pursuit. The traffic cops must have been rubbing their hands at pulling such a high-speed merchant. Just a shame, I thought, that they hadn't pulled our target when he'd sped by!

Our tracker driver jumped out and shot back to the police car, ID in hand, and quickly explained that we were on high-speed surveillance. And then added, 'Oh, and by the way, there's six more of us due past soon.' The traffic cop's smile dropped as – right on cue – we all screamed past like a formation of low-flying rockets.

Making up the lost time was difficult, even at this speed, and we didn't really get close to Peter until he turned off the M25 and on to the M1. We had gone from Folkestone to Northampton (slowing only for the toll) with every driver practically having his foot flat to floor. The traffic had been good to us through the night and luckily every car performed well, as did the drivers.

But did we get what we were after? Well, only just. Two of our cars caught up enough to get within visual range of Peter, just as he entered Northampton, and they managed to keep with him right up to a premises that was previously unknown to us. So we did get his new address. The result of the night was humble, but important: two photographs, one with him getting out of his car with a bulging sports bag and the second of him opening his front door with a key. We had the information that we were after – the home base for a drugs runner.

But the thing that most amused us that night was the fact that it was one of our pursuit cars that got pulled by the police and not the villain's car that had half a million pounds in cash and two pistols in it.

Some targets took a lot of working on because they had anti-surveillance techniques and were very vigilant. It would have obviously been the most elementary mistake, on our part, for a target to spot us. So we used whatever vehicles fitted into an operational area. When working in north London in the Green Lanes area (one of our major stomping grounds for Turkish heroin gangs), we would blend in with the locals by using either BMWs or Mercedes-Benz. If our target was a City man and spent much of his time in central London, then we would sign out a private hire car and a couple of white vans and use those as tracking vehicles. If the target lived in the countryside, we would use Land Rovers, Subarus and motorbikes. The biggest advantage of using motorbikes was that they could make up ground at tremendous speed, a definite boon when you happened to lose sight of the target. We'd often position the bike at the rear of our convoy of tracking vehicles. The life of the biker was not an easy one as they often had to be out in all weathers.

The other position in the convoy that most officers wished to avoid was that of the surveillance or 'obs' (observation) van. It was often slow and ponderous to drive and had very little in the way of passenger comforts. Guys in the tracker cars usually had to leave the van behind during high-speed surveillance, only to see it again hours after we had stopped. When using an obs van, the driver would attempt to place it in the best possible position for the observation of the target. Sometimes this would mean a surveillance driver going out in the early hours of the morning in one of our cars to take up the required position and keep the parking space until the van arrived. Once in position, the obs-van driver would lock up the vehicle and abandon it for a much more comfortable surveillance car. But in the back of the van there would remain a second and often a third officer who were tasked with the surveillance. The rear windows were one-way glass. Within the van we would have a powerful radio link and cameras (both still and video); if you were very lucky, there might even be a portable toilet. A winter assignment in the van was often only survivable if you packed up some warm clothes to take with you. The real killer time to be in the van was during the summer. The summer sun had a habit of turning the van into a slow cooker. A very hot day would result in such a loss of body fluids that later on they had to be immediately replaced in the pub.

The use of the van was twofold. First, it could be used as an early-warning device for the rest of the surveillance team, giving updates as to the position and possible movement of the target. Second, and most importantly, the van was there to enable an officer to take evidential photographs and films of targets, cars, premises and even meetings.

One July morning, I was given the prestigious job of van officer on a large Excise job. The job had been handled by one of the Excise investigation teams until one of the suspect lorry drivers was involved in a shooting. The bad guys weren't after the driver but the load of booze that he was carrying in the lorry. Unfortunately, the driver fought back and the gang took a dislike to this attempted 'have a go hero' and tried to blow his head off with a shotgun. He was lucky to get away with his life. So things had definitely turned dirty and heavy, and the Excise team needed officers who didn't mind the risks. As such, myself and my colleagues on the cocaine and heroin teams were brought into the operation.

The sun was already hot at 7 a.m. when I clambered into the back of the Transit van. I had with me, in my kit bag, two towels and at least six litres of water. The day before, I had seen the van officer fall out of the rear of the van after duty: he was barely conscious and so dehydrated he was whisked away to hospital. By 8 a.m., the van had been put into position covering the entrance to a large cash-and-carry drinks warehouse. We knew that lorries loaded full of duty-free booze that were supposed to be heading for Europe were in fact being diverted into the home market. This was no Robin Hood crime: the organizers didn't reduce the price of the drinks but charged full whack and pocketed the difference. As a large percentage of the booze price is tax and duty, you can guess how much the gang were making per bottle. And where there are large criminal profits there are usually large criminals desperate to hang on to them.

By 10 a.m., the inside of the van was hotter than Satan's jockstrap. I had both a stills camera and a video camera set up on tripods and focused on the entrance of the warehouse. Lorries had started to arrive and I had to photograph their number plates then radio the lorries' details back to base. The same thing was happening at a bonded warehouse in the City of London. The case officer collated the information from the observation positions at the bonded warehouse and combined it with the information he was getting from four dirty cash-and-carry warehouses.

By midday, Satan's jockstrap felt like a vindaloo had been tipped into it, and in order to bear the stifling heat I was stripped down to my underwear. I'd already consumed four litres of my water. Suddenly, all hell broke loose when there was a series of massive bangs on the side of the van. For a second, I wondered if I'd been rumbled and was about to get dragged out of the vehicle. Then the loud banging started again, followed by cheering from people outside. I radio-contacted the covering team to send a car round to my position to see what the hell was happening. They soon arrived and radioed through.

'Jon, it's just workers from the factory over the road that are having a kickabout and using the side of your van as a goal! Don't sweat it.'

'Don't sweat it? Not funny, boys. It's hotter than fuck in here.'

'OK, then: cool it. Do you want us to have a word with them and get rid?'

'Well, *I* can't do it,' I said. 'I'm only in my underpants.'

'Really? Weird time to have a wank.' I heard a cackle of laughter down the line.

'*Fuck* you. Just for that you've got first shout at the rehydration session in the pub later.'

'Loving the optimism, Mad Dog, but you'll be no more than a puddle of piss and a pocket watch by the end of the day.'

'Well, just mop me up with a sponge and ring me out into your wife's knicker drawer. Now fuck off.'

And off they jolly well fucked and I was left to gather the rest of the day's evidence. I'd gone into the van the size of a rugby front prop and came out the size of Gandhi.

On mobile surveillance, one of the most widely used items was the aforementioned 'lump', as we called them, or commonly known as a tracking device. (The name 'lump' came from the sound that the device made when it became one with the vehicle.) The 'lump' is the name that all law enforcement agencies use and this piece of kit has its origin in the tracking devices that we used in the 1970s and 1980s. In the early days, the tracker was the size of an average sandwich box and not like the tiny thing that is used in modern surveillance. The original had four huge magnets on its top to hold it tightly to the underside of a car. And, if you think about the amount of potholes and sleeping policemen that are around, you realize that the magnets had to be very powerful (one day, after a job, it took two of us to wrench one tracking device free from the underside of a Transit van).

One evening, our sister team was tasked with lumping up one of our target's BMWs. He had two, a his-and-hers for him and his missus, and both were parked outside his house in south London. The lumping officer, wearing his best black overalls, crawled under the front BMW and tried to attach the lump, but with no success. For some reason, it wouldn't stick. He crawled out again. After legging it back to a surveillance car, he grabbed a screwdriver, muttering the words 'fucking anti-rust proofing' as an explanation of why the tracker wouldn't stick. Then he went back under the car, scraped a small area clean of the rust proofing and placed the lump in position – *lump!* This time it attached smoothly. Job done. But, just as he started to crawl out from under the car, word came over the air that the target and his wife were coming out of their house and heading for the cars. This was the moment to try not to panic. The boys in the surveillance cars were helpless to do anything – they couldn't reveal themselves without blowing the whole gig. The poor officer under the car was now a sitting duck.

He held his breath as he saw the feet of the targets approach. Should he wait until they got in the car and then try to slide out at the back? But what if they reversed – they'd run right over him. Same if he slid out the front. If he just lay there waiting for them to drive off, part of the underside of the car might rip him in two or drag him screaming down the road.

He nervously watched the two pairs of feet stop and then pause on the pavement, and then, luckily for our officer, they moved to the rear BMW – hers – and used that one instead. They drove off and there were mighty sighs of relief all round. And then the case officer's voice came across the earpieces – 'Right, please tell me you lumped the other car as well! Not happy if you haven't!' So, straight back to business as usual.

The following morning, my team took up position on the target's house. I was driving the tracker car and the tracker reader was my colleague, Jayne (who had been in the department for about six years and had worked her way up from a VAT officer to my drugs investigation team). These vehicles we used were known as the 'smart cars', as if they did everything by themselves with no need for human input. It would have been easier if they had. Though then I'd have missed out on the fun and excitement of driving the three-litre, twenty-four-valve Vauxhall saloon that I'd chosen out of our fleet. It was a real beast of a motor with tons of power.

We'd stood all the cars quite far back from the address as we had a very good signal and there was no need to risk 'showing out' (getting spotted). So we didn't even need to be in visual contact distance. At about ten in the morning, the blip on our screen started moving, which meant that the target had come out and moved off. We were off too as we started the surveillance. It wasn't difficult because we had a clear signal, so we spent the first few hours following without ever actually seeing the BMW in front of us except as a blip on our computer screen. Then it started raining, not your normal pitter-patter but full-on stair rods. It wasn't too long before we got stuck in traffic and the target's distance increased to an unacceptable one. We were sat there in traffic, rain drumming on the roof, the road like a river, the wipers working overtime, the powerful engine of the car rumbling under the bonnet but with nowhere to go.

We called in other cars to make up ground just as I spotted a gap in the traffic and put my foot down. The engine roared, the front end rose slightly and we were free. I gave the old gal some welly in order to try to claw back some of the lost ground. But, just as I hit the throttle and we shot down the road, a bus suddenly pulled out into the space ahead of us. We were now speeding towards what was essentially a large metal wall full of petrol – a double-decker bus with the face of a wide-eyed passenger in every window. I took evasive action, slammed the brake down, the ABS system juddered into life and we ended up sliding sideways at 85 mph, heading for the bus on a road that was more water than tarmac. The worst possible thing had happened: we were aquaplaning – water film forming between the tyres and the road so that we were no longer touching the road at all. Jayne started screaming so badly that I couldn't hear the radio. We all reflexively braced in anticipation of a big impact. Then just before we became one with London transport, I flicked the steering wheel and floored the throttle. Full power raced to the rear wheels, the fat back end of the Vauxhall swerved around, the car straightened up, and we shot past the bus in long waves of tyre spray. In the rear-view mirror I saw the bus driver lowering his arms from his face.

After a while, Jayne stopped screaming and decided to give me a little friendly advice. 'The next time I want you as a driver, Jon,' she shouted, 'it will be for my *fucking hearse!*'

After hours of further surveillance in heavy rain, the target finally stopped in the Lakeside Shopping Centre. They did like to shop, these big-time criminals. Must be all that spare cash they had lying about the place. I suppose you've got to get rid of it somehow. We flooded the place with officers, only to discover that we had spent most of the day following the target's wife! I found the target car in the car park by following our tracking blip until we were on top of it, and saw that it was her BMW and not his. Jesus. That bastard lumping officer – if he had lumped the right car and been dragged down the road when they drove off, we wouldn't have wasted a day and had a near-death experience.

You win some. You lose some. You fuck some up.

17. Getting into Drugs and Going on the Knock

My first drugs job as a qualified investigator was a heroin importation into Harwich. A Dutchman called Eric had been stopped as he drove through Customs controls. It was what we called a cold pull, namely, that there was no specific intelligence on him or his car. A cold pull is done on an officer's experience and suspicion.

The car was thoroughly searched, as was Eric, but nothing was found. The only suspicious thing was that Eric had a one-way, cash-paid ticket (a pretty rare occurrence and often a good indicator of a smuggling run) and that was it. But the stopping officer was still not happy. Eric's reason for travel was unconvincing and he was visibly shaking.

The officer had three options: send the driver on his way, reduce the car to nuts and bolts in a full search or call in a dog. With the officer still suspicious and a dog being on station at that time, the decision was an easy one. It took the drugs dog all of five seconds to indicate the presence of drugs as he sat in the boot of the car barking and covering the carpet in slobber and dog snot.

With the dog out of the way, the car hall team got down to what they were good at – pulling a car apart. But tonight their job was going to be easier than usual because as soon as they pulled up all the carpeting in the boot – there it was: drugs heaven. Through the bulkhead behind the rear seat were lots and lots of lovely packages that, on testing, proved positive for heroin. In total there were thirty-two packages, or 16 kg of very pure heroin that could be cut down and made into very many wraps, and worth more than I would earn in ninety years (give or take a pay rise or two). So Eric, for the foreseeable future, was in the gentle hands of Customs.

A find of this size was immediately notified to ID central control and, from there, they notified the heroin team officer on duty, which just happened to be me.

It was now eleven o'clock at night. I picked up my partner and we flew down to Harwich from central London. When I say 'flew' I mean we drove; and when I say 'drove' I mean we drove fast; and when I say 'fast' I mean that I know a speed camera on the A12 flashed me at 134 mph. We were, unsurprisingly, soon at the port and going over the car and Eric's paperwork with a very fine-tooth comb. The concealment was very good. The bulkhead that the officers had seen was, in fact, false. Someone had cut out a rear bulkhead from another same-model Audi and welded it eight inches in front of the proper one, and then glued in the carpet. They were also clever enough to leave the car for a few weeks so that the smell of glue and welding had dissipated – that was another telltale sign smugglers often neglected to cover.

As I chatted with the car hall team about Eric, the car's alarm system activated. It took us a good half-hour to turn it off and gain entry to the Audi again. This was no Halfords special-offer alarm: this was a system worth more than the ageing Audi itself.

Far be it from me to give advice to any potential smugglers out there, but you'd have thought it obvious that, if you're going to embark on a fairly long European cross-border journey, you should have a plausible story ready regarding your reason for travel. Not poor Eric. During my interview with him, he said that he was driving to Britain because . . . wait for it . . . in Amsterdam he had met a man in a pub.

Now, at this point, I should mention that the person Eric was talking about was actually the World's Most Wanted Man. Yep, a good 50 per cent of captured smugglers, dealers and drugs runners always started their explanation of their exploits with the words 'I met this bloke in a pub'. He certainly got around, this bloke, and if we could only find him we could have stopped most of the world's smuggling trade overnight.

So, Eric 'met a bloke in a pub', a few weeks before, and they'd got talking and within a few hours they had become firm friends. Strangely, Eric couldn't remember his name. The chap had said to him that he should come to England and they would meet up for a few drinks. So here he was.

'Right. So where does this chap live, Eric?'

'London.'

'And where in London does he live?'

'I'm not too sure.'

'You don't know, do you, Eric?'

He thought for a minute. 'No, not too sure, but I should be able to find him.'

'And how are you going to do that, then?'

Eric pondered. 'Well, London's not that big, is it?'

You can see that if there is a high rate of depression in Customs officers it is because they have to interview – at tedious length – gibbering idiots. So I started turning the screw in the next inquisition until Eric told us that, before catching the ferry, he had spent the night at a hotel that was local to the port and that it must have been during the night, when he was in bed, that someone put the drugs in the car.

'So, you went to bed and in the night a couple of very good mechanics managed to disarm your state-of-the-art alarm system, removed the carpet in your boot and carefully measured your rear-seat bulkhead, found an exact match in a scrap yard, then returned to your car and in the middle of the night welded in the false bulkhead and then filled the gap with a few million quid's worth of heroin. Is that what you are telling me, Eric?'

Eric smiled and, as if I'd just accidentally given him a good alibi, said, 'Yes – that's it!'

Later, during the resultant court case, my interview with Eric was read out to the jury. So, as you can imagine, at least they got a laugh out of their jury duty. Which is more than poor Eric did as he was soon heading for nineteen years at Her Majesty's pleasure. And I had my first investigation job under my belt.

Incidentally, during the court case, the original intercepting officer that had stopped the Audi at Harwich could still not put his finger on why he had suspicions about Eric. I knew exactly what he meant; it was like a sixth sense that you built up during your career regarding who you suspected. But, in this case, I like to think it was simply because he was called 'Eric'.

It wasn't just cars driven in from Europe that were used as vehicles for smuggling; at the airports, I'd obviously encountered the use of planes, but here in the Investigation Division, we got to see the use of boats too.

Cutter boats – that is, a medium-sized boat sanctioned with official authority – have been used in the Customs service for hundreds of years. The maritime arm patrols British waters and stops and searches hundreds of boats every month. Despite our rich naval past, we didn't have as many cutters as some of our European neighbours but what we lacked in numbers we made up for in quality. They were an expensive fleet to run and man, and their deployment was usually planned months in advance.

We had been following a gang of cannabis smugglers who had been using local fishing boats to do their dirty work by bringing in the gear from a mother ship. In the trade this is called 'coopering'. But the fishing boat crews turned against their part-time employers when they found out that they weren't smuggling tobacco (as they had been told) but were importing drugs. One of the boat captains was so angry that he phoned our free drugs phone line and left us some workable intelligence. (And it made a change from jokers ringing up our free drugs phone line and asking when they could pick up their free drugs.)

Now the gang had no fishing boats to use, they had to do the job themselves and so they used some of their enormous profits to purchase a RHIB (rigid-hulled inflatable boat), which is a kind of high-speed cross between a speedboat and an inflatable boat. The trouble was, they were better drug buyers than they were sailors and so on a couple of runs they had to throw the drugs overboard before they sank. These bales of drugs later turned up on various beaches and the members of the public who found them handed them in (or, at least, the ones we got back were handed in).

So myself and my colleagues in Investigations put our Intelligence teams to work on the gang and we soon had a few names and addresses to work with. Our job now was to build up patterns of lifestyle on these new targets, follow them, photo them and check out whoever they met, etc. It didn't take long for us to have a good picture of how the gang worked and what they were up to.

But these things take time and investigations sometimes take months, even years. Luckily, a few weeks into the operation, I received a great update from the Intelligence team. Two of the gang's cars, one towing a large RHIB, had been seen going on to Mersea Island, which is the most easterly inhabited island in the UK and is just off the Essex coast. Their move to the island had happened only a couple of hours earlier. We scrambled immediately. Mersea was only about twenty miles away from our HQ. With any luck, we thought, we could catch them in the act.

While we were shooting to the island, I contacted the maritime team, explained what the situation was and requested a cutter to move into position, north of Mersea. This would cut off their sea escape if they decided to flee that way. The maritime team said that it would be no problem as they had a cutter in the area. Our next call was to the police to ask if they could put in a control point on the access way on to the island. All was going swimmingly; it looked like we might have the whole thing sorted and sewn up.

We arrived on the island and plotted up in a good position to be able to view the two cars and the by-now empty boat trailer (the RHIB was gone), as well as covering all the possible exits. As usual in surveillance, it was now a matter of playing the waiting game. Again, we were lucky: within the hour, we spotted the RHIB on the horizon – it was heading at speed to their meeting place on the coast of the island, in all likelihood for another consignment pick-up. I contacted the maritime team again in order to call in our cutter boat to move in and cut off the escape route out to sea. However, when the guy at the maritime HQ answered my call and then asked me a question, I knew our luck had definitely run out:

'OK. How close into the Liverpool docks do you want the cutter to move?'

'What do you mean Liverpool docks? This is Jon Frost calling. Are you sure that you have the right job?'

There was a slight pause at the other end. 'Yes, yes, I'm quite sure. Officer Frost requested a cutter to position itself to the north of the Mersey.'

So our cutter was actually 300 miles north and on the other side of the country, near Liverpool. No way to get another one scrambled in time now. Our luck returned, though, when we observed that the drugs gang were just doing an engine trial on their boat. We moved away with our tails a little between our legs, at least content that no one knew about the cock-up apart from us and the maritime boys, and they weren't likely to brag about it. Meanwhile, some poor bastard had to skipper the cutter boat all the way back home. Sometimes investigations ended in even more unexpected ways.

Another fan of the RHIB mode of drugs transportation was a career criminal called Shaun Fletcher. He was a nasty piece of work and he worked full time. Born and bred into a London criminal family, he was the elder of two brothers, and both were so close to being human pitbull terriers I wouldn't have been surprised if they cocked their legs to piss.

After making money selling drugs as a doorman at London discos, he'd decided to move up the narcotics ladder and cut out the drugs middleman that he'd been using, and that he'd been losing money to. Fletcher was a martial arts expert and would use his skills on anyone that upset him. And, as most of the time he was high on amphetamines, people seemed to upset him quite often. Fletcher was like a nasty, drug-propelled and steroid-fuelled whirlwind that left in his wake chaos, cracked skulls and cleaning bills.

He started his new smuggling venture with a friend but it

wasn't too long before Fletcher teamed up with, believe it or not, an ex-choirmaster who had changed careers radically and was now importing cannabis from the Netherlands in his speedboat. Nice. From master of the choir to drug buyer.

Both Fletcher and his new partner in crime, Evans, were known to us. We had intel on them and had done some reccies and surveillance but without ever being able to catch them at it. So it was now a matter of watching and waiting for their next move. Being in Investigations was sometimes like the front-line soldier's description of war – long, quiet periods of fuck-all-to-do followed by loud, intense periods of people trying to fuck you up.

We waited about three months, and then our control centre received an anonymous call relating to Fletcher. The caller stated that he had been approached to move a large quantity of cannabis resin that was coming in from the continent that week. His contact was Fletcher and all his dealings were with him only. That fitted the picture as we knew that Shaun was a 'hands on' chap; he was either too drug-addled or too arrogantly confident to put the usual distance between himself and the drug consignments, which is what most dealers did so that they had a buffer between themselves and what would become the evidence to send them down for years. (And the fact that he had been shopped by one of his 'colleagues' proved that, in the criminal underworld, fear wasn't as good a motivator as respect. Unpredictably violent criminals were often wanted out of the way, even by their own kind, and were never missed after they were gone.)

Evans, our singing smuggler, was the boat driver. The RHIB was, we learned, his boat and his retirement present to himself. How these two unlikely partners in crime had first hooked up, God only knew, but I couldn't imagine it was at choir practice.

Through manipulation of the informant, we eventually got even more detailed information of the kind that we were after. Fletcher and Evans would make landfall at a certain beach in Kent the following week, at around two o'clock in the morning. That was when we would carry out the knock.

'The knock', as we called it, was our equivalent to what the police called a strike or what the military would call an attack. In other words, it's Customs' own phrase for a law enforcement pounce, grab and arrest – bang to rights.

There are many kinds of knock. The most common is the pre-planned knock, where, because of intelligence gathering from surveillance and undercover work, ID know in advance what they are going to do. This is bread-and-butter stuff.

A 'rolling knock' is where the fun is. For example, if I was doing an undercover bootleg cigarette job, we would never know what was going to happen. Was the lorry going to be unloaded into storage? Was it going to be redirected? Would the main men be there? Would it turn nasty? Would we need an escape route? Lots of possibilities and unknown quantities. But when the bits fell into place, we would knock the job.

Usually, there is only a two-minute warning before a knock is on, and that's when you'd squirt adrenalin through every pore. Every officer would scramble for handcuffs and note-books at the same time as moving into a position to knock.

When the ground commander finally gave the word, the world would go into a blur as cars, officers, members of the public and professional criminals alike all went flying in all directions. We mastered the art of leaping from moving cars and, believe it or not, I'd even seen a driver do it, such was his eagerness to be in on the knock and take someone down (I forget where the car ended up . . .). Which just shows what the imperative is – arrest everyone and secure everyone and, quite often, shout at everyone (psychological intimidation was often vital); secure goods, secure evidence, protect the public and, in the pursuit of all this, it often meant bollocks to Customs officers' personal safety. But then we knew what we'd signed up for.

The department decided to issue body armour about ten years ago but even then it was a pool item – that is, too few items between too many – and, anyway, you wore it only if you wanted to. Even doing undercover work, I would rarely end up wearing anti-stab protection as the bloody stuff would get in the way even though you couldn't see it.

We were never officially issued batons or any other form of self-defence weaponry but we didn't let that stop us – most of us didn't want to go up against violent career criminals with little more than our dicks in our hands and the Lord's Prayer. So we tended to carry 'a little something': extendable metal batons, truncheons, blackjacks, etc. During the later under-cover CROPs jobs in the countryside and rural locations, I would carry a Ghurkha kukri knife and a dagger, which was a concealed wrist dagger/thrusting blade, first used by Second World War Special Operations Executives.

It was not unknown for Customs to use SO19 – the undercover armed police unit from the Metropolitan Police – when knocking a major drugs gang; the SBS (Special Boat Service) for boat and maritime jobs; and the SAS (Special Air Service) for other operations. But these forces, no matter how specialized, secretive or powerful, would always be under our command.

As for additional surveillance equipment, we would often be what they now call 'first adopters', which meant we would often get to test and deploy things like night sights or infrared sights prior to the special forces. The police would then get access to it after a few years.

Sometimes, though, we didn't need anything more sophisticated in terms of equipment than a size-ten boot and a battering ram.

One instance of this was when my team and I were at Heathrow Airport. We had just followed one of our targets from Sutton, south London, to Terminal 3 and watched him board his flight. It was a nice and easy job. Now we'd await his return and welcome him and his drugs package with open arms and a closing cell door.

We were just about to head back to London when the senior officer of the local investigation unit called us into his office. He had a job on and could we help? Well, anything beat driving back to the office and ploughing through the waiting piles of paperwork, so we agreed.

The situation was this: at lunchtime, the uniform boys had pulled a known drug dealer in the green channel as he arrived from Spain. The Intel officers had done some homework on this chap and had discovered that, while in Spain, he and another Brit had travelled over to North Africa and back three days before they arrived home at Heathrow. A full baggage and body search discovered 1.5 kg of cannabis oil. Proper cannabis oil was very rare, and it was even classed as a Category A drug because of its transdermal properties, that is, it could pass through human skin. It was worth its weight in gold in the right market.

Unfortunately, Intel had discovered that this chap's mate had arrived at Gatwick at ten o'clock that morning and the Customs staff there hadn't stopped him because there was no interest in him at that time. What the senior officer wanted of us was to spin down to the arrested man's address and carry out a full house search under PACE (Police and Criminal Evidence Act). We had all our search kits in our cars, so it was on.

By six o'clock that evening, we were all outside the target address. I had what we called the Enforcer – a 50 lb steel door ram. If the door wasn't opened straight away, my aim was to take the door off its hinges. Sometimes on a knock we had literally to . . . knock. We did – no answer. I drew back the enforcer and was about to release carnage when the door swung open and there stood the chap who had arrived at Gatwick that morning. He quickly turned and ran into the living room and I followed, as fast as the 50 lb steel girder in my hands would allow. As I reached the living-room door, he emerged, shouting, and going for my head with a full-sized crowbar. I knew where this was going better than he did. He leaped at me with the crowbar heading for my skull. Mid-air is not the best place to meet the Enforcer. I swung it and he caught it full in the chest. I heard cracking and guessed that his ribs had gone. He flew back, hit the wall and collapsed in a moaning lump.

We all stepped over the body and into the living room, except for 'Big' Alan (our rugby-playing brick shithouse) who grabbed the target by one ankle and casually dragged him into the living room like a caveman lugging his latest kill. There, in front of us, lay another kilo and a half of cannabis oil. Bingo. Five minutes later, there was a knock at the front door. Alan wandered out into the hall and answered the knock. Standing there was what can only be described as every single stoned-hippy cliché gathered together in human form: tie-dye T-shirt, sandals, curtains of long hair, nose ring and a broad stoner smile. Hippy Neil from *The Young Ones* incarnate. He spoke . . . and didn't disappoint.

'Oh . . . hey, dude. Wow, man, you're a size. So, is the gear here, my brother?'

Any neighbours watching this scene would have then observed what looked like a large monster paw reach out from inside the house, grasp Hippy Neil's head *whole* and yank him swiftly inside, leaving behind only the smell of patchouli oil and, on the doormat, a single wobbling sandal. And, if the neighbour's window had been open, they might have also heard a small, startled yelp.

What they wouldn't have heard was what Big Al said just before the moment of hippy lift-off – 'Hello, son. Come on in and join the party!'

But for every light-hearted knock that we went on – and, by our standards, someone coming at me with a crowbar was fairly low down the list – we also had the jobs against the career criminals like Fletcher. His drugs drop on the beach was looming up in our very near future.

So, all this in mind, we prepared for the knock on Fletcher and Evans. And, sure enough, at the appointed time and place, their speedboat arrived and the two smugglers offloaded approximately one ton of cannabis resin. Just as they were covering it over with sand, we made our move. It was the most satisfying part of the job: when months or even years of investigation, surveillance, tracking, trailing, tapping, recording, cross-referencing, researching and (worst of all) waiting all came to fruition. No wonder officers got hyped up in the minutes just prior to the knock; they had good reason. None of us really fully knew exactly what situation we were about to run out into – the black holes of a double-barrel shotgun pointing at you, perhaps. We could only best-guess what would be waiting and hope we were prepared. But a career criminal drugs runner at risk of going back inside for a ten- or fifteen-stretch was not the kind to come quietly.

At the signal, myself and thirty other officers leaped out of cover, screaming blue murder, and descended on the beach like a squad of marauding black-clad devils. Evans, drawing on all his experience in the hardened world of teaching children to sing together pleasantly in church, immediately dropped straight to the ground like a sack of shit at a Sack of Shit Dropping to the Ground Contest. The sight of Her Majesty's Customs and Excise storming the beach seemingly made him rediscover his love of praying on his knees. Fletcher, on the other hand, was off like a greased whippet, accelerating like a professional sprinter and vaulting the cannabis load like a gymnast. He dived headfirst back into the boat, which was still bobbing in the surf. From the speed at which he'd shot away from us, it was easy to see why amphetamine was also called 'speed'.

Fletcher roared away in the RHIB, but we had planned for this possibility and had our own Customs cutter boat sitting off the coast. The cutter turned and set off after the fleeing craft but unfortunately it was like watching a hippo chase a cheetah – the power-to-weight ratio of the RHIB was superior to our own craft, especially with Fletcher's boat now lightened of its heavy load; and so, within a couple of minutes, the little speedboat was just a memory and a fading wake in the water. Fletcher, unfortunately, had slipped through our grasp and was gone. That beach at that moment was probably home to more pissed-off Customs officers per square foot than anywhere else in the world.

We tried to track him down, of course, but even he wasn't reckless enough to emerge into daylight. It wasn't until quite some time afterwards that we were contacted by a police regional crime team. They had found our old target, Fletcher, and were we interested? Like Canadian Mounties, we were pissed off if we didn't get our man, and we never forgot it. So we invited the police case officer to our office to tell us the tale.

Apparently, Fletcher had been getting quite a rep in the Netherlands for the supply of speed and ecstasy. A reputation that was starting to interest the Dutch police. He had managed to start his new business from the proceeds of selling Evans's speedboat. From there it was easy for a man of

Fletcher's ability to build up the right contacts, and soon he was shimmying his way back up the crime tree. The only worry for him was the Dutch authorities. And one morning, when he received a tip-off from an official source that the police were going to turn him over that night, he grabbed everything that he could and made for the coast. Once there, he stole another RHIB and headed for home, hoping that we had forgotten all about him. Mid-channel, he contacted his brother to meet him at a beach in East Anglia. The dutiful brother was there on time, and they had soon unloaded Fletcher's gear from the boat into the car, including £500,000 worth of ecstasy tablets.

In celebration at arriving safely and being undiscovered, Fletcher popped three or four tablets and decided to drive. His brother was furious and the two argued as they sped through the East Anglian countryside. Fletcher was hitting 100 mph when the car left the road and met a large oak tree coming the other way. Nothing stops a speeding car more dead in its tracks than a thick tree. There's no 'give' in a deeply rooted oak – it's like slamming into iron. Neither man was wearing a seat belt in the old car, so the younger brother was fired straight through the windscreen like a human rocket, punching a hole in the windscreen like a cannonball. Fletcher also shot forward, straight into the car's steering wheel, which cut into his head at the bridge of the nose. It being an old car, the steering wheel was made of solid metal (covered only in thin plastic) and so, as it met Fletcher's skull at extremely high speed, it sliced right through his head, from front to back – neatly flipping off his skull-top like a pan lid.

Our police colleagues said that it was not a pretty sight. Then they showed us the police accident scene photographer's pictures to prove it. Fletcher had taken so much ecstasy and finally got so off his head that the actual top of it – still covered in tufts of hair and blood – had finished stuck upside down in a pat of cow shit in a field in East Anglia.

18. Pricking Michael Jackson's Bubble

On a list of things that are bad for your health – such as getting hiccups while juggling chainsaws or tickling your dentist while he's drilling your filling – add to the list this one: it's never a good idea to threaten a Customs officer. You'd think that would be pretty obvious to most for the clear reason that, if you're already being questioned, then to a certain extent you're already in the crosshairs, so why make things worse?

It's never a good idea to complain too much in a restaurant *before* your food's arrived – you never know what the chef might send back out to you from the unseen, dark recesses of the kitchen (is that really just mayonnaise?). Best to wait until at least you've had dessert. Similarly, it's best to wait until you've walked away from and out of hearing distance of an HM Customs officer that could snap on a rubber glove and introduce you to the dark arts of the strip search.

On this basis, I try to never piss off the guy that's cutting my hair (available weapon: scissors), the barber giving me a wet shave (available weapon: razor) or the doctor due to give me a prostate exam (available weapon: finger in arse).

Sometimes discretion really is the better part of valour. It could save you a lot of bad haircuts, nicks on the neck and sore bottoms.

It follows that even worse than threatening one Customs officer would be to threaten a whole country's Customs service. I mean, who would do that? Well, during one of the stranger occurrences of my career, this actually happened.

On a US TV show, Michael Jackson was promoting his new live tour of Europe. He was asked if his pet chimp, Bubbles, would miss him while he was away. 'No,' he said. 'I'm taking him with me. And British Customs can't stop me.' Oops.

This was now a case of professional pride versus a very public challenge. The threat was taken seriously; one thing any professional service hates, as much as members of the general public also hate it, is the idea that someone thinks they should get preferential treatment: it offends all notions of fair play. So all ports and airports got direct HQ orders to seize Michael Jackson's stage kit and 'examine thoroughly'.

The next day, all the stage kit arrived at the airport and was put into cargo sheds. No one could enter without Customs clearance. That night, baggage officers and cargo officers joined forces (a rare thing in itself, which gave an indication of how pissed off everyone was) and set about Mr Jackson's stage kit. Every speaker, mixer and lightbox was taken apart in the hunt for a possible hiding place for Bubbles. Nothing was found. But every bit of kit had to be reassembled and tested. The tour crew were not happy. No word came through, however, about how Bubbles viewed the whole affair. And, to make matters worse, every European Customs service did the same as us. All of them were determined not to be made a monkey of by the chimp-owning singer. And it didn't end there.

Quite some time later, long after we'd forgotten about the monkey business, a colleague and pal of mine, hippy-lifting Big Al, arrived in the office at Charlie Hotel with a very interesting-sounding invite. He leaned on my desk; the desk sagged.

'All right, Jon? Wanna come with me and Terry? We're just off to shoot someone.'

I replied without hesitation, 'OK.' It had, after all, been a slow day.

Al smiled, gave the thumbs up, and then he straightened up and my desk returned to its original shape.

We picked up a couple of other officers, Dave and Paul, on the way, and then went out to Thames Quay on the south side of Custom House, opposite HMS *Belfast*, which sat moored on the Thames.

Now HMS *Belfast* is a pretty impressive sight – 11,550 tons of steel and guns; a 600-foot-long Second World War battle-ship bristling with armaments. Pretty difficult to upstage that, you might think. And you'd be right. But right next to HMS *Belfast* was something new, something that hadn't been moored there before, something that had never before been seen in London or anywhere else for that matter. We all looked up at it in slight disbelief, speaking to each other while never taking our eyes of it.

'It's un-fucking-believable,' said Big Al.

'No, it's actually worse than that,' said Terry. 'It's un-fucking-believe-a-fucking-bull.'

'It's a bloody liberty is what it is,' said Dave.

'It's certainly looks as big as the Statue of Liberty,' I said.

Paul chipped in, 'Did they really open Tower Bridge for it?'

'Too right they did,' I said. 'How else would they have got it to float this far down the Thames?'

'The cheek!'

'Really un-fucking-believable.'

Big Al was particularly unhappy that this thing had been moored right outside our offices. He took it as a personal affront. 'Right, lads,' he said, clapping his hands together, 'be back here tonight at 9 p.m. And wear black. We're gonna have to go extra-secret coverts ops on this.'

Luckily, none of us had to be out on duty that evening and no one was lost to a late call-out. We couldn't think about anything else for the rest of the day. Sometimes, walking through Custom House, you'd catch a glimpse of it outside through one of the south-facing windows.

Hours later, we were all there, back at the riverside at the appointed time, all dutifully present and correct for the secret meet. All dressed in black. A car flashed its lights at us and then turned and reversed nearer. Big Al got out and opened the boot of the car. We all looked inside, looked at each other, grinned in unison, then looked back inside the boot. It was full of rifles, guns, catapults and crossbows, with ammunition for the guns and bolts for the bows. We all reached in, eagerly took our weapon of choice and then turned and faced our target.

There it stood: a forty-foot-high fibreglass statue of Michael Jackson.

In order to promote his new album, *History*, it had been floated down the Thames, through Tower Bridge – which, of course, had to be opened for it – and moored outside our own Charlie Hotel, right next to HMS *Belfast*. So, next to a battleship that had fought Nazi convoys and that had also, in 1944, carried the King of England, there now stood a big fibreglass model of the King of Pop. It did all look rather odd and more than a little bit ridiculous. And this literal monument to one man's ego looked even more ridiculous floating next to a battleship that during the war would have been manned by men too modest to even talk about it afterwards.

To make things worse, the statue was, apparently, one of nine such monstrosities in major cities around the world. So we decided that the one in London was going to be the only one that was welcomed by a late-night, five-man firing squad. Well, think about it: if we could detain billionaire friends of the Queen of England, as I'd done at Stansted, and if we could successfully put the brakes on a chimpanzee called Bubbles, then I didn't see why British Customs officers shouldn't redecorate the King of Pop.

So, for the next few hours, we threw everything we had at it: every air-rifle pellet and airgun bullet, every crossbow bolt and arrow, every high-powered and brightly coloured paint-ball, every water bomb, and every catapulted rock and missile we could whistle through the night air.

And, in case you're wondering, we had decided, early on, that the highest point score would go – naturally – to who-ever could knock off the nose. We didn't quite make the Michael Jackson statue history that day, but at least repeatedly shooting him gave us a little bit of a bad, dangerous thrill.

19. The Yardie Coke Smuggler and the Future Mrs Frost?

Jade, a beautiful German girl, eighteen years of age, arrived at Harwich from the Hook of Holland. She was to become the centre of my first cocaine case. She was pulled by the bench staff as Intelligence had discovered that she was travelling on a cash-paid, one-way ticket. Within ten minutes of being stopped and questioned, she broke down and admitted that she was carrying cocaine. She was taken to a cell and strip searched; she was wearing a bodysuit (very much the same design as the body armour that you see the police wear), which contained fifteen kilos of pure Colombian nose sherbet.

I got the phone call ten minutes later as I was the duty officer on that week, and I was at Harwich within half an hour. With the capture of a smuggler, the investigation service swung into a fast and well-tested routine. While I was driving to the port, my senior officer was making available as many investigators as he could. The reason for this was to enable what we used to call a 'live run'. This meant we would get the smuggler's agreement to carry on with their delivery instructions but under the tight control and surveillance of ourselves. Historically, this had produced amazing results with some of the UK's greatest drugs hauls and arrests. Sometimes you had to follow the rabbit down the hole to get to Wonderland.

If I was quick enough and if she agreed, we could get the operation moving within thirty minutes. But I found out the trouble with the plan when I got there: the young woman, Jade, was petrified. She really didn't want to go through with it, she said, as her boyfriend and his mates would kill her. It was hard not to feel a little sorry for her because she was clearly both naive and bullied. I gave her the standard answer: 'Don't worry, there are more of us than them and we will look after you.' This just made her burst into tears again.

'No, they are Yardies! They carry lots of guns and knives. They don't mess!' she said.

She had a point. Yardies, indeed, 'don't mess' – meaning that, when it comes to settling scores, they aren't shy. I gave Bob, my senior officer, a call on his mobile to update him. Jade was not going to play but she had told me her instructions and I thought we might be in luck. I explained the situation and its background.

Apparently, six months earlier, Jade's friend had taken her to a club on Reeperbahn in Hamburg. There she had met the owner of the club, a British guy who had been in the Army and decided to stay in Germany at the end of his service. He and Jade got on well, although at forty-five he was much older than her. They made a strange couple but Jade, being young and impressed by the guy's money, fell for him. The guy's name was Nevin Bull and, as we found out later, Jade was just one of many whom Bull had got close to – most were now prostitutes working in his club.

But it seemed that luck was on Jade's side, in some perverse way. They stayed as a couple for a few months and Bull asked her to go on holiday with him to Jamaica. She said she agreed immediately as she had never been abroad before and her family had roots in Jamaica. But, once there, Bull totally changed. He would leave her locked in her hotel room for days as he left her to 'go do business'. Then, when he did take her out, it was to a Yardie club where she was paraded nude in front of Bull's associates. Some of them had tried to rape her but she had managed to fight them off. Bull, she said, never batted an eye. In the last few days of the holiday, Bull took her to another hotel where they were to meet what he called 'the tailor'. Thinking that Bull was going to buy her a new dress, she was willingly measured and the tailor left, telling Bull that it would be ready in two days. Five minutes later, four Yardie gang members arrived at the hotel room and she was locked in the bathroom as Nevin and the men discussed something that Jade couldn't hear.

After the four left, Bull unlocked the bathroom door and led Jade into the bedroom where he told her his tale of woe. His club was losing money hand over fist and he had used the last of his own money for this holiday. The four men had lent him some money a few months before and now they wanted it paid back, and if it wasn't repaid in the next few days then both he and Jade would be shot, cut up and dumped at sea. He said that the men had said that, if Bull was willing to do something for them, they would write off the debt. He told Jade that, if she carried something back to the Netherlands for them, they would both be all right.

Now anyone with any sense and experience could see this was a classic softening-up technique used by men like Nevin Bull who were used to manipulating vulnerable people, especially women. It's how most of the young women he now had working as prostitutes for him had first fallen into his world. The only reason Jade hadn't already been brutalized and passed around the other gang members was because Bull knew he had to maintain her feelings for him in order to facilitate using her as a drugs mule.

Jade had been totally taken in, although the story was, to us, clearly nonsense (of course, she had actually been measured by the tailor for the drugs bodysuit). The thing behind her apparent naivety was love: she was madly in love with this character, although it was apparent he showed her little in return. So she believed his story. She also thought that, if she carried out the run, they would be together forever. It was both saddening and pathetic to hear how she believed it to be true.

For the drugs runs, she was duly fitted with the bodysuit full of drugs and put on a plane to Germany. Her instructions were for her to go to her flat in Hamburg, pack a small holdall, making sure that she had no paperwork linking her to either Bull or Jamaica, and then get the train to Amsterdam and then on to the Hook of Holland (buying a cash-paid ticket for the ferry to Harwich). Once in Harwich, she was to take the train to London and then get a taxi to an address that Nevin Bull had written in her diary. At this address, she would meet up with him again and he would take the drugs to another London address before the two returned to Hamburg together.

At eight o'clock that evening, some strangers arrived at the address in London. They were actually my drugs team, backed up with some uniformed officers from Harwich and a couple of police officers to keep the peace (and also to be used as human shields if the Yardies reacted badly). The door was answered by a young blonde woman who was removed from the doorway in a firm but polite way, and then the team went steaming in. Thankfully, there were no armed Yardies in the house so Bob, the ground commander, and the police breathed a silent sigh of relief. What was there was Nevin Bull and his best mate, Paul Morrison, sitting at the dinner table each eating a bowl of soup. They were both arrested and transported to Harwich for questioning. Morrison was later released and would appear again, with his wife, as a witness for the defence.

Right from the start, Bull refused to admit knowing Jade. He even refused to admit that he had been in Jamaica. He stated that he had just driven over from Hamburg to visit an old friend in London. He would stick to this story right up to the trial. So, what did we have on him?

His passport was found hidden under a bed at the London address with the Jamaica stamps in it showing that he had arrived from there into Heathrow that very morning, having left two days after Jade. Our drugs liaison officer had got his hands on the booking and payment details of the hotel in Kingston that the two of them had shared for three weeks plus

CCTV video footage of Bull arriving at Heathrow. Then we had the great evidence of Jade's diary in which Bull had written down the London address. Another great piece of evidence came in the form of a wrap of cocaine that I had found in Bull's wallet. Now, we couldn't go into court and state that because he had a wrap of cocaine he must be a smuggler but, bugger me, it does make a jury think.

The final nail in the coffin was Jade herself, and the evidence she could provide to the whole affair. But, to start with, it was really hard work. Her on-call solicitor, Bill, was well known to me. We had legally jousted on many a case before. But what you could say about him was that he had a human side and that he was realistic about defending a person who had so much evidence stacked against them. Some solicitors would cause all kinds of shitstorms to try to get their client off, only to have them get a longer sentence in court when they were found guilty. This is always the way: if you're found guilty in court after a not-guilty plea, you get a longer sentence than if you had pleaded guilty at the start. A good, pragmatic brief should realistically assess their client's chances of double-screwing themselves with an indefensible not-guilty plea.

Bill had been with Jade from the first interview and was well aware of how she had assisted us. He had also brought in a German interpreter called Mrs Hess so that there were no misunderstandings during the interviews. Unfortunately, Mrs Hess was an elderly German lady who was not too on the ball with law enforcement techniques. She had a habit of jumping down my throat when she thought I was being rude and, in return, she was much ruder back than we could ever hope to match. Even Bill had to laugh whenever she started barking at me in her strong German accent. That earned him a bark and an evil stare of his own.

Over the months leading up to the trial, Mrs Hess became a surrogate mother to Jade. Every time either Bill or I visited Jade, Mrs Hess had to be there by her side. It was really quite sweet how she wanted to protect her, but also easily understandable because the young woman was clearly very naive and out of her depth. Bill and I joked about telling Mrs Hess the full horrors of Nevin Bull's treatment of her young charge and then locking her in a room with him. But we decided we'd rather see Bull convicted of trafficking than Mrs Hess convicted of murder.

Normally, once we had arrested, interviewed and charged an individual, that was the last we would see of them before the trial, but in this case it was different. If Jade was to be the coffin nail that I hoped she would be, then I needed her to turn Queen's Evidence, which meant she would have to stand up in court against Bull. To do this successfully, she would have to give me a full, no-holds-barred witness statement of everything that had happened since she met Bull in his club. And here the problem arose. No matter what Bull had led her into, she still thought she was in love with him. I would need Bill and Mrs Hess's help to try to change that. As it turned out, fate lent a hand in the form of Holloway Prison.

Most of the public are unaware that there is a huge number of foreign female smugglers in UK prisons and, in Holloway Prison's case, many of them are linked to the Yardie gangs.

One thing that you can accurately say about criminal communications is that their system seems to be so much faster than BT. Within the first three days of her being on remand, Jade had already received four death threats. Bill was straight on the phone to me.

'Jon, you got her in this shit, you get her out,' he said. 'If we help her now, I'm sure that she will play ball come the trial.'

It was questionable whether it was my fault as I wasn't the one that had got her into drug smuggling – but I could see his point regarding the trial. So I did two things together that would enable her safety. First, I contacted a certain police team based at Scotland Yard. These were the supergrass boys, the officers who could make someone disappear and start a new life. I explained the situation and they jumped at the chance to help (knowing that Customs would foot the bill). Second, and with the help of a nice letter from a judge that I approached, I got Jade moved to a female prison near Sheffield. It made it a swine of a trip up there to interview her, or for her to come to court in Essex, but at least she was safe, and to make double sure of that we had her housed in the hospital wing where she could be watched.

Two days after the move, Bill, Mrs Hess and I arrived at the prison and met Jade in a closed room and not in the open visiting area. I explained the Queen's Evidence rules and that Bull was saying that he didn't even know her. She was still worried. For two hours, I tried my best, along with Bill, but we were not gaining ground. I decided I had to try a shock tactic.

'Jade, look, get this into your head: Bull is going to see you go down and then he'll be off, back to Hamburg and into the loving arms of one of his other girls. He's put you in the shit and he's quite happy to leave you there. And you're going to be there for the next twenty years.'

Bill tried to appeal to her in a much gentler manner but I responded with more of the brutal truth. 'And make no mistake,' I said, 'in all that time that you're inside, you'll only ever see your parents and family twice a month, if that. That's if you get to see them at all. But, if you want to throw your life away, that's up to you.'

'That's enough, Jon, I think, for now. We need to let Jade think about things.'

We left the room and Bill turned to me and shrugged. 'The old good cop/bad cop routine. Think it'll work? Do you think she gets it now?'

I said that I wasn't sure, but it would be better for her if the routine did work in persuading her to save herself rather than sacrifice herself for a professional criminal. We both now needed a fag so we walked outside and, at the prison door, we each lit up a much-needed smoke.

'So what do you really think?' I asked Bill.

He said, 'I think I'm sexually attracted to Mrs Hess.'

'Is it the moustache?' I asked. 'Because I see what you mean. It's quite sexy.'

'It is, but, if she ever cuts it into a little square Hitler one, it'll be all over between us . . .'

Two cigs each and many Mrs Hess jokes later, we turned to see Mrs Hess standing in the doorway, glaring. 'You are both bastards,' she told us firmly. 'But . . . she says she wants to do it.'

It was with great relief that, when we returned over the next few visits, we managed to get the full story. Then there was a small but very unexpected twist. On one of my last visits, Mrs Hess suddenly grabbed my arm and squeezed it. She said, 'Have you noticed that Jade has changed?' I said I had to admit that she was much chattier and seemed to enjoy the visits. 'No, you idiot,' Mrs Hess said. 'She's in love with you!'

Well, that could be inconvenient, I thought. It was obviously just a case of someone transferring strong feelings to the person they felt was 'saving' them, and in this case Jade had decided that was me. Still, I'd rather she mistakenly believed she was in love with me than someone like Bull. The next time I saw him, I told Bill the news, and he just asked if that meant it left the way clear for him and Mrs Hess.

We were quietly confident about the court case, but I knew that, even in the highest courts in the land, things can go tits up. What juries hear is never really the full story – it is only what the law lets them hear. The full story is always known by the defendant, often by the police or Customs, sometimes by the defence, and rarely by the prosecution. The jury were last on the list of people who got to know the full facts. Before a case comes to court, large lumps of it are hacked away by the barristers. Interviews are chopped and changed by them and certain facts are removed for different legal reasons. Items such as telephone taps and information from CROPs officers or undercover agents are often usually known to the judge and investigators only. Deals are struck between defence and prosecution, witnesses are cancelled, and so on. Then there are certain things that go on during the case that normal jury members have no idea about, such as the defendant's criminal past. The defence can only claim that their client is of good character if they have no record, so, if they don't say anything along these lines, you can tell their client *does* have a criminal record. But you are never told straight. It was sometimes a question of listening to what was not said.

On the other hand, judges are fun. I love them. Some are as mad as a bag of hot ferrets and others are as strict as a sergeant major. There are still many judges sitting who have no idea of the world outside their legal lives. They seem to follow the same paths in life: private school to university and then into chambers, followed by becoming a QC and then on to being a judge. No time spent with ordinary people, which is why many judges don't understand them. The only so-called common people that they get to see are either in the dock or in the witness box, so their view of 'the man in the street' is very strange. And the judges certainly don't want to live on that street, wherever it is.

We had a very simple drug-smuggling case going through one of the Home Counties courts. The judge was ancient (even by judges' standards) and was hanging on to his job by his old fingernails. Our case depended mainly on evidence gleaned from pager messages between the smuggling gang. The judge had never heard of pagers before. To get around this, we employed an expert from a pager company to give evidence, in children's terms, as to how the pager system worked. The poor chap was in the box for over an hour and, in the end, it was decided that we would carry out a demonstration. I passed the judge my pager, the expert then phoned the pager control centre and gave them the message; they in turn sent the message to my pager, which the judge was now holding. Within a few seconds, the pager started bleeping and vibrating. The judge put it to his ear. 'Hello! Hello! Are you there? I can't hear a damn thing,' he said. Quickly, the court usher pointed out to the judge the message on the screen of the pager. 'That's all well and good,' said the judge, 'but I still can't hear the person on the other end.'

It's blatantly obvious to all that the one master rule for court is 'Don't piss off the judge'. This could also be said of magistrates. Customs is unusual in that it has a legal power that the police lack – a thing called the right of audience. This basically means that officers can appear in the magistrates' court as solicitors for the department. I ended up doing it hundreds of times throughout my career. This form of legal work is often the making or breaking of many officers. I knew some that would feign illness to get out of doing it. But, once you have twenty or thirty appearances under your belt, it becomes quite good fun and is a great grounding for Crown court. You have to learn very quickly that the opposition's job is to make you appear stupid and to lead you into traps. Once you know this, you will become a force to be feared in the witness box.

One of our local county judges was a real tartar. During court sessions he was a natural-born bastard and I loved him. He had a soft spot for Customs officers as long as we displayed the character of a Crown-commissioned officer. I was once accused by the prosecution of planting evidence on their client. Now this was a touch hopeful as a defence because we had arrested their client with four kilos of cocaine, body-packed to his torso. I would have had to be Harry Houdini to plant that evidence on him. The judge was so incensed with the accusation that he made the prosecution barrister apologize to me in open court and in front of the jury. Suffice to say that the barrister was my nemesis from that day forth.

This judge just kept surprising us, trial after trial. He was less than complimentary when one of our top officers appeared in front of him sporting a beard, earring and ponytail. But far worse than this was when we had a young officer in the witness box who had changed religion. Our officer had caught a smuggler almost eight months earlier and then, in the time between the arrest and court, he had met a girl and fallen in love. The girl was of the Muslim faith and he loved her so much that he converted to Islam. Now in court, his witness statement had been written while he was Christian, but now he stood in the witness box as a Muslim. The judge was furious and, being a Christian man himself, he could not contemplate how this could have happened; the officer got one of the worst maulings that I have ever seen a judge give anyone. It may have been the Queen's court but, seeing as she wasn't there, the judge was going to have things entirely his way.

Barristers do the job because the job is there to be done. They defend the guilty and frustrate the innocent, often making them feel guilty. From what I had seen over the years, it was just a game to most of them, albeit a very well-paid one. The trouble that law enforcement has is that one week they could be working for you, prosecuting in a big case, and then the following week they could be defending against you. This means that anything they learned from you while prosecuting could then be used against you while defending. Not really fair, that.

But, out of the great possible mess that could have come from all this, we actually have a good justice system that most (but not all) of the time works.

A great game we invented for criminal interviews or giving evidence in Crown court was one we called 'word wizard'. All officers concerned would agree on a subject (for interviews) or a single word (for court). Our task was to then somehow find a way of saying the phrase or word. With interviews you had a big chance of getting lots of words in, for example, if the subject was animals: 'It's warm in here, don't you think it's getting a little otter?' The Crown court version of word wizard may have seemed easier because you only had to get one word in, but the words chosen were usually complete bastards. For example, words that we had used include 'Rumpelstiltskin', 'lawnmower', 'herpes' and even 'skid mark'. The main point, of course, was not to get caught or make yourself look like a complete numpty. Not easy when you're trying to squeeze Rumpelstiltskin into a sentence.

The Jade/Nevin Bull court case eventually came around and was to last over three weeks. Some of the Jamaican evidence was missing and I was tasked with travelling out there to bring it back personally. But the drugs liaison officer in Kingston informed me that he'd been informed that there were a number of Yardie hitmen waiting for my arrival. I was still ready, willing and able to go out there, but my senior officer put his foot down firmly and stopped me.

The case was presided over by Judge Fox, who was widely regarded as one of the most strict judges to walk the earth. I happened to be extremely lucky as the judge knew me from other cases and I'd often heard him chuckling during my giving of evidence, especially my responses to defence questions (I never liked being backed into a corner by the defence and I usually made that clear).

Mr Adams, counsel for Nevin Bull's defence, announced in court that I must have planted the cocaine in Mr Bull's wallet. Mr Bull was, he said, a law-abiding citizen who had served his country in the Army. They then called the Morrison family to give character-witness evidence for Bull. First, Mrs Morrison, who tottered into the witness stand in a very short skirt and a blouse showing ample bosom.

Following her evidence, Judge Fox leaned forward and asked her to explain her profession as he hadn't quite grasped what she did. Mrs Morrison explained that she was a rep for a company that carried out cosmetic tattooing such as permanent eye-liner and lip-lining. 'Hmm, I see,' said Judge Fox. 'What an incredibly strange thing to want done to oneself.'

Mrs Morrison stated that she'd had it done herself and, as an example, smiled at the judge and opened her eyes wide. Judge Fox leaned forward a little, studied her for a few seconds and then loudly announced his judgment to the court: 'Don't take it too personally, Mrs Morrison, but, frankly, you look dreadful! No further questions. You may stand down.'

Mrs Morrison, who didn't even realize she was there to be judged, didn't so much stand down as almost keel over sideways with shock. One of the security guards stepped forward and helped her regain her balance and then quickly led her away as she started spluttering.

See, I did say he was strict.

Next up was Paul Morrison, whom we had arrested at the same time as Bull. I had discovered that he had a few Yardie connections but couldn't tie him into the drugs operation. He was quite a strong character witness, giving credence to much of Bull's story. All our QC had to do was destroy him in the eyes of the jury.

'So, Mr Morrison, your wife works but you stated to the jury that you are unemployed and have been for a few years, is that correct?' asked our QC.

Morrison, being very cocky (a foolish move in the witness box), said, 'Yeah, that's right. Have to do a bit of wheeling and dealing to keep a roof over our heads.'

'I see, Mr Morrison. I'm also informed by the case officer that you have a fair-sized house with five bedrooms. Is this correct?'

'Yeah, well, we like to call it home.'

'I see. And, Mr Morrison, I also understand that there are only the two of you living in this *smallish mansion*.'

'Yeah, that's right, just me and the missus. Plenty of room for visitors like when Nevin comes over to see us.'

'Do you drive, Mr Morrison?'

'Yeah, been thinking of doing some cabbying but most of the time I just run about for some mates.'

'Yes, I see. And how did you and Mrs Morrison arrive at court today?'

'In my old banger,' said Morrison.

Our QC flashed a quick smile at the judge, who knew exactly where this questioning was going.

'Really? Well, Mr Morrison. I was sitting in Park Street car park this morning in *my* old banger when I noticed a brand-new red Mercedes-Benz park across from me. I should say that it was about four months old and my friend the case officer informs me that it's worth in the order of £55,000. And who should alight from the vehicle but you and your lady wife? Your car, Mr Morrison? *Your* old banger?'

It only takes a short exchange like that to destroy a witness's credibility in front of a jury. It was fun watching these court capers when you weren't on the receiving end. But it could be hellish to be in the firing line when you were giving evidence.

Earlier in the trial, we had put Jade in the box. She looked small and defenceless as she told the jury the story. Some of the women in the court cried, I assume at her naive love for Nevin Bull. Judge Fox, who had already seen her full statement, seemed to take her to his black heart and shielded her from most of the defence's harder attacks. She did really well, explaining that she knew what she had done was wrong and was expecting to be punished for her part in it. I could see how that went down well with the jury because it made it look as if she was not just giving evidence to save herself. Although it wasn't a lie on her part – she really did expect to get sent down.

After three weeks, the jury was sent out. They were back after thirty minutes with a clear guilty finding on Bull. Jade had already pleaded guilty five months earlier. The judge then did a strange thing and broke for lunch before sentencing. Meanwhile, I was over the moon, another one for my 100 per cent guilty record of drugs-case convictions. The court usher caught our QC and me just as we were making off for lunch. 'Judge Fox will see you in his chambers now, gentlemen, if you please.'

We arrived in chambers to watch the judge tucking into his lunch of two hard-boiled eggs and a glass of red wine. He looked up with a well-practised scowl. 'Well, gentlemen, where are Mr Nevin Bull's pre-cons?'

I explained to the judge that regarding the pre-cons (previous convictions), I had been in contact with the Royal Military Police (RMP) early in the investigation and they had told me that Bull did have a military record but the details were kept in Germany and as such they had no access to them. Only a UK judge could get the details.

'Well,' said Judge Fox, 'I'm a judge, so make your phone call.'

I hurriedly phoned RMP Berlin and I was speaking to the duty officer, explaining the request (which he remembered), when the judge grabbed the phone from me. 'Hello. This is Judge Fox, I want to speak to your commanding officer.'

The CO was on the phone within minutes only to get a dressing down by the judge for not supplying me with the case details. As a result, we had the fax of Nevin Bull's courts martial details within ten minutes. He had been found guilty of running prostitutes and drugs while serving in Germany. Which neatly put paid to the defence's 'Army hero' line.

At sentencing, the judge was more than happy to hand Bell a twenty-nine-year sentence. As for Jade, she was sentenced to the time that she had already spent in prison. And that same afternoon, the supergrass boys from Scotland Yard whipped her away to God knows where to start a new life under a new name.

And so concluded my very first cocaine case.

20. Ghosts, Heart Attacks and Half-arsed Evidence

As with any job, if you do it long enough, you get to see strange things occur and working in Investigations was no different. There was one strange, reoccurring thing that was also very spooky, even though I'm sure that there was a technical answer to it. It happened while we were working on the heath in Blackheath, south London. It was rumoured that the large open heathland was used as a mass burial pit during the Black Death in the Middle Ages. Although many trenches had been dug in the past, no mass graves have ever been found . . . yet. But the myth still exists and when we were doing surveillance work there the heath had a very strange effect on us. Our technical kit and radios were state of the art but they instantly stopped working. Our car tracking devices would go dead and our radios wouldn't transmit or receive. The second we reached the far side of the heath, everything came to life again. And it wasn't just a onc-off occurrence: it happened every time we crossed the heath. If any of the targets that we were tracking had learned this information, they would have just needed to head for the heath to make it easier for them to lose us.

It was also strange how being in the wrong place at the wrong time could sometimes provide unexpected results.

One of our car crews had been deployed on surveillance in the centre of Liverpool. They were attempting to make ground on their target's car but they were approaching a zebra crossing when an old lady unexpectedly stepped out from the pavement. Our driver slammed on the brakes and the car's ABS cut in, juddering the car to a halt just in time. But, as they came to a halt, there was a large bang at the back of the car, the sound of shattering glass very close at hand and glass flying around inside the car. Our car had been hit in the boot by a motorbike. The bike hit at such speed that the rider was flung over the handlebars, over the car's boot and straight through the rear window. His helmeted head ended up well and truly wedged between the two rear head restraints. Strangely, the biker seemed unhurt, not even a cut or a bruise, but he was trapped. He was trying frantically to free himself, but his head just would not move – which was unlucky for him because the next vehicle to arrive at the scene was the police car that had been chasing him after he had stolen the motorcycle. So, Customs lost its own target but had the small compensation of acting as an inadvertent roadblock for the police to catch a bike thief.

Sometimes on a drugs raid, things were not always as they seemed. We had gone in on a knock, fast and hard, at a house we'd had under surveillance that was the delivery address for Afghan heroin; the occupant had received the dummied-up packages about ten minutes before we hit. With the aid of my special access-all-areas 'key' – that is, the boot on my right foot – I kicked in the back door and it shot off its hinges. We were in. We all ran into the hall and then pulled up dead in our tracks and froze on the spot. There were five of us but there could have been twenty-five for all the good it would have done us, we still wouldn't have gone any further. There, in the middle of the hall, standing its ground, was a giant English mastiff. Not many breeds of dog would put the fear of God into a gang of Customs officers mid-raid but this was one of them. Both Julius Caesar and Hannibal had used these beasts as war dogs with good reason and none of us wanted to be the first casualty of war. Or even the second.

It was a densely muscled beast and, at that moment, very alert and twitchy. As were we. The dog looked us all over, up and down, left to right. Terry, to the right of me, spoke quietly out of the corner of his mouth.

'Fuck me, Jon, it looks like it's checking out who's the most tasty.'

From behind me I could hear the telltale sound of a couple of the lads slowly racking their expandable steel batons into place. I didn't say anything but I thought, good luck with that – this big toothy bastard would probably use one of those batons as a toothpick to dislodge our tattered flesh. At that point, the hound from hell braced itself, opened its mouth and boomed out a loud, deafening, rumbling bark. Twice. I'm sure I heard one of us whimper, but I don't know who it was and it was never spoken of again (in fact, it might have been me). And then the most shocking thing happened: the hound lay down on the carpet and rolled on to its back.

Terry was the front man of our pack and he immediately fell to his knees. I couldn't tell whether he was praying or just fainting in stages. What on earth was he up to? Then he started to wave us all past as he began rubbing the dog's tummy. The dog was loving the attention.

We filed quietly past the two of them like a line of men tiptoeing out of a minefield, leaving behind the poor bastard on the ground trying to defuse a bomb. When we got to the living-room door, we turned to Terry. He stopped tickling the dog's belly and started to get up but as soon as he did the dog-bomb started ticking again, that is, it slowly started growling very deeply. Terry quickly sank back down to the floor and resumed his tickling duties.

Inside the living room, our target was in the middle of trying to stuff the heroin packages under the sofa. We nicked him on the spot and treated him to a pair of HMRC locking wrist jewellery. With the target now slumped on the sofa, cuffed, we carried out a full house search. All the while, Terry kept the dog entertained on its back in the hall, preventing it from jumping up and having a nibble on any of us.

As we filed out the front door, our suspect looked down on his dog with a sorry expression. 'Bloody great guard dog he is!' We had to agree, though Terry was in two minds: the beast seemed playful enough but, as soon as his stomach was not being tickled, the low growling began again. We took our smuggler to the car and then, when we looked back at the house, we all burst out laughing: through the open door all we could see were the whites of Terry's pleading please-don't-leave-me eyes.

As I loaded our arrestee into the car, he told us that we couldn't leave behind Chops (the beast). He said that the other members of the drugs gang knew how much Chops meant to him and they would hold him hostage to ensure that he didn't talk to us. Or that they'd kill Chops in an act of revenge. On top of this, the dog was worth a fortune in the breeding world. Apparently, young Chops was actually worth more than one of our surveillance cars parked outside – which, I figured, meant he was worth about five-grand per dog bollock. On the plus side, I knew that, if we or the police kept Chops safe from harm, there would be more chance our suspect might turn chatty when we interviewed him.

We all had a quick chat and decided to bring Chops with us. I volunteered to go and rescue Terry because I already had something in mind. Back in the house, he was still keeping Chops happy on his back on the floor. Upside down, the dog's big black lips fell away from its teeth and they were a scary sight to behold. I figured that one lucky thing was that the dog was so frightening that, if the thing bit you, you'd probably die of shock before you got to experience being eaten alive. I stood over Terry and the animal, Terry's right hand still automatically scratching the dog's belly. This was too good an opportunity not to milk.

'Terry. Good news.'

'What's that?' he said eagerly.

'We've found out the dog's name.'

Terry glared.

'Yeah,' I said, 'he's called Chops.'

'Are you fucking kidding me?!'

'No. He really *is* called Chops,' I said. 'But . . . there's some bad news.'

'What's that?'

'We have to bring Chops with us.'

'Sod off!'

'We do. But there's some more good news.'

'What's that?'

'Our suspect says you can stop tickling the dog's belly.'

'Thank fuck.'

'But . . . there's some more bad news.'

'What's that?'

'If you stop tickling him, he'll probably bite you.'

'Oh fuck . . .'

'But there *is* some more good news.'

'Yeah?'

'There is a way to stop Chops eating you . . .'

'Which is?'

'You have to wank him off.'

Pause.

'Oh. Fuck. You. Jon.'

'No, Terry. Not me. The dog.'

We eventually got the slobbering animal in the car – and also the dog. But Chops wouldn't go in the back – he was having none of that. His owner pointed out that Chops would only travel in the front passenger seat (and I guess no one had ever argued with him about that). Apparently, he liked the view from the front seat and it made him look important. I could understand that. So Terry took him round the front of the car and in he jumped. Once he had the seatbelt on, old Chops looked quite regal in the front. I had to agree, that's definitely where he belonged. Even better was the fact that Terry's driver, Dave, was a dog hater – they scared the shit out of him (I think it might have been Dave that whimpered) – and now he was sitting right next to the Mike Tyson of hounds.

I was now standing at the front of the car, looking back at it. Through the windscreen, I saw Dave turn his head very slowly to the left to look at the dog; I saw Chops – seatbelt on, spit dripping from his lips and teeth – turn his head to the right and look at Dave; I saw Dave turn his head very slowly back to me, looking out at me with those same please-don't-leave-me eyes. Of course, I immediately burst out laughing. Now the hound was safely locked in the car, it was really funny, in that way that it's always funny when it's happening to someone else.

My last sight of the car was it driving slowly away with Dave pressing the right side of his face hard against the driver's window, and Chops sitting in the passenger seat like Lord Muck. And I'm pretty sure the dog was grinning.

Occasionally, we ran into human beings who made it seem as though dealing with big slobbery dogs like Chops was the better alternative. In the case of a chap named Mac Taylor, it wasn't a question of *if* we arrived to nick him, but just *when*. Mac Taylor was a security official for a large shipping line and prior to this he was a police sergeant who had overstepped the line too many times and had been sacked. The problem about being a sacked copper is that your pension is gone (unless you're sufficiently far up the professional food chain that your bosses give you the option of rebranding your imminent sacking as 'early retirement', and then as a reward for your incompetence you get to live out your days on a taxpayer-sponsored retirement plan).

Naughty Mr Taylor had moved from being a dirty cop to a dirty importer: he had been facilitating illegal importations. It didn't seem to matter to him whether it was drugs, fags, booze, porn or firearms; it was all money in the bank for him. As with the African witch doctors selling their ineffective juju spells, Taylor sold the services of a band of crooked dock workers. But these were very effective. It was very much like a rip-off gang at an airport but much more technical. Within the gang, there would be a crane driver, a driver for the container trailer (the maffy), as well as shift-leaders and administration staff. All of them were bent and on the payroll under Taylor's control. Taylor had already been overseas a number of times to source transhipment countries and there was little doubt in our minds that he was also selling the services of his criminal enterprise abroad.

We arrested him and interviewed him. Then my colleague Paul and I drove him to the local police station. For the first time in his life, he was the one on the receiving end of wearing some very fetching Hiatt silver wristwear (Hiatt being the handcuff maker of choice for law enforcement agencies). We used local police custody offices to charge offenders so that they would slip smoothly into the court system. Taylor was going to be charged and then he would be in front of a magistrate first thing in the morning for a bail hearing and for the magistrate to push the case up to the Crown court.

We all arrived at the police station and entered the custody office. Paul walked Taylor to the charge desk and, addressing Taylor, the custody officer said, 'Hello, mate, long time no see.' It was obvious from this point that the custody sergeant and Taylor were old friends and had possibly even served together.

I started to walk around to the side of the custody officer's desk so that we could go through the paperwork together but before I got there he jumped up quickly, thrust out his left hand and grabbed me by the windpipe and, with his right hand, raised his baton. 'Where the fuck do you think you're going, shithead? Get back round the desk before me and my baton tell you your future!'

At this point, Mac Taylor held his hands up and jangled the handcuffs to show that he was actually here under arrest, not on business. The sergeant, who had not noticed the cuffs, now sussed that he had made a mistake and that it wasn't me that was the arrestee. Without so much as a shrug of an apology, he released my throat and put his baton back in its harness. He then carried on as if nothing had happened. For the next half-an-hour, he was what we term 'a total shit'.

Having never seen a Customs smuggling charge before, this custody sergeant refused to accept it, so I had to call for the duty inspector. He in turn informed the sergeant that everything was in order and that he should proceed. Eventually, we had Taylor charged and locked up. I stood by the door of the interview room and called to the custody sergeant, 'Can you please pop into the interview room for a second, sergeant?' He snapped back that he was too busy. I was rapidly losing the little patience I had left.

'I didn't say come into the interview room *or* carry on with what you are doing – I meant get in here now!'

With hand on baton, he sauntered into the interview room. I asked him if he'd sit down, but he turned on me again and said he was going to stand. The end of my tether being reached was announced by a loud noise that sounded suspiciously like me saying, 'SIT. FUCKING. DOWN!'

He sat fucking down.

'Now, having seen the way that you treat what you think are prisoners,' I continued, 'let *me* tell *you* your future'. This definitely got his attention, which immediately made me wonder if there was some dodgy business link between him and Taylor. 'I can plainly see that you and Taylor are old mates and, as we continue with this investigation, if I or my colleagues should find any mention of you or come across your telephone number, you'll be spun off your desk and into an interview room quicker than slippery shit off a shiny shovel. OK, sunshine?'

Paul and I felt better as we left the police station knowing that we were leaving behind a little Hitler that we had just done a Winston Churchill on. I rubbed my neck where the bruises were beginning to appear and thought about the fact that, if we found any evidence linking the desk sergeant to Taylor's activities, his neck would end up being at far greater risk than mine.

* * *

The whole of my Investigations team ended up in the car hall at Dover docks. The uniformed officers, under our instruction, had pulled an old Mercedes that had driven through Europe from Turkey. The search was relatively simple as we knew where the gear was hidden. The uniforms emptied the boot, lifted the spare wheel and hey presto – ten kilos of the distinctive brown powder of Turkey's finest smack.

We bundled the driver into an interview and explained the ways of life to him. Or, at least, the way we conducted the business of drug busts. He was 'encouraged' to cooperate, which he was happy to do. There's a huge difference between serving twenty years in jail and four years with time off for good behaviour. The driver, a Mr Khan, said he was to deliver the gear to an address in London where he would receive his payment from the main man. His instructions were to call the main man once off the ferry.

'Right, then, you'd better do it,' Dave told him.

Khan made the call and we recorded it. We knew the mobile number that the main man was using had been used before on other Turkish heroin jobs. So we knew we had a chance to get a heavy repeat offender. We bedded Mr Khan down in a nice fluffy cell for the night and we retired to the hotel to plan our attack. The following morning, with the operation planned, checked and re-planned, we were ready to go. Back at the port, Khan was instructed to call the main man again and tell him that he'd had an accident in the car. He was also to say that he was in hospital with suspected concussion and that he couldn't leave until the following day. Khan's phone call was a real bit of Oscar-winning acting. The main man fell for it. Khan then arranged to meet his boss the next day at the car park where he said he'd abandoned the damaged Merc, next to a large hotel, near the Dover seafront.

So, we'd managed to buy ourselves a day's grace. Dave and Chris, another of the lads on this job, took the Merc out for a little drive. To fit in with Khan's story, it had to look as if it had been in an accident. They didn't tell us exactly what they had planned but they did have a sledgehammer in the boot and smiles on their faces. First, they drove a couple of miles into the countryside and found an unemployed tree. Dave jumped out and Chris promptly drove the Merc into the tree. From the driver's seat, Chris looked out at Dave, who stared back at him, looking wide-eyed and surprised. Thinking he'd done much more damage than intended – and stranding the car out in the middle of nowhere would have been a real problem at that stage – he quickly jumped out and only then did he see the cause of the surprise: a three-kilo package of heroin had fallen out from where it was stashed under the front bumper.

Chris said, 'Crikey. Result!'

Then to make it look like the car had been in a rear-end shunt, Dave took the sledgehammer out of the boot and smacked the rear bumper. 'Smack' being the appropriate word because another three-kilo bag of heroin dropped out from under the rear bumper and into the road.

Chris cheered, 'Do it again, do it again!'

'Bollocks to that. With my luck, Lord Lucan might fall out.'

They got the car back to the port and this time the uniforms did a full search without us interfering. No more gear was found. But it was strange to think that, if the Merc had at some point genuinely been involved in a big rear- and front-end smash, it would have resulted in the air being filled with clouds of heroin powder from the exploding bags. Try claiming for that with your car insurer.

We parked up the Merc in the middle of the half-empty car park. It was an ideal position, covered by three CCTV cameras and two of our own. We were not going to miss a thing. At one o'clock, Mr Khan was slipped into the front passenger seat and we took up our positions, all within instant knock distance. At 2.30, the main man of this drugs-importation operation arrived and parked near the exit. This gave him a chance to have a good gander around the car park before approaching the Mercedes. Our senior case officer suddenly exclaimed, 'My God! Look . . .' We all peered closer. 'It's bloody Del Boy!'

He was right. Far from being the super-cool figure that drug dealers are sometimes portrayed as in crime dramas, our boy wore a large brown sheepskin coat, a tweed flat cap, gold chains and, to complete the picture, was chuffing on a big fat cigar. The only things missing were Rodney and Granddad sat nearby in a yellow three-wheel Reliant. We watched 'Del' as he had a wander off towards the Merc. He peered in, saw Khan and jumped into the driving seat. The damage to the car had obviously convinced him the story was true.

We gave them a couple of minutes to reacquaint them-selves, then the commander called the knock. Chris was off like a gundog. He definitely wanted the main man. He ran to the driver's door, which he flung open. Leaving no room for resistance, Chris grabbed our target by the hair with both hands and dragged him out of the car and on to the ground. Then, with both knees pressed into the target's back, he bent back his arms and cuffed him. Job done . . . if not done a bit more *enthusiastically* than was perhaps strictly necessary. Still, we'd seen other arrestees quickly turn violent when we'd pulled them, so to us it was a case of all's fair in love and drug busts.

But Del Boy was incensed. 'Get the fuck off me!'

'Now, now, old son,' said Chris, getting to his feet. 'Remember – who dares wins!'

'Fuck you. These cuffs are fucking killing me!'

Dave chipped in, 'Come on, you know it makes sense!'

And, despite every *Only Fools and Horses* catchphrase being thrown at him on the drive back to the station, our own Del Boy never realized why we were using them.

Many months later, in court, Chris had to defend his arrest actions. Our own surveillance video of the op was now played in court for all to see. The defence counsel stared hard at the video as the jury watched all the action unfold. When our target first appeared on screen, walking across the car park, a few of the jurors looked at each other and you knew they were thinking only one thing – 'Del Boy!' Chris had his head and eyes lowered. The defence counsel struck. 'So, officer, having seen your violent attack on my client, what are you thinking now?'

Chris looked up, looked at the judge, looked at the jury and looked at Del Boy as he sat in the dock. 'Well,' said Chris, in a loud, clear voice, 'I was just thinking how bloody lucky I was that he wasn't wearing a wig!'

Customs one, defence counsel nil. Actually, make that Customs two, because Del Boy got sent down for a ten-stretch. You might say that only fools smuggled horse.

Both the port of Dover and the heroin from Turkey kept us very busy because of the established connection between the two: Dover being a chosen gateway for the drugs gangs. Once, the rest of the team were down at Dover waiting for a lorry full of heroin coming in from Turkey, but I was already busy with a call I'd got from Heathrow Airport. It was a very busy Friday afternoon so it took me two hours to get to the airport. When there, I was fully briefed by the local team. They said a Mr Shah had arrived from Islamabad that afternoon and had been stopped in the green channel. He had reason to be: a search of his large suitcase revealed 15 kg of very pure heroin, wrapped up in a couple of blankets. He was now in the interview room but hadn't been questioned further. He had informed the search officer that he didn't speak English very well.

I grabbed a local uniform officer and entered the interview room in my standard unamused Customs officer mode. 'Mr Shah, my name's Mr Frost. You are still under caution and I will be recording anything that you say. Mr Green here tells me that you don't want a solicitor, is that correct?'

Shah sat back in the chained-down interview room seat. 'Yes, yes, that's right. I have nothing to hide. I want to tell the truth.'

'I see that your English has suddenly improved. Do you still want an interpreter?'

Shah admitted that his English was quite good. He told me

that he was a gold trader in Pakistan and that he and his brother often travelled to America via the UK to trade in gold. But this time was different; he'd had a heart murmur a few weeks ago and was off to a hospital in New York to have checks carried out. A search of his briefcase revealed various forms from a hospital in New York and on face value it appeared that he was telling the truth. The trouble was the contents of his suitcase, and that I didn't believe he was carrying 15 kg of heroin so it could be used on himself as an anaesthetic should they decide to operate.

I charged Shah and had him locked up on remand until the trial. At this point, the investigation started. Every area had to be explored to find out the how and the why. Shah and his brother lived in Rawalpindi and, when the Pakistan drugs authorities paid an unannounced visit, it was no surprise that the brother was away on business. The authorities found some matching blankets to those that we had found wrapped around the heroin. They also found a telephone book containing English mobile numbers underlined in red. Sometimes such numbers could be real gold dust, but in this case it turned out that the phones were pay-as-you-go and the numbers had been ditched.

Once we had a prisoner in custody, the real hard work started: that of putting a legal case together. We didn't just pass all the paperwork up to a legal department; no, the case officer had to put the prosecution together himself, hopefully with the help of the rest of their team. Every prosecution case consisted of reams of statements from witnesses, such as the intercepting officer, any other officer that may have assisted them, interviewing officers, the translator, transcribers, the government chemist, fingerprint specialists, lab workers, etc. The list was long. And, even though many statements that you took would never be seen or heard in court, you could be sure that, should you miss a statement, it would be that same one that was demanded by the defence lawyers. The taking of these UK statements was time consuming, but the very worst job was getting (or trying to get) overseas statements. In most instances, the case officer would have to put in for something called a *commission rogatoire*. This was permission, linked to an international agreement between law enforcement bodies, allowing a case officer to gather evidence in a particular country. We called them 'comrogs' and they were nightmares to get in a hurry. To get a comrog for Spain could take up to eight months, but one for South Africa could take a couple of weeks. It seemed strange that judges in our courts would never accept that overseas police and Customs could have different priorities or work to a different timescale. I'd even once heard a senior judge state that he would write to the 'slovenly' country himself because, in his words, 'That will get the buggers moving!' Which was typical of the detached and sometimes delusional thinking of many judges who seemed to still think most of the world was within the British Empire. In the case of this particular judge, his letter worked so well that 'the buggers' managed to lose all of our overseas evidence, never to be seen again.

In Mr Shah's case, I was lucky. All my overseas evidence was in Pakistan and the Pakistan Narcotics Agency was on the ball. I received everything I wanted within weeks, plus more. Shah had been stopped at Islamabad Airport by a Customs officer and his passport had been checked and stamped. His defence was that the drugs must have been placed in his suitcase by some behind-the-scenes baggage handler, and he said that his passport stamp proved that he'd had his baggage searched. His defence counsel demanded that we fly the Pakistani Customs officer to the UK to give his evidence in person. Our barrister – representing the Crown – explained that this was of great expense to the British public and that the case officer, Mr Frost, had thought of another idea. He was right, I had thought of another idea – and one that would only cost £1.50 rather than the cost of a return flight for the officer.

My bright idea was to contact the Narcotics Agency in Islamabad and ask the duty major to bring the airport official to a phone in their office. Within fifteen minutes, the offending Customs officer was on a hands-free telephone, giving his evidence across thousands of miles to an open court in England. Both defence and prosecution barristers questioned him. He admitted that he had stopped, questioned and stamped Shah's passport but there was, he said, no way that he could have searched his baggage. Shah's defence rested on his contention that his bag *had* been searched and the drugs planted then. But the Customs officer insisted he did not conduct a search. Both barristers had their heads in their hands until the judge asked a simple question.

'So, Officer Minda, how can you be so sure that you didn't search this man's baggage?'

'Simple really, sir,' stated the Customs officer, his voice sounding distant and echoing slightly over the phone's loudspeaker. 'I know because Mr Shah travelled on a Thursday . . . and I *never* search bags on a Thursday.' The jury and the judge all fell about laughing.

The following day, the jury was sent out and came back within fifteen minutes with a guilty verdict. Shah got eighteen years.

While I was packing up all the paperwork at the end of the trial, I had a chat with the court usher. 'That was a quick decision by the jury,' I said.

The usher winked. 'Quicker than you may think, sir. They told me it took them only one minute to decide and the next fourteen minutes to have a cup of coffee.'

Three years later, I would receive an upsetting phone call from the Home Office. Could I supply the Immigration Service at Heathrow with Shah's passport as he was flying back to Pakistan in a week's time because of ill health? At first, I was furious as I'd always believed that smugglers should always serve their term and not use supposed health problems as an excuse to shorten their time. We'd seen it happen before. But in this case it turned out that Shah did have heart problems that had reoccurred and over the three years it had got to a point that he only had a few months left. Our prison service didn't want him dying on them, hence the ticket home. His heart finally gave out on the flight home. History doesn't record whether or not it was a Thursday.

It's funny how often heart attacks seemed to crop up in our line of work – and I don't just mean among dog-phobic Customs officers having to deal with large hounds called Chops. An officer friend of mine, Peter Marsh, had been in the Collection Investigation Unit while I was working in the Investigation Division. The unit dealt with smuggling within their own local areas. Peter's local area was East Anglia, where I would finish my Customs career.

Peter had been given a prestigious VAT job, and we all assisted on the surveillance for a few months. It didn't take us too long before we had built up quite a case against a Mr Warner and his wife. They were running an illegal computer-supply company and pocketing very large quantities of VAT. After it had come to our attention, the morning finally arrived when it was decided that we would knock the company. Team one would arrest Mr Warner at his business premises and team two would raid his house and arrest his wife. I was in team two.

We arrived at the home address in Harlow at about eight in the morning, which was actually a late start for a raid, but this was hardly a hardened drugs gang – more like a couple of middle-aged fraudsters with hardening arteries. The plan was for both knocks to go in at 8.30 a.m. so that one target couldn't warn the other. Unfortunately, there was a change in the plan when Mr Warner arrived at his office at 7.45 a.m. and then came out of his office and headed for his car. Peter, not wanting him to get away, instructed his team to start the knock early and immediately raid the business premises and arrest Warner.

Rather than the loud and sometimes violent raids carried out by Customs, this one was a rather sedate affair; Peter calmly walked Mr Warner back to his office, sat him down and explained clearly why he was being arrested. Mr Warner nodded, grimaced, and then had a heart attack and dropped dead on the spot. A few seconds before, he had been a slightly worried-looking man with beads of sweat on his forehead; now the chair contained a slumped corpse with blue lips and skin like wet wax.

Just before myself and team two were due to carry out the knock on the home address, I received a phone call from Peter explaining what had happened. Peter informed me that our raid should be held back until he could arrive and break the bad news to Mrs Warner.

Thirty minutes later, team one arrived at our location and Peter briefed us all that the knock was suspended. He then went into the home address to break the bad news, accompanied by a Police FLO (Family Liaison Officer), who are specially trained to deal with bereaved family members. The liaison officer had limited chance to put their training into practice as, when informed by Peter of her husband's death, Mrs Warner burst into tears and then clutched her chest and dropped dead on the spot.

With the sight of Mr Warner dying still so fresh in his mind and with the chances of his wife also having a heart attack seeming so remote, for one weird moment, Peter later said, he thought Mrs Warner might be faking her own heart attack. It sounds extreme but, by this stage in our careers, we had seen people try anything to avoid arrest. However, in this case, Mrs Warner was indeed suffering from a bad dose of death.

It was probably the strangest end to a raid that we'd ever experienced. We concluded that the Grim Reaper must have been having a very slow day on that day and so had decided to speed up the harvest.

* * *

Investigation officers can be great show-offs, sometimes, when it came to successful cases. And I must admit that I was no different from the rest. Just as a footballer might brag about a goal he scored or a boxer might go on about a knockout he delivered, so law enforcers like to do the same. A good place to revel in the acclaim of your peers was the Government Forensic Service (GFS). At some time or another, and usually the sooner the better, you had to get your seized gear to the experts to be examined and officially designated. The GFS was happily housed in the Forensic Service labs and, unlike the unrealistic lab boys on shows like *CSI*, the real forensic guys barely step outside their 'office'.

On arrival at the GFS labs, you sat in a large waiting room with other police and Customs officers from all over the country, each of us clutching some vital evidence that needed testing for an official classification so we could proceed with the case.

I was having a pretty good day when it came to bragging rights because I'd turned up carrying forty kilos of pure heroin in see-through seizure bags. Most police officers would never see this amount in their whole careers so the coppers in the room were impressed; the other Customs boys there, less so. But then, they were carrying less than I was today so I was Top of the Pops. There were questions and requests for a closer look, so I sat there and told them about the seizure and that this was actually one of our smaller cases. There followed a number of appreciative ums and ahs from the captive audience. Ten minutes later, I was joined by a couple of Investigation colleagues from a specialist cocaine team and they brought with them fifty kilos of coke. The ums and ahs started all over again.

All of us had arrived early so that we could get our evidence booked in and then shoot back to the office so we were still waiting for the reception team to open up the lab and start work. It was always a little nerve-jangling carrying around a couple of large bags that you knew were worth a few million pounds each. And so we were always quite glad to get them signed over to the labs.

After our little evidence-comparison contest, we started to chat among ourselves. I started to talk to a young copper sitting next to me who was from Manchester and had a large freezer box in his lap.

'So, what's in the box? Anything interesting?'

He shrugged and said, 'Oh, it's nowt as exciting as yours. It's just somebody's arse.'

The room went dead silent. I smiled and nodded and tried not to look too impressed. But I knew I was failing miserably so I just gave in.

'Did you say "somebody's arse"?'

'Well, it's a buttock, actually. We think it could be a left one, but, if you hold it the other way up, it could be the right. Dunno, really.'

He lifted the freezer-box lid and in seconds every officer in the room was in a scrum around it. Dry ice smoke billowed out of the box and, when it dissipated, there, peeking out of the ice and staring us all in the face, was an actual man's arse cheek.

'We came across it after a really big, vicious gangland fight in the city centre last night. It's a clean cut so we think it was cut off by someone wielding something extremely sharp, like a samurai sword. The trouble is, there was no one left about to reclaim it. We've warned all the local hospitals to keep an eye out for anyone who comes in with such an injury. Or –' he looked up as he closed the lid '– anyone who has trouble sitting down.'

Even I had to admit defeat and concede that, in the game of evidence Top Trumps, the Unidentified Arse from Manchester had won the day.

21. Addicted

I'll let you in on a little secret: busting drug dealers could get very addictive. Sure, you start out on the soft stuff – pulling over a doper coming back from Amsterdam with a spliff in his sock. But before you know it – and despite all the warnings about weed being a gateway drug to the harder gear – you're itching for something stronger: a cocaine bust, maybe; and then, when you get one of those, you just want another one – and then even more cocaine confiscations. Finally, it gets to the stage where nothing can satisfy your craving for a drug bust except heroin – a nice, big, juicy heroin seizure. It was very true what they said about heroin – and this seemed to be the case whether using it or confiscating it – it was very more-ish.

What most people don't realize is that, if taken correctly and with no impurities added from bad 'cutting', it is possible to live a comparatively normal life on heroin – though that situation is in itself pretty impossible to recreate because it is based on the unattainable ideal of the user getting a constant supply of unadulterated heroin. It is the other substances that are added to it to reduce the purity of the drug that can be a danger in themselves. I had discovered heroin cut with brick dust, baby powder, Vim and even rat poison. The big problem is that, by the time the user has purchased it from their dealer, they have no idea what it is cut with or how many times it has been cut before reaching the streets. Cutting agents such as brick dust are not really designed to be injected into the human body. It will be classed as an invader and as such the body will attempt to defend itself against this alien intrusion; but, in the long run, the invader usually wins and the user gets septicaemia.

So there is a case to be made for the regulation of drugs, or a synthetic substitute, for registered addicts in order to take the power away from drugs gangs and in order to try to stem the tide of criminal activity committed by desperate users.

But it was never my remit to say whether taking drugs was right or wrong – and making that judgement doesn't really change anything anyway: taking drugs is just something that some people do. My duty was to stop it entering the country and hunt down those that arranged and participated in the commodity's smuggling. Drugs gangs invariably were involved in other damaging criminality and the damage tended to spread outwards. The only ones who seemed to benefit were the local luxury-car dealerships where the most successful drug dealers laundered some of their profits by turning up with sports bags full of cash bricks and buying Ferraris and Bentleys outright.

One such lucky lad was a guy we'd been tipped off about by the telephone drugs line that had been set up for members of the public to ring with information. We started following the guy in order to glean some information. He was no slow driver and he made sure our tyres were kept warm whenever we followed him. This meant we had to use fast rotations of the '55 car' (the following car) in order for him not to get suspicious about one car being behind him too long, and also judicious use of our 55 bike, as a motorcycle could follow more easily in traffic and was also less likely to be identified as suspicious.

Our target took us all over and we ended up following him around London and up to Birmingham, Leeds and Liverpool. He really did get around for someone on the dole. He was either a very conscientious job hunter or perhaps someone who we should watch further. When we traced him to his own three-bedroom house, which also had another car – a new convertible BMW – parked outside, we thought that we might be on to a good thing. Even though the pattern of his behaviour was familiar to us as that of someone expecting a delivery soon, our original source of the information about him told us that, as far as they knew, the drugs were not due into the country for another month. So we backed off the intense surveillance and installed lighter, local surveillance around London until nearer the time of the drugs drop.

The first sign that we should have followed our own gut instinct about the timing of the drugs delivery rather than believe the source's information came in an unusual way. One day, while we were following the guy as he drove around in his BMW with a mate, he turned off into a Ferrari dealership and didn't emerge for an hour. When he did come out, he was at the wheel of a brand-new red Ferrari. He roared off into the distance and we knew then that the drug delivery he'd been expecting had obviously already successfully arrived and he'd already sold it on. And this new bright-red toy for himself was his way of 'washing' some of the cash.

So, again, repeat after me the mantra of not only law enforcement agencies but also the human race: you win some, you lose some, you fuck some up.

I got another sample of the sweet taste of a good drug bust when an investigation of ours involved us sitting on the King drugs gang for about a month, waiting and observing. Members of the gang would regularly take day-trips to Amsterdam but, when we stopped a couple of them on a routine pull at the airport, they were clean. We had the details of Andrew King, the believed boss, and we had put his house under surveillance for a couple of days. It appeared to us that he must have left his wife as he never went near his house and there seemed to be a new man in his wife's life. There was a slightly worrying aspect to the case in that one of the criminals on the payroll had a private pilot's licence. Light aircraft were a pain in the arse: they flew low to avoid radar, they could land almost everywhere and, if they didn't want to touch down, then the gang could fling their drugs importation out of the door at a predetermined place. We had all this at the back of our minds all the time. I didn't think for one second that King had employed the guy with the pilot's licence just because he was an amusing conversationalist.

King wasn't as easy a target as the rest of his gang. He never drove north to see his wife and most of the time he deployed anti-surveillance techniques. Now, many people can do anti-surveillance manoeuvres to avoid being followed, but it doesn't work unless you know what you are looking for and you don't know this unless you are trained in it. It was a real pain to us as we had to be extra careful, just in case. I must admit that King kept us entertained with his multiple trips around roundabouts and reversing back down motorway slip roads to try to lose anyone tailing him. He also did most of his work at night, visiting potential dealers, buyers and moneymen.

Night surveillance can be a bit of a task and knackers you out very fast due to the high levels of concentration needed. We eased this slightly by lumping up his car with a tracker and drilling his car lights. The drilling worked like this: one of us would sneak up behind the target's car when it was parked up and, using a small portable drill, bore a small hole in the rear off-side brake light. The hole was barely visible to the naked eye in the day, but at night it caused a bright white dot to shine out in the middle of the red tail-light cluster. Following this bright white dot at night was so much easier because it distinguished the target car from other cars on the road, and it allowed us to back off a bit and leave a bigger space between the target's car and our 55 car.

So, if you now notice that your car has got a small hole drilled neatly in its rear-light cluster, you're either a smuggler (and we're on to you) or you've bought one of their old cars. (In which case, check in the glove box and under the seats too – you might find an old joint.)

After a couple of weeks trailing Andrew King's gang, we managed to get a phone-tap authority so we could now get some more up-to-date intelligence. This went well and the information we gleaned meant that we didn't have to sit in observation and surveillance on the gang every single day and night; we could now turn up when something important was happening, such as an arranged meeting or a money handover.

We knew we were getting close to the smuggling run. King was talking about pick-up dates and places, and the pilot was putting out feelers to hire a light aircraft. At the news of this, we all inwardly sagged and thought, 'Bugger it! A bloody light aircraft job' – every investigator's nightmare. But King's actions cheered us up a bit when he started looking at landing strips in Kent. Some were private and some were unused. What was of help was that, at each site, King would phone the pilot and describe the strip. By the end of a busy week split between the pilot and King, we had got info on the strip to be used and the aircraft that had been hired and paid for.

Behind the scenes, in preparation, we had lots going on. The RAF were brought onside for the mid-air radar tracking, air traffic control would work in league with the RAF, and we would be informed the second the plane dropped off-radar and came in to land. We also had two more teams of surveillance officers on standby so that all of the gang could be controlled. And we had the Kent police ready and waiting to assist. It was a law enforcement and high-tech surveillance orgy and, hopefully, only the bad guys would get screwed. What could possibly go wrong?

After a tense wait, the light aircraft finally came in at altitude, registering on the RAF radar, and was tracked by them until it dropped height and went off-radar and under the detection system. Air traffic control notified us of this. So now we knew it was on – the landing was imminent; the light aircraft would soon emerge from the low cloud. We were all waiting nearby in vans and cars, out of view of course, and also careful to be hidden from being spotted at height by the pilot.

The aircraft finally appeared, the distinctive buzz getting louder as it dropped and approached. Finally, it touched down and taxied over to a hardstanding area. Waiting for it were two escort vans, small but fast, probably tuned up for a quick getaway if needed. We had discussed when was the best time to knock this job and it had been decided that we would do it midway through unloading. That way we could try to nab everybody in one place, with no chases or getaways. King was merrily telling his gang what to do over his mobile phone.

At a given signal, we went in: the knock was on! All our vans and police cars screamed out of cover and shot at high speed on to the small landing strip, before screeching to a halt in a wall of tyre smoke to form a blockade; every vehicle spat out its officers and they hit the ground running, batons out, shouting and charging down the gang members. It was all going like clockwork until Andrew King, in shock and panic, decided that he didn't really want to be nicked today and so made a blind dash for it. His getaway lasted all of ten feet as his dash took him running straight into the airplane's still spinning propeller. Nearby officers and gang members all groaned and covered their faces – both in horror and to block the blood spray. Shiny, wet bits of Mr King span all around the vicinity.

How he did it, I will never know, but with some good paramedic first aid and a fast ambulance, King survived and made it to hospital, where the immense bleeding was stopped and he was sedated into a controlled coma.

As the rest of us dealt with the gang and their interviews, Paul, our senior officer, headed up north to talk to King's wife and break the bad news. Paul was very diplomatic and explained to her that Andrew had been in a severe accident but he was still alive. What he needed from Mrs King, he said, were details about her husband for identification purposes.

'Sorry to have to ask these questions at a time like this, but does Mr King have any tattoos?'

'Yes, he has a pair of lovebirds tattooed on his left arm.'

Paul phoned one of our officers who was keeping an eye on King at the hospital and passed on this information. There was a slight pause while checks were done at the other end. But the answer came back: 'No.' No lovebirds.

Paul shook his head at Mrs King, and tried again. 'Does Andrew have any more tattoos?'

'Yes, he had a small tattoo of "The Saint" on his right hand,' she said, now getting more upset.

Once again, Paul passed the information to the hospital officer. There was another pause, some more whispering and then: 'No.' Nope, no Saint tattoo.

Paul shook his head at Mrs King and she started crying all over again. Like Paul, she was now thinking that, if all King's tattoos had disappeared, just how many of his body parts had been chopped off by the propeller blades?

It all came to a horrible climax when she told Paul that her husband had a long scar above his knee on his left leg. Surely that must be there. Once again, Paul passed on the info and once again the answer came back: 'No.'

At this, Mrs King howled and collapsed on the floor in tears and Paul nearly collapsed too when, just at that moment, Mr King walked in through the front door.

There was no doubting it, they did look very much alike: the real Andrew King, who had just got home, and the fake Mr King who was laid out in the hospital. The real Mr King had had his passport stolen while on a business trip to the Netherlands and this was no doubt where the fake Mr King – our drugs boss – got his hands on it and adopted his identity. Chances were that the passport had been stolen to order because of the resemblance.

And no wonder our 'Mr King' had never travelled north to see his wife: it wasn't his wife at all. The only ID we had ever seen was the passport after we had the fake Mr King stopped at Customs during the early days of the operation.

The real Mrs King was overjoyed to get back the real Mr King, and all in one piece rather than several separate ones.

And it's fair to say that, for their services during the raid, all Customs officers were fully decorated. Especially those stood near the propeller.

22. CROPs: The Art of Using a Clingfilm Toilet

There was one thing that shocked people more than anything else about the work I did as a Customs officer. And that was the investigations where I worked as a CROPs officer. That meant Covert Rural Observation Positions. It was about as far away from the image of a black and gold uniformed officer standing in an airport as you could get – and most members of the public don't even know that Customs officers do this kind of work. And those who do know think they are a little bit crazy for doing it. Even for those in the trade, CROPs officers are thought of as nutters who risk their lives every time they are deployed. Sometimes, I was one of the nutters. I was still working for the Investigation Division but would be called to go on a CROPs 'adventure' as and when required.

CROPs is regarded as such a danger because the main role is to set up observation positions as close as possible to a target address, whether that is a house, a farm, a landing stag or so on. These are the rural locations used by criminal organizations and drugs gangs as hideaways, meeting places and drop-off points for their gear. But, because of the rural positions, normal urban surveillance is impossible. So, as CROPs officers on surveillance, we had to dress and act as you would imagine SAS soldiers would on a field deployment: camouflaged, silent, dug in, totally independent and self-sufficient.

The golden rule was that we should be able to remain concealed to a trained soldier at twenty paces and concealed to a civilian at ten paces. The major difference between Customs CROPs and the police force's version was that our rural surveillance ops were much more hardcore – we would remain dug in for days on end, if needs be, whereas the police would do short-term deployments for hours. Due to this extended exposure to the weather and to the risk of discovery, we trained and exercised with the special forces. We would also try out new techniques in the UK that the special forces were trialling, and then pass on our findings back to them so they could put them to better use in Northern Ireland, Afghanistan or Iraq or wherever they happened to be deployed. Whenever an ex-special forces soldier came over to the dark side and joined the Customs CROPs teams, we'd make sure we'd test ourselves and our skills against them – we always came out on top. Customs CROPs officers had such a good reputation that we were sometimes in demand from various bodies such as the secret services. But our primary employer was, of course, Customs.

CROPs officers were predominantly from a military background that wanted to continue using their expertise. I'd started off in the Army so I already had the initial training required; and I also had the desire. I'd travelled through the ranks and services of HMCE, so CROPs work was a natural development and a needed challenge for me.

Every deployment required different skills and intricate planning, the briefings of which could go on for hours. For example, if myself and a colleague were to stake out an area in the middle of the countryside that we suspected was being used as a drugs drop, we would carefully map out the surrounding area, choose the best spot for observation that was also the best spot from which not to be seen, calculate our required time there and then, from all that, choose our kit. This would be a Bergen (military rucksack) filled with high-energy food supplies (all cold as heat and smell is a giveaway), drinks, surveillance kit (binoculars, sights and scopes), cameras and zoom lenses, camouflage gear, spare clothing items (thermals), weapons of choice (kukri knife and an SOE dagger for me) and odd sundries such as clingfilm (which, if we had to, we shat into in order to hide the smell: the crap-and-wrap).

You can see now why most Customs officers didn't want to become an Investigative CROPs officer and thought we were a little crazy to volunteer. Sleeping rough in mud and water while dug in a ditch in the middle of nowhere, day and night, in the freezing cold and suffering wind, rain and snow, while eating cold rations, crapping into clingfilm and observing at close quarters hardcore criminal gangs who if they found you would want to kill you is, I can see, not everyone's idea of a good time at the office.

I absolutely loved it.

The adrenaline surge was incredible, as was the sense of satisfaction when you withdrew from a job with surveillance photographs of a consignment drop that you knew would be used as evidence to crack open a smuggling organization.

As difficult as CROPs missions could be, it was always a relief when one came around if the current investigation case-load was low. On this occasion, I was having a slow week: no surveillance going on, half the team on holiday and I had a pile of papers to get ready for court. My phone rang about midday.

'Hi, Mad Dog, fancy a dirty weekend away?' It was Peter Holland, a great CROPs officer from one of our northern offices and someone who'd known me long enough to use the 'Mad Dog' nickname I'd picked up in uniform.

'Peter, I'm just too busy to play at the moment,' I said.

There was a bark of disbelieving laughter at the other end of the line. 'If that's true, then I must be talking to an impostor and not the Jon I know who loves a bit of CROPs work. So, get your arse in gear and you and Nick put your kit together and get up here for 20:00 hours.'

After a little unconvincing resistance, I agreed. I gave Nick, one of my fellow CROPs officers, a shout and asked if he'd like to go out on a rural surveillance op. Two minutes later, Nick was at the end of his desk with his giant Bergen rucksack.

'I'll take that as a definite yes, then,' I said.

As CROPs work was deemed a job more for the mad than the sane, as soon as we started getting our kit together people would tend to move away from us to give us room. Nobody ever asked where we were going or what we were investigating because they knew we couldn't say. We would automatically switch into a military mode of behaviour with its accompanying language and sense of humour. During the packing of our kit, we morphed from Customs investigators to CROPs officers. The difference between us and most other forms of law enforcement officer was that when we hit the ground there was a possibility – depending on the risk of the job – that we wouldn't come home.

It took us a couple of hours to get all our kit together. We never really knew what we might need so we'd just take everything that we could pack into a Land Rover. We arrived at our northern office in the early evening, just in time for the briefing. There were eight other officers in the room as well as the head of office and the case officer. CROPs briefings were always held in secret, away from officers not involved in the operation, so there was no risk that they could give evidence about our actions in court.

The briefing took just over two hours, which wasn't too bad by our standards: sometimes the briefings could be more than double that. This operation was to be the culminating action of a six-month surveillance job. The targets were importing large amounts of cannabis resin from the near continent. They had previously used lorries and cars via the passenger ferry into Dover, but for some reason they had been spooked and decided to change their MO. Information gained from phone calls and informants led the operational team to believe that the next importation was the following morning at a remote airstrip, about forty miles away. Most of us had been involved in light-aircraft jobs before and we knew how dangerous they could be.

For this one, myself, Pete and a new CROPs officer, Den, were the ones on the ground – or as Pete put it: the ones in the shit. Nick would be what we termed the silver commander at our remote HQ, with the other five officers covering such jobs as medic, communications and transport. As far as the operational team went, our contact would be with Nick only. We used a different radio channel to the back-up officers as we couldn't afford to have their chatter blocking up the airways if things started to get hot.

I spent the next hour with Pete and Den getting our operational kit ready and going over the routes in and out of the area as well as the emergency pick-up points should they be needed in case of injury.

We hit the ground at one in the morning when we were dropped off by Land Rover by our back-up team as near to the target zone as we dared take a vehicle. We jumped out and then disappeared into the darkness. And there's no darkness like countryside darkness; it's not like an urban environment at night where there is still quite a lot of light pollution from towns and cities. Out in the rural wilds, it was what you might call *dark* dark.

The three-mile route towards our target – the small aircraft landing strip – was over fields and ditches, through hedges and trees, and even through a couple of small but freezing cold rivers; the rivers were the only thing that slowed us down as water isn't the quickest medium to wade through at night, especially when carrying heavy kit bags that you can't afford to get wet. Pete and Den had already checked out all the routes a couple of days before to try to ensure there would be no nasty surprises. By sunrise, the three of us were nicely settled in a thick hedgerow with deep channelled ditches both front and rear. It had been decided that, on the aeroplane's arrival, Pete would take the video camera and move down the ditch to a point twenty metres to our left, and I would crawl into a forward position with the stills camera. Den's job was as a permanent lookout to scope for any signs that we might have been spotted. The role of lookout is very important in that we were putting our lives in their hands. Having said that, it was now in the early morning and we needed to recharge for the following day, so, content that we were well dug in, we were asleep in a matter of minutes.

The next day was really crappy. There was a steady drizzle that penetrated everything and a light fog had rolled in. Within a few hours, most of our kit was soaking wet and, to make matters worse, whenever we'd take it in turns to catch up on a bit of sleep, we'd each get kicked by the others for snoring. Nick came on the radio every half-hour to check on our condition and to give us an update on the smugglers. We couldn't afford to miss a single radio check because, if we did, our back-up team, who were camped a few miles away, would take it to mean that we were compromised and in trouble, so they would scramble to rescue us.

The fog was bad news. It meant that the drugs gang couldn't land at the farm strip, and they were also fogged in over in the Netherlands. So, another night in the CROP. Unlike the police CROPs officers, we would always deploy with the knowledge that we could be out in the field (literally) for days on end, with our post-op pick-ups always at night. So, even if a job went down at nine in the morning, we wouldn't get picked up until midnight. Home comforts were non-existent. Cold food was the order of the day (and low-fibre food was preferred as we all prayed that one of the others wouldn't need a crap). We would piss in plastic bottles and, if needed, crap in clingfilm and take the whole lot home with us. On the occasions when we were in tight, dug-out CROPs, then our partner would have to drop his trousers where he lay and drop his guts right next to you. But it meant we would stay hidden and alive.

The weather critically delayed everything. Two days later, we were still there: sleeping rough, eating rough, getting cold, getting wet, talking crap, trying not to crap, trying to remain hidden no matter what. We didn't want to blow it now. Eventually, the rain stopped and Nick was on the radio: the drop plane had finally left the Netherlands and was heading in our direction. Our mobile surveillance team were moving into our area but were on a different radio channel. Pete clicked his radio on to their channel and listened to them getting ready for their part of the knock.

The plan was this: from the spotting, unloading and the departure of the plane, the operation was in our hands. Then the plane would be followed on radar to its destination in the Midlands where the pilot would be arrested and the plane seized. Meanwhile, at our end, whoever met the plane on the ground was to be allowed to leave the airstrip, then knocked.

Pete and I got our respective camera kits ready – spare film, lenses and batteries in certain pockets so we could get to them quickly – and, finally, my Ghurkha blade (just in case).

If we were spotted by the gang, they would see three guys in camouflage pointing something at them and probably wouldn't know we were just shooting them with film, not bullets. And they might act accordingly. Though if they turned out to be fully armed, our knives and batons would do absolutely sod all.

Thirty tense minutes passed before we got the 'heads up' from Nick. A motorway maintenance van had driven past the entrance to the farm, slowly, twice, and was reported as heading back again. Two minutes later, the van arrived, dead opposite us, on the other side of the grass strip. Pete and I slid into the water- and muck-filled ditch and slithered to our respective camera positions. Covered in camouflage and shit from the ditch, I started shooting pictures. We used an expensive but standard Nikon FM2 camera. The reason for this was that it worked wet or dry, frozen or cooked (something that couldn't be said about all high-tech cameras).

At the sound of a plane's engine, I swung around and started shooting the red and white Piper as it landed and taxied up to the van. For the next ten minutes, Pete and I shot away as the pilot unloaded 200 kg of cannabis resin and the van driver and his helpers slung it into the van. All the gang on the ground regularly looked around as if scanning for signs they were being watched, but, although this was the time when we were most exposed, as we tried to get evidence, we managed to remain hidden. As these actions were taking place, Den gave us a running commentary over the radio. We would need all these details later when we wrote our witness statements.

Then the smugglers shook hands and the plane was away, followed shortly by the van. Job done – both theirs and ours.

The pilot was arrested when he landed in the Midlands. And, ten minutes after his departure, the van driver had to stop because of a bad road accident on his route – an 'accident' our surveillance team and the local police had set up so that the van couldn't try to make a break for it. As soon as the van pulled over, the driver was unceremoniously dragged from it at gunpoint. Those involved were later put away for nine years each.

One unforeseen consequence of this CROPs mission was something that happened four years later. Myself and Pete were in Custom House and sitting in on a training-room lecture about how good remote-control cameras were and how they were superior to the traditional, old-fashioned CROPs-officer-operated cameras. The lecturer clicked through a series of photographs taken six months earlier by the new remote camera kit. They showed a red and white Piper aircraft, a motorway maintenance van and the unloading of 200 kilos of cannabis resin. Pete and I exchanged puzzled looks. The lecture ended and then Pete and I had a few quiet words with the lecturer and pointed out where the photos had actually come from and that the multiple angles and changing viewpoints in the pictures could only come from the mobility and decision-making of an 'old-fashioned' human being, not from a remote-control fixed camera. The pictures would never be shown again.

Pete and I left the room feeling somewhat vindicated. We didn't like to think we'd crawled through mud and bramble hedges and slept in dirty ditchwater for three days just so some bloody high-tech camera could get the credit.

Though, when singing the praises of real live officers over remote camera devices, we did, admittedly, leave out the bit about crapping in clingfilm.

23. Holidaying on Heroin

Covert loads – an illegal thing hidden in a legal thing – come in every shape and size and can be absolutely anything. In the case of the UK's largest ever heroin importation, the cover load was bentonite. I have to admit that, like most people, I had no idea what this was and had to take to a dictionary to find out. To save you the trouble, in case you don't know either, bentonite is an absorbent clay most commonly used as cat litter. It just happened that the main man behind the heroin-smuggling attempt owned a bentonite quarry in Turkey. Which was nice. Whether he had this quarry before deciding to smuggle or whether he purchased it to assist in the smuggling attempt, we didn't know. But successful big-time drug dealers could certainly turn over enough money to buy their own small islands, let alone a small quarry. And there was a very good reason why bentonite was used as the smuggling agent.

The importation of the drugs themselves was a long, drawn-out operation. We had the main men, Dave and Ali, under constant surveillance for nearly fourteen months, which was one of our longest surveillance gigs. It is a testament to the surveillance tradecraft we had been taught that, in all that time, none of us was ever spotted.

We had good intel that these fellows were two of the big boys when it came to Class A importations so we knew the time was well spent. If we brought them down, we'd be blowing a pretty big hole below the waterline in HMS *Heroin*'s regular dockings in the UK. So we watched Ali shopping with his family every week, we watched him ice skating with his daughter, we watched him when he went abroad with his secret girlfriend and we even followed him on holiday with his family in the UK.

One particular week of surveillance ended up going down in Customs folklore.

We were in position on the target house at 7 a.m. on a beautiful July morning. We had a full surveillance team of eight cars in the surrounding area of the Ali's home. This was just the normal level of surveillance in this particular job, which reveals just how important it was. If we were correct, we thought that today he would go shopping with his wife and later take his daughter to the ice rink in north London. But by 10 a.m. we'd had neither sight nor sound of our target, which was surprising as he was very much a creature of habit.

Becoming concerned, the case officer contacted our headquarters in London and asked them if they could 'ping' Ali's mobile phone and find out his whereabouts. The 'ping', as we called it, was the electronic triangulation of a mobile phone signal between different signal masts, thereby identifying the phone's location. We waited twenty minutes before control contacted us back and informed us that Ali was now in St Ives. We wondered what he was doing in the town of St Ives, near Cambridge.

'No, no!' replied control. 'Not St Ives in Cambridgeshire. He's in St Ives in Cornwall!'

Well, that meant he was now nearly 300 miles away at the very tip of south-west England. Even with all the surveillance we had in place, he'd still managed to elude us somehow. However, we thought his escape from our grasp was more by accident than design because we were still quite sure he wasn't on to us.

We were more than aware that our boy had many contacts in Wales so we hoped that this trip had been taken to find an out-of-the-way meeting point for them all to get together. Without having to issue any orders, the case officer waved at us as we all shot past him in our cars. It was now a question of who could get to St Ives first. It was a matter of pride and a matter of driving at speed but with skill. I was with Rob, my team partner, and we decided to take the stance of the tortoise and let the others hare away. By the time we arrived in St Ives, we were second in the convoy and this was down to good map-work by Rob and, all modesty aside, some crack-ing driving by me (courtesy of my advance-driving tutor Clive's great teaching).

St Ives isn't the biggest holiday destination in the world; it's quite small and quaint. Which made it easier to find our quarry. But then we knew that the smaller the place, the more difficult it is to track someone without being rumbled. We managed to identify our target's vehicle in the car park of a small hotel near the cliffs. Then one of our footmen officers spotted Ali in the town with his wife and daughter. This rang a few alarm bells. We thought that, if you are going to have a drugs meeting with some of the nastier members of society, i.e. other drugs gang members, you don't take your wife and kid. Even we didn't think that Ali was cynical and nasty enough to dupe his family into coming with him on a 'holiday' while he was really using them as cover. There had to be something that we were missing. We found out what that was a couple of hours later when our boy phoned a contact in Wales to say that he was to be unavailable for the next week as he had taken his family on holiday. The trip then was genuine.

So what were we to do? We couldn't commute 300 miles every day to Cornwall to keep up the surveillance, and the more local team from Bristol were tied up on their own job near Birmingham. Which just illustrates how investigation teams rarely work within their own areas; the job may start at a port or airport within their jurisdiction, but often ends up on the other side of the country where the established target actually lives.

In our case, Ali was on holiday and we couldn't just let him wander around the coast of southern Britain without a Customs presence. Despite what we might think, in the end, we wouldn't put it past him to use the holiday as an excuse to also meet up with some of his 'business colleagues'.

So we were to have a holiday as well, following him and his family wherever he went for the next eight days. The one rule that we could not break was that we should always remember that our target's wife and child were not part of this operation. They were innocents (we had no evidence of any involvement by the wife). So, for example, if our target escorted his daughter to a playground, we would have to drop back, as this was the rule, but we still had to try to keep one eye on him at all times, just in case his mobile phone should ring. This was absolutely vital, as proof of mobile phone use had become a central plank in prosecution case evidence.

In the case of mobiles, we had to record in our notebooks the time that any call was received and the time that the call was ended. In court, when mobile telephone evidence was used by the prosecution, the defence barrister would often state that we could not prove that their client was using that particular telephone at the time. If we could provide evidence of the use of the mobile telephone at the time of a particular call, then we could place telephone and target together at the correct time. This may sound petty, but this is the way that the bad guys played the game in court – with a lot of spin on the ball. We had to have our own ways of getting that ball back over the net.

Ali had chosen one hell of a week to go on holiday: the weather was absolutely glorious. We had a very particular problem with summer surveillance: we would have to swap between being the driver and the passenger every day or suffer the consequence of having a beautiful tan on just one arm. Jobs like these sometimes made up for the ones where we would be sitting all night in a freezing car (with no heater on because we couldn't run the engine), starving, dying for a piss, exhausted and trapped with a fellow officer who farted like a bull elephant on a diet of beans. I say 'sometimes made up for . . .' because we had far more of the night-time freezing-and-farting jobs than the sunny holiday ones.

Another hell that we had to suffer on the St Ives operation was staying in some very expensive hotels. Though, I hasten to add, not by our choice. This was the absolute peak holiday time and as such every single reasonably priced hotel was chock-full. This meant we had to go upmarket and stay in the only hotels that were not full – the posh ones. This was the very first time in my career when we were staying in a hotel that was actually better than the target we were following. My hotel in Torquay overlooked a beautiful bay in which you could watch dolphins playing in a perfectly still sea.

If, during the day, Ali took his family to the beach, we would do our best to stick to the rules and only have a couple of officers covering him. For the rest of us, it was heaven: we closed down our cars and lay out in the sun, eating ice cream and breathing in good karma. These breaks also enabled us to get to a supermarket and pick up much-needed clean underwear, shorts and T-shirts – after all, we had left in an unexpected hurry. A fellow surveillance officer made an expensive mistake in St Ives. During lunch, he spilled soup over his only pair of trousers and desperately needed a new pair. He got his driver to pull up by a clothes shop near the front and, with the engine revving hard, he dashed inside. He grabbed the first pair of trousers that he saw in his size, put his credit card on the counter and asked the assistant to be as quick as possible. He almost fainted when he saw that the slacks cost £150 – unluckily, he'd chosen the most expensive shop in town. His driver was by now sounding the horn, desperate to be on the move, so for him there was nothing he could do but pay up. (And so pissed off was he when he found out that he couldn't claim them on expenses that he barely took them off for the next year.)

So then, was our enforced holiday really worth it? Too right it was. We managed to provide evidence of Ali on his mobile telephone at the vital moment that he passed information about a container number to his gang regarding the drugs shipment – and this evidence also enabled us to target the dirty container. Plus, we had put in place a fatal blocker to the 'my client wasn't using his phone' defence before it was even attempted in court.

On top of this, I managed to get a stunning suntan. Both arms. This eight-day trip went down in the annals of investigation history, as did we as the officers most liable to win the award for Jammy Bastards of the Year.

But we didn't realize then just how important and critical this whole case was until we actually carried out the knock on the container that Dave, Ali and their pals were importing. What was waiting for us was beyond even our wildest dreams: a UK-record haul of 400 kg, nearly half a ton, of heroin. We made the news headlines.

The concealment of the drugs was very clever. And this is where we return to our old friend bentonite/kitty litter. The density of the bentonite was very, very similar to the density of the heroin, so it was incredibly hard to identify one from the other via X-ray (though I daresay shooting them into your arm would have revealed a big difference). This meant there was a high chance that the heroin would not be discovered if the container was X-rayed at the port. Luckily, we had intelligence that told us when and where the drugs were to be imported, right down to the vital container number. But the bentonite theory was well founded because the local officers had to X-ray the container several times before they actually found the drugs. Personally, I thought that instead of sniffer dogs they should have just brought in some 'pisser cats' to identify the dodgy kitty litter.

So this well-run and ambitious drugs gang had been severely wounded. In order to ensure that his company appeared legitimate, Ali had even made a number of previous importations, all delivered to an address in South Wales. All of these importations of cat litter, 30 tons of the stuff, had already been delivered and filled the large warehouse to the brim.

Following the successful arrest of the whole gang, we had to start cleaning up what was left behind. Now, whether or not it was a punishment by one of my bosses because of some insubordination, I couldn't say – it was! – but I ended up being tasked with disposing of the kitty litter. I was sent to the warehouse in South Wales. But 30 tons of *anything* is difficult to dispose of. We could not flood the market with cheap litter as that would be wrong. We didn't want the bottom to fall out of the cat-crap material market, did we? So what was I to do with all this stuff? I had a couple of days in South Wales to ponder the question.

I asked the locals in the pub and the other warehouse users if any of them had any idea what to do with it. Some of the ideas they came up with really are not printable; other ideas were so stupid that they were actually quite clever. The owner of a local golf club offered to take all of the bentonite off my hands for nothing. He thought that he might be able to use the litter in his fairway bunkers. Trouble was that when bentonite is wet it turns into wet clay. I was actually all for the idea because I loved the idea of completely screwing up the lives of golfers. Who wouldn't? But I knew this would just lead to my getting into even bigger trouble.

I was also approached by the owner of a stable who thought that the dust could be used on his all-weather track. Once again, the resulting wet clay would have slowed his horses down to a crawl and may even have injured them. The stuff was useful when it was dry but when it got wet it was no use to man nor dog nor horse. Just cats. So what about selling it to zoos for the massive cat-litter trays they must use for their tigers? I thought I better not follow that one up . . .

It was the case officer on the investigation that saved my bacon when he delivered the news that, unbelievably, the defence barrister for a number of the arrested smugglers had decided that the cat litter was to be kept as evidence! This was 30 tons of moisture-intolerant rock dust, which would have to be stored in dry conditions at taxpayers' expense. And the reason given for this was that the defence team might want the jury to see the original concealment in person. Why on earth did the defence think that we spent lots of money on taking pictures and videos of the concealment from every available aspect? Maybe they thought we just did it for fun. However, we played along rather than give them some excuse to object to the investigation. We didn't want to fall at the final hurdle.

My problem now was how to move 30 tons from South Wales to the East Midlands so we could store it for the court case. In the end, we made use of that great secret weapon that is always at the forefront of the war against drugs – the forklift truck. Yep, I had it all lifted into a convoy of large articulated, curtain-sided lorries. It took three days, with bentonite dust spilling everywhere and filling the air. I inhaled so much of the shit that when I sneezed clay fired out of my nose – or at least the bits that hadn't already started to harden in my nostrils. By the time we had finished, I was sneezing out clay bullets.

Strange, I thought, how I'd spent most of my career identifying, questioning, searching, interviewing, following, arresting and charging people who, for recreation, spent their days inhaling various illegal and expensive substances for pleasure . . . and here I was snorting nothing more exotic than cat-crap dust.

As I drove at the head of the three articulated-lorry convoy that was carrying evidence of the largest heroin seizure yet made in the UK, I thought about how it was a bloody good job that I didn't have a feline pet of my own waiting for me when I got home. There was the possibility that it would try to shit on my bentonite-stuffed nose. And because by now I was so thoroughly sick of anything to do with cats I would have booted it squarely up the arse.

24. No. 1 with a Cocaine Bullet

On an undercover CROPs job on the Isle of Wight, we'd had a run-in with some crime squad officers on the island who nearly cocked up an investigation of ours. The surveillance on the mainland was being conducted by both Customs and police, but on different targets. There were regular daily briefings between the case officers and the ground commanders of both groups so that everybody knew their jobs, so avoiding any 'blue on blues', which was the police codename for what the Army called 'friendly fire' or, in other words, shooting your own.

On the Monday, it was agreed that Customs CROPs would deploy on the island to carry out recces and close-target recon. There were to be no other Customs or police surveillance officers anywhere near: just ourselves and our back-up teams. CROPs work is dangerous at the best of times so we didn't need our airwaves messed up by any surveillance boys. From surveillance of the previous two days, we were 90 per cent sure that all the main targets were on the mainland and hadn't yet got to the island.

We deployed at one o'clock in the morning. It was dark, cold and clear and, thankfully, there was no moon to give away our movements. One of our teams was closing in on part of the target address to check out the household security system when a call came through saying that a car had un-expectedly swung into the long drive of the target premises, almost illuminating the team with its headlights. They dived for cover and sent out a danger message over the radio. All the teams, including mine, stopped dead in their tracks, and then we disappeared into the nearest undergrowth. Could this be the target or one of the gang turning up without warning? We all knew we could really be screwed here.

The car stayed in the same position for a few minutes, giv-ing one of our teams the opportunity to get its registration and note that there were three people in the car, all males. No weapons could yet be seen. The team radioed the details to our ground crew who ran checks on the car reg. And, lo and behold, it was a police surveillance car from the regional crime squad that was working alongside us. It couldn't have been a mere mistake or a wrong turn, because they would have to have taken a ferry to get to the island. The following morn-ing, the three officers were standing in front of both their own and our governors for what we called 'an interview without coffee' and what everyone else called 'a right fucking bollocking'. Blue on blue, indeed.

Ultimately, that mission had turned out a good result. And a month later we were now heading back out to the Isle of

Wight for what would turn out to be our biggest job yet – Operation Eyeful. We had no idea yet but a record-breaking 400 kilos of cocaine worth £90 million was heading our way. It was appropriate in a way that it was being brought to the Isle of Wight because the island had a rich history of smuggling; as well as taking salvage goods from shipwrecks, historically the locals had also made a living from smuggling goods from France. But, this time, they were coming from a bit further afield.

What we did know was that it was being organized by a big-time smuggling ring run by a drug trafficker called Michael Tyrrell and his British wife Julie Paterson aka the 'Cocaine Queen'. Tyrrell was from the West Indian island of Antigua and was well known there and in the United States for his criminal activities, especially with an associate called Frederick Fillingham, although the US Drug Enforcement Administration (DEA) had been unable to touch him. Paterson was no decorative gangster's moll – she owned a yacht charter company and was a yachtswoman herself with three Atlantic crossings under her belt.

Between the three of these characters, they seemed to have everything sewn up: Tyrrell had the drug connections; Paterson owned a yacht charter service; and Fillingham was a boat builder and sailor. The perfect combo for drug-smuggling operations by sea then.

We'd had the drug organization under surveillance for months. Whenever they were in the UK, Tyrrell and Paterson were kept under close surveillance and were observed buying equipment in preparation for their next big job. It would be interesting to see if a trafficker who had managed to elude the mighty power of the DEA would have as much success against a small island called Britain. We did once have the world's greatest Navy fleet so we'd have to see if our rich maritime history was deep enough in our DNA to be able to bring the Cocaine King and Queen to book.

My involvement began humbly enough with my driving our CROPs Land Rover down to Southampton. It was the day before my birthday, so I wasn't too happy. I soon cheered up as I saw my mate and colleague, Puddy, waiting for the Red Funnel line ferry to the island. He was his normal chirpy self. 'Hello, me old mucker. What the fuck are we doing in this God-forsaken place?'

He was quite right. Large commercial docks are not the places that romantic stories about smuggling are made of. We knew the job we had been called back to the island to carry out was going to go down soon and CROPs were an essential part of the operation, but we didn't know much else. I would love to say that the ferry trip was smooth, but it wasn't. Puddy scowled at the waves: 'If this keeps up it's going to be one bastard of a night for a boat landing.' And he was to be proved right.

We joined up with the rest of our merry band of CROPs officers at a secret location. Only the people who needed to know knew that we were there and what our mission was: CROPs was always a very secretive part of an investigation. Very few people could identify us, even in the broader investigation team. Outside the investigation, hardly anyone in Customs and Excise even knew of the cadre's existence. We did jobs that people didn't talk about. It was as rare as snooker ball fur for us to appear in court. Even in the drugs-drop aircraft job we did before, all the jury knew of us when it came to court was that the pictures had been taken by an officer 'in a position to observe'. There was no specific mention of CROPs. And, in this latest instance on the Isle of Wight, it was so bloody secretive that even we didn't know yet what it was; we weren't in a position to observe anything, not even our own involvement.

Once we were all gathered and the kit had been unloaded, we got together for a briefing. Before the briefing started, my mind drifted back to the last annual CROPs meeting we'd had a few months earlier. We were told that the bad guys had just learned how to be a little worse by improving their CROPs-officer-hunting techniques. Previously, the better gangs had employed soldiers and ex-Marines to hunt us down, but now things had got more dangerous, thanks in part to the Cold War. The officer taking the annual briefing produced a very strange piece of kit for us to look at: Russian by design and manufacture and definitely military, our colleagues in military intelligence had managed to get it on the black market. They had known of its existence but never before been able to get their hands on one. It was, to put it bluntly, an OP hunter – designed to identify observation positions or even hidden tanks or artillery spotters. And, since the end of the Cold War, there had been no more need for this technology so someone had started selling them off to the criminal underworld. And what exactly was this piece of kit that, months later, I was still thinking about and even fearing?

It was a device with a computer-controlled passive laser that would scan 180 degrees to its front in search of a reflective surface, which was the kind of telltale surface not usually found in the countryside. This surface could be a camera lens, a tank sight, a weapons scope, etc. Once the device identified a target, the passive laser would concentrate its search down to the exact position of the reflection and zoom in so as to build up a picture of the reflective surface. If it was a non-military target, the laser scanner would then restart the scan. But, if it was what it classed as a legitimate target, the operator would engage the secondary, full-power, non-passive laser. Using the scan and targeting, the main laser would lock on to the target and fire. This main laser was very powerful. And, we were told, if the laser locked on to a camera, scope or binoculars being used by a CROPs officer, it was powerful enough to burn a hole right through the lens, the device you were holding and then your head in a single shot. If all the other dangers and indignities of CROPs work weren't enough, we now had the thought of possibly facing something that could burn you an arsehole in the back of your head.

Thoughts of the laser retreated a little as the current briefing got underway. At the start, the point was made that the job would either go down that night or the following night, depending on the offshore weather. I looked over at Puddy and he winked back. The situation was this: a yacht had been loaded with a very large amount of cocaine on the southern Caribbean island of Bequia. It had spent the last couple of weeks at sea and had narrowly missed a mid-Atlantic hurricane. It was now approaching British waters and we had it on satellite. The beaching point for the drugs was to be an ex-coastguard/Excise house at Orchard Bay, on the south side of the Isle of Wight. We had known this destination for a little while as the house and its small harbour had already been under surveillance for a few weeks. There were to be three CROPs ops covering the north, the east and the west of the bay. Each CROP was to be two-manned and the remaining officers were to be transport and covert ops control. We, the CROPs teams, would operate on our own radio channel but other Customs units could listen to us to get a grasp on what was happening and what the timescales were.

So, with 150 Customs and police officers on the island that night, it looked like we were going to be the radio station of choice (though not forgetting that, because of our secret status, none of these 150 would have any idea who or where we were).

I was teamed up with Pete and we had the CROP location in the west. Mick and Shane had CROP east and Larry and Simon CROP north. Pete and I would have the first drop-off of the night as we had the longest to travel to reach the target. As for every CROPs job, we broke down all our kit, tested it, re-tested it, then put it all together again. This was to be an in-and-out job, no overnighting for us, so the kit was light. Every officer had a radio and individual call signs. This was for evidential reasons as every radio call was recorded, the transcriptions of which assisted us later in compiling our witness statements. We also carried spare batteries, large first aid kits, lots of water, camouflage kit, Mars bars, large items for self-protection and special kit. In my case, the special kit was a state-of-the-art thermal-imaging camera. This was a super piece of what we called 'shiny kit'. But the camera did have one big drawback and that was its eight-by-eight-inch TV screen, which lit up the darkness like the brightest beacon. As such, I had to also carry a large ground sheet under which I was going to cocoon myself. Looking at the bright screen would also impair my night vision for a few seconds when I looked away. Pete was going to have to be on the ball. If our CROP was rumbled while I was using the camera, I would be temporarily blind and he would have to get me out. Not to mention the added danger that if by some chance I left that large screen exposed (even when it was switched off) then it would make a big, juicy target, as would my head, for anyone who had one of those ex-military Russian lasers.

It was a couple of miles' patrol into our surveillance position. Ours was a new observation position that hadn't been recced on our previous visit. It turned out that we would be precariously perched on a cliff edge with a long drop to our right and the coastal path to our left. There was just the right amount of cover to camouflage both of us, so we started making the spot a little more comfortable. In the pitch dark, in which we often worked, we had to know where all our kit was just by touch. We had to become versed in a kind of techno Braille. But we even had some things, such as knives, tied to us on bits of rope. That made them much easier to find. If I needed a weapon, I didn't want to be relying at a time of high tension only on my sense of touch in the dark.

By 11.30 p.m., we were all in position. I was checking out the area with my thermal-imaging camera when I saw a large figure approaching CROP east. I radioed Mick and Shane the warning and they 'went dead', cutting all communications and lying inert. The large figure was actually one of the gang checking the area for signs of any unwanted visitors or snoopers . . . in other words, us. He started hitting the undergrowth with a stick and shining his torch into holes and bushes. Things were getting increasingly tense. In a situation like this, it was hard to know how near to let the enemy get to one of our troops without intervening. You just hoped they were braced and ready to spring to their own defence if they were discovered, but, at times like this, you had to go into such a lockdown mode that you weren't always best prepared to jump into action.

The stick thrashing and torch searching went on for what was probably a good five minutes but felt like half-an-hour. Then, apparently satisfied, he moved away, back to the house. We all breathed again.

It got to midnight and I became a year older, balancing, as I was, on the edge of a cliff on a coastal island with professional bad guys wandering around the area looking to do damage to my poor cold, windswept body. Happy birthday to me. I knew I could have been in warmer and safer places, but probably nowhere more exciting.

By 1.20 a.m., it was game on: a yacht called the *Blue Hen* appeared in the bay. Hopefully, it would be carrying the mother lode. It had to be a big job for all this work, but we still had no idea of the exact contents. The gang in the house obviously did, though, because they started to signal the yacht with torches. The yacht moored up about 800 yards out of

Orchard Bay and some of the gang members took a small boat out to meet it and help load up the drugs bales on to the yacht's own inflatable boat. I watched everything with the thermal-imaging camera and gave a running commentary of information on movements and descriptions, passing all info down the line so the ground force could accurately plan and coordinate their attack.

One element that was beginning to hamper everyone involved – drug smugglers and law enforcers – was that the weather was progressively worsening and becoming wilder. The wind was getting up and the waves were starting to lash the coast.

After unpacking the consignment from the yacht, the gang then headed for the island. And here was where we had our first piece of good luck and their first piece of bad: the outboard motor of the inflatable died mid-journey, meaning they had to divert and land about half a mile away at Woody Bay. This new turn of events meant that they now started unloading the bales of cocaine on the beach that was directly behind Pete and me. This in turn meant that they would be using the coastal path between the house and the new beach. And this in turn meant a shitload of unexpected heat for us – we would be lying next to the new main thoroughfare to the gang's hideout.

They started unloading the gear, and, each time a gang member went to the beach or struggled back up the cliff with a bale, they were only about six inches away from my head. We were now in the thick of it in the worst possible way. But I thought I'd be damned if one of them was going to take me out on my birthday: I decided that, if we were found, it would be a jump down the cliff and into the sea for me before I would let them catch me. And hopefully I'd grab on to one of them and take him with me.

Taking the bales up the cliff was time consuming and exhausting for them. But then one of the gang eventually mended the outboard motor of the inflatable and, in doing so, was able to transfer the remaining bales to their planned beach drop. One of the gang members (it turned out to be the boss, Tyrrell) jumped into their van to try to use it to collect the last few drugs bales. We watched the last bales being dragged up the first beach. We knew that part of the operation was nearing the end as the gang member shouted out, 'Ain't any of you fuckers going to give me a hand with these last two?' At the point when Tyrrell got in the van, word we'd all been waiting for finally came over the radios – the knock was about to be called! Now it was time for the others to have some fun.

First, our cutter, which was sitting out to sea, was ordered to get ready to take out the yacht. Next, officers were made ready for the knock. The trouble at this point was that control HQ was not getting back all the conformation responses that they needed. Then a bright spark realized why: with our CROPs control's permission, the case officer came on to our channel and ordered all troops to get back to their channel and be ready for the knock. It was then that we realized that every Customs officer present had been sitting on the edge of their seats, listening in to our radio commentary. We had provided the tense narration for the whole night's events. Seconds later, the knock was called and all hell let loose.

A Customs high-speed RHIB came out of the darkness of the sea and roared right up the beach (so far that it got stuck for a couple of days); our cutter slewed alongside the yacht and disgorged further officers who jumped aboard like ninja pirates; and a hundred other officers hit the target address, kicking in doors and slamming startled bad guys to the floor, arresting the gang and seizing a huge haul of Colombia's finest marching powder worth £90,000,000. As we found out a little later, we had just watched the single biggest cocaine importation on British soil, and we had filmed it and given a full running commentary.

But the job wasn't over yet. We still had to pull out without being seen (even by our own guys), which was easier said than done with Customs and police officers flying in every direction, looking for someone to nick. Adrenaline was high and night-time visibility was low; I didn't want to be mistaken for a bad guy and coshed to the ground. But as we pulled back along the coastal path we received a worrying radio call. One of the gang was missing and there was a chance that he was going to be on our route out. I fired up the thermal-imaging camera again and off we went. Within 20 metres, I hit a heat source, only a light one, but it was there. Pete approached it as only an ex-commando like him could – knife first. There was a worrying silence. I watched the eerie white-glowing heat-image of him in the night-vision camera, watching to see if there would be any other similar signs of someone waiting to jump out at him.

Eventually, he re-emerged out of the dark carrying a discarded wetsuit that had still been giving off enough body heat for the camera to pick up. We radioed our find to control and then off we went again. After 20 metres, I found another heat source. Off went Pete again into the dark. With no sounds of murder, Pete returned this time with a fuel can, half full. Pete and I had a quick chat and decided to leave the search for discarded evidence to the uniforms. We set off again with Pete leading. All of a sudden, there was a sharp cry of 'Fuck it!' and Pete disappeared. This wasn't a situation for the camera – nothing for it but for me to bring out a torch.

Pete was on his back, swearing like a trooper and holding his shin. He had gone arse over tit after hitting a bloody great outboard motor in the middle of the path. We radioed in the find. I sat next to Pete as he continued to rub his leg. He sighed and said, 'Let's get out of here, Jon, before we trip over Shergar's body and find Lord bloody Lucan on this sodding path.'

The morning was now bright and we were finishing off cleaning our kit and getting it packed away. News of the job quickly broke and it was already all over the airwaves and TV screens by 8 a.m. There were pictures of the house and of the yacht. The gang's hideout on the island turned out to be a seafront development bought by Tyrrell and the part of Orchard Bay where they had tried to land was the private beach to the development. The news bulletin also featured all the arrests and details of a drugs haul of huge proportions. The news organizations were used and briefed by law enforcement agencies in order, of course, to broadcast our success and to help scare off anyone thinking about trying the same sort of operation. I'd be surprised if the latter part of that worked on anyone planning a big smuggling job; one thing they had in common was that they all thought they never would get caught.

We all headed off to bed, exhausted by expending large amounts of nervous energy as much as by the physical graft of cliff climbing and gear carrying.

In the end, Operation Eyeful netted the then largest UK cocaine haul – almost half a ton of Colombian cocaine – leading to the gang receiving a total of 145 years of jail time, including the twenty-four years given to Julie Paterson, one of the longest jail sentences ever handed down to a woman drug trafficker. Paterson, who was living with Tyrrell in Parham, Antigua, but was from Norfolk, had not only prepared the *Blue Hen* yacht for sail but she had also briefed the yacht's crew on the use of navigational equipment and advised them on landing sites. Michael Tyrrell, husband of Paterson and King Cocaine to her Queen, was sentenced to twenty-six years imprisonment. The American member of the ring, Frederick Fillingham, who was already on the run from the US authorities due to his breaking a fifteen-year parole for earlier drug-smuggling convictions, was also caught, convicted and sentenced. He was the one who had recruited the crew and also used his skills to adapt the yacht for carrying the drugs across the Atlantic.

Tyrrell, Paterson and Fillingham had been part of the gang I'd observed on the beach through my night camera; all three were later found on the island, hiding in the grounds of a local holiday complex and where, in the words of a news report, 'they were arrested by Customs officers in the early hours . . . Assistant Chief Investigation Officer for Customs and Excise, Jim Fitzpatrick, said: "This gang tried to smuggle a huge quantity of cocaine into the UK and have received jail terms that reflect the seriousness."'

I was later told by the officer who was handcuffed to Tyrrell in the arrest car that, as they drove him away from the scene and on to the Red Funnel ferry, Tyrrell looked out of the window and said to no one in particular, 'I guess that this is the last time I'll get to see the ocean.'

The officer's reply was a grunted: 'Not unless you take up fucking tunnelling.'

I was to later find out that this record-breaking drug bust was featured in an article on Wikipedia about Michael Tyrrell, which detailed his organization and his eventual arrest during our own Operation Eyeful. Though there was absolutely no mention, I noticed, of *my birthday*.

That's the thing with working undercover – all guts, no bloody glory.

Epilogue: Thrills and Spills . . .

Dealing with a wide range of people on a daily basis, as I had done as a Customs officer in uniform and out, certainly revealed to you the truth of the saying, 'There's nowt as funny as folk.' Too bloody right. From men who filled the lining of their overcoats with smuggled live monkeys to those that had 'BOLLOCKS! GOOD!' tattooed on their arse, there was little human weirdness you weren't regularly exposed to. Sometimes I'd felt less like a Customs officer than a black and gold uniformed gatekeeper to a lunatic asylum that was offering free room and board.

When I'd worked at the airports, I'd sometimes thought, what if, as an experiment, we all just gave up this job and abandoned the idea of any border controls at all? Would there be an even bigger conga line than usual at the airport of passengers wanting to take advantage of their new freedom: walking through holding hands with monkeys and with rucksacks full of snakes, cages of squawking parrots, bags of tarantulas; cases of dodgy medicines, pirated pills, illegal prescriptions and poisoned booze; suitcases of heroin, bags of cocaine, cartloads of cannabis; armfuls of machetes, swords,

338

handguns, rifles, semi-automatic weapons, machine guns, grenades, plastic explosives and ostrich eggs?

And the answer is (obviously): yes. Yes, there would. The queue would be around the block and right up the Blackpool Tower, and the Channel Tunnel would be choked to capacity with everything from Russian gangsters to rabid hamsters.

And that was just what we found in the airports.

Going out undercover and on investigations just exposed you to a whole new level of what we might charitably term 'advantage-taking'. Or what we could also more accurately call hardened professional criminal activity. Times ten.

So spare a thought for the poor old Customs officer. They're only trying to stop the country becoming overrun with marauding villains leading gangs of chimpanzees covered in tarantulas riding packs of rabid dogs that are so high on speedballs of cocaine that they can't shoot straight or remember which suitcase full of heroin on the carousel is theirs. Not that this would really matter too much because the more ambitious ones would be driving convoys of lorries full of the stuff through the ports or landing their own airplanes full of it at Gatwick.

And there are those other villains, possibly much worse even than all of that, coming back from Spain wearing flip-flops and a sombrero. Talk about threat to society.

So, from working in airport uniform to then progressing to plain-clothes Intelligence work and then on to undercover Investigation, it all gave me a real sense of the scale of things – from the smallest offence to the largest assault; from an incident down the road to an operation planned on the other side of the world.

And it also revealed how much of the world wanted to come to our funny, soggy, foggy little island – and how many of our own citizens who left wanted to come back.

Now, almost all of the people that encounter Customs are perfectly fine and they contribute their own little bit to the whole bigger bit we call society. But some of the other ones that we beckon over to our desk with a finger, or have reason to search the boot of their car, or have evidence that leads to a raid on their flat . . . well, let's just say that sometimes you really do need someone who's going to say, 'Hang on, sunshine. I don't think you really should be bringing that in here.'

And the parade of these people is never-ending. And I knew there were still many more to come in my career. I went on to become an Anti-Corruption Manager and a National Intelligence Co-ordinator in South Africa, as well as working as an investigation and intelligence specialist for SOCA, the Serious Organised Crime Agency. You see, that's the thing about serious, organized crime – it is very serious and very organized.

(Note: I did actually put in for a transfer to AMCA – the Amusingly Messy Crime Agency – but they couldn't accept me because I've just made it up.)

As in any job, the thing that often got me through were the laughs, or the ability to laugh even in grim situations; the response to the things we saw was often to develop a kind of gallows humour. A good example of this was when we lost one of our own.

In any profession, you lose loved ones or close friends. In our job, it often came out of the blue: sometimes it was in the line of duty and other times it was the duty that did for them. Both in the police and Customs we had a drinking culture, all part, I think, of coping with the things we had to see. I once asked my doctor why he didn't have a go at me for smoking, and he said that, with a job like mine, smoking was often safer than going to work. I presume he thought the same about the drink. During my time in Intelligence, we often had to 'liaise' with our law enforcement cousins. In our case, we would liaise with the airport Special Branch on an almost daily basis. Both ourselves and the Branch had hidden bars in our respective offices and we certainly used them.

Charlie was a very well-liked and respected officer. He had served overseas and had been in most departments of the police force. He was on the final lap towards retirement and he'd earned it. Charlie had recently been feeling a bit off colour and, as such, he had visited his local GP. The doc had performed the normal tests. His wise but unwanted advice was that Charlie should cut down on the booze. Charlie decided to take the most extreme of measures and immediately stopped drinking, full-stop. Six days later, he was last seen by his wife, watching TV. He never made it to bed: his body just shut down.

As he was a serving officer, the funeral was a full uniform affair. Those of us from Customs who had known and respected Charlie joined the ranks of uniformed police officers making their way from the chapel to the graveside. His coffin was borne by six officers and the Union flag was draped across the lid.

As they passed us, the coffin route took in a small grassy slope, which was still damp with morning dew. One of the bearers slipped slightly on the slope and a deep voice, belonging to his best mate, boomed out across the mourners. 'Careful now, lads, we don't want to *spill* him.'

Acknowledgements

I would like to thank the following people for their help with my first attempt at book writing and for my somewhat strange career:

My agent and the most polite gentleman I have ever met, Andrew Lownie of the Andrew Lownie Literary Agency; Charlotte Macdonald and the wonderful staff at Constable and Robinson; Mike Puddicombe for being a good mate in good and bad times; my parents, Pamela and George for always being there when I needed them and sometimes when I didn't; Marcus Georgio who had the hardest job of all, making my scribbling readable.

Colin, Robin, Dangerous D. and the Reverend G. who made the madness of surveillance seem so fun.

Geoff Yerbury MBE, a master Customs officer, inspiration for a whole career and friend in South Africa.

Steve Paskin, who kept me sane but drunk in Pretoria and Joburg.

Peter Pinch, the best SIO in the business.

And finally . . .

Ann Cadwallader – who dragged me out of madness, always believed in me, wiped up the tears and joined in with the laughter, but most of all . . . says nice things about my cooking. I will always love you.